Collins

CONCISE REVISION COURSE
CSEC®
Human and Social Biology

T0340469

Author: Anne Tindale
Reviewer: Shaun deSouza

Collins

William Collins' dream of knowledge for all began with the publication of his first book in 1819.
A self-educated mill worker, he not only enriched millions of lives, but also founded a flourishing publishing house.
Today, staying true to this spirit, Collins books are packed with inspiration, innovation and practical expertise. They
place you at the centre of a world of possibility and give you exactly what you need to explore it.

Collins. Freedom to teach.

Published by Collins
An imprint of HarperCollins*Publishers*
The News Building
1 London Bridge Street
London
SE1 9GF

HarperCollins *Publishers*
Macken House, 39/40 Mayor Street Upper,
Dublin 1,
D01 C9W8,
Ireland

Browse the complete Collins Caribbean catalogue at
www.collins.co.uk/caribbeanschools

10 9 8 7 6 5 4 3

ISBN 978-0-00-854162-0

Collins Concise Revision Course: CSEC® Human and Social Biology is an independent publication and has not been
authorised, sponsored or otherwise approved by **CXC**®.

CSEC® is a registered trademark of the **Caribbean Examinations Council (CXC®)**.

British Library Cataloguing in Publication Data
A catalogue record for this publication is available from the British Library.

The publishers gratefully acknowledge the permission granted to reproduce the copyright material in this book. Every
effort has been made to trace copyright holders and to obtain their permission for the use of copyright material. The
publishers will gladly receive any information enabling them to rectify any error or omission at the first opportunity.

Author: Anne Tindale
Reviewer: Shaun deSouza
Publisher: Dr Elaine Higgleton
Commissioning Editor: Tom Hardy
In-house senior editor: Julianna Dunn
Project manager: Peter Dennis
Copy editor: Jess White
Proofreader: Roda Morrison
Illustrator: Ann Paganuzzi
Typesetter: QBS Learning
Cover designers: Kevin Robbins and Gordon MacGilp
Cover photo: Shutterstock
Printed and bound by Ashford Colour Press Ltd

MIX
Paper | Supporting
responsible forestry
FSC™ C007454

This book contains FSC™ certified paper and other controlled
sources to ensure responsible forest management.

For more information visit: www.harpercollins.co.uk/green

Acknowledgments

P11:Eric Isselee/Shutterstock, P11:Robert_s/Shutterstock, P11:Tatiana Belova/Shutterstock, P11:Feathercollector/Shutterstock, P11:Stephen
McSweeny/Shutterstock, P11:Vitalii Hulai/Shutterstock, P11:Wim van Egmond/Visuals Unlimited, Inc./Getty Images, P11:Anat Chant/Shutterstock,
P11:Matt9122/Shutterstock, P11:Roland Birke/Getty Images, P22:Anne Tindale, P25: Jeff Rotman / Alamy Stock Photo, P25:Brian A Jackson/Shutter-
stock, P27:Billion Photos/Shutterstock, P27:Peangdao/Shutterstock, P27:Alexander Prokopenko/Shutterstock, P27:leonori/Shutterstock,
P25:leonori/Shutterstock, P27:JPC-PROD/Shutterstock, P28:BURGER/PHANIE/Alamy Stock Photo, P28:MAURO FERMARIELLO/SCIENCE PHOTO
LIBRARY, P45:Microgen/Shutterstock, P46:Wikrom Kitsamritchai/Shutterstock, P54:PROF. P. MOTTA/DEPT. OF ANATOMY/UNIVERSITY LA
SAPIENZA, ROME/SCIENCE PHOTO LIBRARY, P90:ARZTSAMUI/Shutterstock, P102:Southern Illinois University/Science Photo Library, P102:Addy-
vanich/Shutterstock, P102:Image Point Fr/Shutterstock, P102:Areeya_ann/Shutterstock, P128:Jian Hongyan/Shutterstock, P120:Alila Medical
Media/Shutterstock, P122:elenabsl/Shutterstock, P141: DR M.A. ANSARY / SCIENCE PHOTO LIBRARY, P160:Ildi Papp/Shutterstock, P160:Dmytro
Tyshchenko/Shutterstock, P161:eranicle/Shutterstock, P166:Sambulov Yevgeniy/Shutterstock, P168:anishankar Patra/Shutterstock, P172:grebcha/Shut-
terstock, P177:ChiccoDodiFC/Shutterstock, P172:Francisco Rodriguez Herna/Shutterstock.

Contents

The pathway to success

About this book

This book has been written primarily as a **revision course** for students studying for the CSEC® Human and Social Biology examination. The facts are presented **concisely** using a variety of formats which makes them **easy to understand** and **learn**. Key words are highlighted in **bold** type and important **definitions** which must be learned are written in *italics* and highlighted in colour. **Annotated diagrams** and **tables** have been used wherever possible and the relationship between **structure** and **function** is continually emphasised. Some **diagrams** are marked with a **star** (★); these are diagrams that are specifically identified in the syllabus as ones that students should know and be able to **label**, the important labels to learn being those highlighted in **bold** type. **Questions** to help test knowledge and understanding, and to provide practice for the actual examination, are included throughout the book.

The following sections provide **valuable information** on the format of the CSEC® examination, how to revise successfully, successful examination technique, key terms used on examination papers and the School-Based Assessment.

The CSEC® Human and Social Biology syllabus and this book

The **CSEC® Human and Social Biology syllabus** is available online at **http://cxc-store.com**. You are strongly advised to read through the syllabus carefully since it provides detailed information on the specific objectives of each topic of the course and the format of the CSEC® examination. Each chapter in **this book** covers a particular topic in the syllabus.

- **Chapters 1 and 2** cover topics in Section A; **Living organisms and the environment**
- **Chapters 3 to 9** cover topics in Section B; **Life processes**
- **Chapters 10 and 11** cover topics in Section C; **Heredity and variation**
- **Chapters 12 and 13** cover topics in Section D; **Diseases and their impact on humans**
- **Chapters 14 and 15** cover topics in Section E; **The impact of health practices on the environment**

At the end of each chapter, or section within a chapter, you will find a selection of **revision questions**. These questions test your **knowledge** and **understanding** of the topic covered in the chapter or section. At the end of Chapters 2, 9, 11, 13 and 15 you will find a selection of **exam-style questions**, which also test how you **apply** the knowledge you have gained and help prepare you to answer the different styles of questions that you will encounter in your CSEC® examination. You will find the answers to all these questions online at **www.collins.co.uk/caribbean**.

The format of the CSEC® Human and Social Biology examination

The examination consists of **two papers** and your performance is evaluated using the following **two** profiles:

- **Knowledge and comprehension**
- **Use of knowledge**

Paper 01 (1 ¼ hours)

Paper 01 consists of **60 multiple choice questions**. Each question is worth **1 mark**. Four **choices** of answer are provided for each question of which one is correct.

- Make sure you read each question **thoroughly**; some questions may ask which answer is **incorrect**.

- Some questions may give two or more correct answers and ask which answer is the **best**; you must consider each answer very carefully before making your choice.

- If you do not know the answer, try to work it out by **eliminating** the incorrect answers. Never leave a question unanswered.

Paper 02 (2 hours)

Paper 02 is divided into **Sections A** and **B**, and consists of **six compulsory questions**. Each question is divided into several parts and is worth **15 marks**. The answers are to be written in **spaces** provided on the paper. These spaces indicate the length of answer required and answers should be restricted to them. Take time to **read the entire paper** before beginning to answer any of the questions.

- **Section A** consists of **four** compulsory **structured questions** whose parts require short answers, usually a word, a sentence or a short paragraph. The questions usually begin with some kind of **stimulus material**, often a diagram, which you will be asked questions about.

  One question will be a **data analysis type question**, which will provide you with some form of **data** that you will be expected to answer questions about. The data might be in the form of a table or a graph. If you are given a table, you may be asked to draw a **graph** using the data and may then be asked questions about the graph. Make sure you know how to draw graphs (see page ix).

- **Section B** consists of **two** compulsory **structured essay questions**. These questions require a greater element of **essay** writing in their answers than those in section A. They include **authentic scenarios** that will allow you to demonstrate knowledge that you have gained through experience.

The marks allocated for the different parts of each question are clearly given. A total of **90 marks** is available for Paper 02 and the time allowed is **120 minutes**. You should allow between 15 and 20 minutes for each question. This will allow you time to read the paper fully before you begin and time to check over your answers when you have finished.

Successful revision

The following should provide a guide for **successful revision**.

- **Begin your revision early.** You should start your revision at least two months before the examination and should plan a **revision timetable** to cover this period. Plan to revise in the evenings when you do not have much homework, at weekends, during the Easter vacation and during study leave.

- When you have a **full day** available for revision, consider the day as three sessions of about three to four hours each, **morning**, **afternoon** and **evening**. Study during two of these sessions only, do something non-academic and relaxing during the third.

- **Read through the topic** you plan to learn to make sure you **understand** it before starting to learn it; understanding is a lot safer than thoughtless learning.

- Try to understand and learn **one topic** in each revision session, more if topics are short and fewer if topics are long.

- **Revise every topic** in the syllabus. Do not pick and choose topics since **all questions** on your exam paper are **compulsory**.

- **Learn the topics in order**. When you have learned **all** topics **once**, go back to the first topic and begin again. Try to cover each topic **several times**.

- **Revise in a quiet location** without any form of distraction.

- **Sit up to revise**, preferably at a table. Do not sit in a comfy chair or lie on a bed where you can easily fall asleep.

- Obtain copies of **past CSEC® Human and Social Biology examination papers** and use them to practise answering exam-style questions, starting with the most recent papers. These can be purchased online from the CXC® Store.

- You can use a variety of different **methods** to **learn** your work. Choose which ones work best for you.

  - **Read the topic several times**, then close the book and try to write down the **main points**. Do not try to memorise your work word for word since work learned by heart is not usually understood, and questions test **understanding** as well as the ability to repeat facts.

  - **Summarise** the **main points** of each topic on **flash cards** and use these to help you study.

  - **Draw simple diagrams** with **annotations**, **spider diagrams** and **flow charts** to summarise topics in visual ways which are easy to learn.

  - **Practise labelling diagrams** that you have been given. You may be asked to do this in your exam.

  - **Use memory aids** such as:
    - **acronyms**, e.g. **GRIMNER** for the seven life processes; **g**rowth, **r**eproduction, **i**rritability, **m**ovement, **n**utrition, **e**xcretion, **r**eproduction.
    - **mnemonic phrases**, e.g. 'some mums buy pretty pink socks' for the six functions of the skeleton; **s**upport, **m**ovement, **b**reathing, **p**rotection, **p**roduction of blood cells, **s**torage of minerals.
    - **associations between words**, e.g. t**ri**cuspid – **ri**ght (therefore the bicuspid valve must be on the left side of the heart), **a**rteries – **a**way (therefore veins must take blood towards the heart).

  - **Test yourself** using the questions throughout this book and others from past CSEC® examination papers.

Successful examination technique

- **Read the instructions** at the start of each paper very carefully and do **precisely** what they require.

- **Read through the entire paper** before you begin to answer any of the questions.

- **Read each question at least twice** before beginning your answer to ensure you **understand** what it asks.

- **Study diagrams, graphs** and **tables** in detail and make sure that you **understand** the information they are giving before answering the questions that follow.

- **Underline the important words** in each question to help you answer precisely what the question is asking.
- **Reread** the question when you are **part way through** your answer to check that you are answering what it asks.
- **Give precise** and **factual answers.** You will not get marks for information which is 'padded out' or irrelevant.
- **Use correct terminology** throughout your answers.
- Give any **numerical answer** the appropriate **unit** using the proper abbreviation/ symbol, e.g. cm^3, g, °C.
- If a question asks you to give a **specific number of points**, use **bullet points** to make each separate point clear.
- If you are asked to give **similarities** and **differences**, you must make it clear which points you are proposing as similarities and which points as differences. The same applies if you are asked to give **advantages** and **disadvantages.**
- **Watch the time** as you work. Know the time available for each question and stick to it.
- **Check over your answers** when you have completed all the questions.
- **Remain in the examination room** until the **end** of the examination and recheck your answers again if you have time to ensure you have done your very best. Never leave the examination room early.

Some key instruction words used on examination papers

It is essential that you fully **understand** what each question is **asking you to do** before you begin to answer. Always look at the **number of marks** allocated for each question and make sure you include at least as many **points** in your answer as there are **marks.** The following **key instruction words** tell you the **type of detail** that you should give in your answers.

Account for: provide reasons for the information given.

Compare: give similarities and differences.

Construct: draw a graph, histogram, bar chart, pie chart or table using data provided or obtained.

Deduce: use data provided or obtained to arrive at a conclusion.

Define: state concisely the meaning of a word or term.

Describe: provide a detailed account which includes all relevant information.

Discuss: provide a balanced argument which considers points both for and against.

Distinguish between or **among:** give differences.

Evaluate: determine the significance or worth of the point in question.

Explain: give a clear, detailed account which makes given information easy to understand and provides reasons for the information.

Give an account of: give a written description which includes all the relevant details.

Give an illustrated account of: give a written description which includes diagrams referred to in the description.

Identify: name or point out specific components or features.

Illustrate: make the answer clearer by including examples or diagrams.

Justify: provide adequate grounds for your reasoning.

Label: add names to identify structures or parts indicated by label lines or pointers.

Name: give the name only.

Outline: write an account which includes the main points only.

Predict: use information provided to arrive at a likely conclusion or suggest a possible outcome.

Relate: show connections between different sets of information or data.

State or **list**: give brief, precise facts without detail.

Suggest: put forward an idea.

Drawing graphs

Graphs are used to display numerical data. When drawing a graph:

- Plot the **manipulated variable** on the **x-axis** (horizontal axis) and the **responding variable** on the **y-axis** (vertical axis):
  - The **manipulated variable** is the factor that is **changed** by the person carrying out the investigation. It will be given in the **left column** of the table of data.
  - The **responding variable** is the factor that is **measured** by the person carrying out the investigation. It will be given in the **right column** of the table of data.
- Choose appropriate **scales** which are easy to work with and which use as much of the graph grid as possible and enter the **variables** along the axes.
- **Label** each axis to indicate the variable that it is showing. To do this, use the **column headings** in the table of data and remember to include any units.
- When drawing a **line graph**, use a **small dot** surrounded by a small circle or triangle, e.g. ⊙, to plot each point, plot each point **accurately**, and join the points with a **sharp continuous line**.
- When drawing a **histogram** or **bar chart**, the height of each bar indicates the value of the responding variable. Draw **vertical bars** of equal width and draw an accurately positioned **horizontal line** to show the top of each bar.
  - When drawing a **histogram** ensure that the bars **touch** each other.
  - When drawing a **bar chart** ensure that **spaces** of equal width are left between the y-axis and the first bar, and between each of the other bars.
- Give the graph an appropriate **title** which must include reference to the responding variable and the manipulated variable.

The School-Based Assessment or SBA

The **School-Based Assessment** or **SBA** is an integral part of your CSEC® examination. It is a single, guided **research project** which all CSEC® Human and Social Biology students are required to complete. It is not carried out under examination conditions and it is worth **20% of your final examination mark**, therefore it is important that you score as highly as you can in your SBA project. **Your teacher** plays a critical role in the management of your project because he/she should provide guidance throughout, and it is really important to start **planning** your project **early**.

The CSEC® Human and Social Biology Syllabus states the following:

Candidates will be required to conduct research in their school or community on a current health-related or environmental issue and its socio-economic impacts in their territory. They will be expected to collect data, analyse and interpret the data and provide recommendations.

You will be required to submit a **written report** on your research project. You may work individually or in a group with other students to gather data; however, you must each produce your own report. No two reports from the same group should be identical, and your report should **not exceed 1000 words**. Your report should be presented **electronically** and it should have the following components in the order listed below. Knowing these components before you begin should help **guide** your project.

- *Cover Page*
- *Table of Contents*
- *Introduction – divided into the following:*
  - ◆ *Background or Overview of the Issue*
  - ◆ *Problem Statement*
  - ◆ *Research Objective*
- *Methodology*
- *Presentation of Data*
- *Analysis and Interpretation of Data*
- *Conclusion*
- *Recommendations*
- *Reflection*
- *Bibliography*
- *Appendices*

The **aim** of the SBA is to assist you in acquiring certain **knowledge**, **skills** and **attitudes** that are associated with the study of Human and Social Biology. It will focus on developing your research, analytical and critical thinking skills. You will receive **formative feedback** from your **teacher** at various stages of your project which should enable you to build self-confidence. Overall, it will help to improve your learning and achievement.

Section A – Living organisms and the environment

1 Living organisms and cells

All living organisms are made of **cells**. Cells are so small that they can only be seen with a microscope and not with the naked eye. From the simplest unicellular organisms to the most complex multicellular organisms, living organisms all share certain **characteristics**.

The characteristics of living organisms

All living organisms share the following **seven** characteristics:

- *Nutrition (feeding): the process by which living organisms obtain or make food.*

  Animals take in ready-made food and are called **heterotrophs**. Plants make their own food by the process of **photosynthesis** and are called **autotrophs**.

- *Respiration: the process by which energy is released from food by all living cells.*

  Aerobic respiration requires oxygen and takes place in most cells. **Anaerobic respiration** takes place without oxygen in certain cells.

- *Excretion: the process by which waste and harmful substances, produced by the body's metabolism (chemical reactions), are removed from the body.*

- *Growth: a permanent increase in the size and complexity of an organism.*

- *Irritability (sensitivity): the ability of organisms to detect and respond to changes in their environment or within themselves.*

- *Movement: a change in the position of a whole organism or of parts of an organism.*

  Most animals can move their **whole** bodies from place to place, known as **locomotion**. Plants and some animals can only move **parts** of their bodies.

- *Reproduction: the process by which living organisms generate new individuals of the same kind as themselves.*

  Sexual reproduction involves the fusion of gametes (sex cells) produced by two parents. **Asexual reproduction** does not involve the fusion of gametes and requires only one parent.

Cells

The **cell** is the smallest unit of **life**. It is the basic structural and functional unit of all living organisms. Some organisms are **unicellular**, being composed of a single cell; others are **multicellular**, being composed of many cells.

Animal and plant cells

Both **animal** and **plant cells** are surrounded by an extremely thin outer layer known as the **cell membrane**, which has jelly-like **cytoplasm** inside. The cytoplasm contains structures called **organelles** that are specialised to carry out one or more vital functions. Organelles include the nucleus, mitochondria, endoplasmic reticulum, ribosomes, chloroplasts and vacuoles. Most organelles are surrounded by one or two **membranes**.

The following are found in **both** animal and plant cells:

- a **cell membrane** or **plasma membrane**
- **cytoplasm**
- a **nucleus**
- **mitochondria** (singular: mitochondrion)
- **endoplasmic reticulum**
- **ribosomes**

In addition to the above, **plant cells** also possess:

- a **cell wall**
- **chloroplasts**
- a large **vacuole**

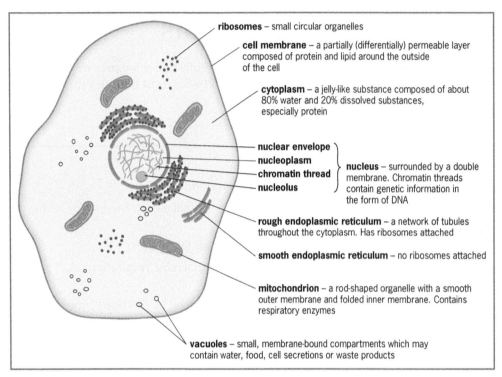

ribosomes – small circular organelles

cell membrane – a partially (differentially) permeable layer composed of protein and lipid around the outside of the cell

cytoplasm – a jelly-like substance composed of about 80% water and 20% dissolved substances, especially protein

nuclear envelope
nucleoplasm
chromatin thread
nucleolus
} nucleus – surrounded by a double membrane. Chromatin threads contain genetic information in the form of DNA

rough endoplasmic reticulum – a network of tubules throughout the cytoplasm. Has ribosomes attached

smooth endoplasmic reticulum – no ribosomes attached

mitochondrion – a rod-shaped organelle with a smooth outer membrane and folded inner membrane. Contains respiratory enzymes

vacuoles – small, membrane-bound compartments which may contain water, food, cell secretions or waste products

★ **Figure 1.1** *Structure of a generalised animal cell*

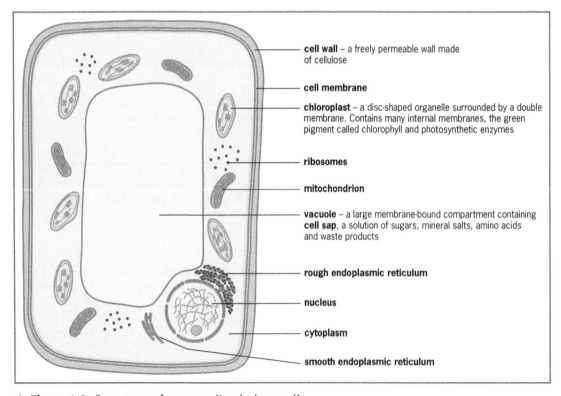

cell wall – a freely permeable wall made of cellulose

cell membrane

chloroplast – a disc-shaped organelle surrounded by a double membrane. Contains many internal membranes, the green pigment called chlorophyll and photosynthetic enzymes

ribosomes

mitochondrion

vacuole – a large membrane-bound compartment containing cell sap, a solution of sugars, mineral salts, amino acids and waste products

rough endoplasmic reticulum

nucleus

cytoplasm

smooth endoplasmic reticulum

★ **Figure 1.2** *Structure of a generalised plant cell*

Table 1.1 *A summary of the functions of the different cell structures*

Cell structure	Function
Cell membrane	Controls what substances enter and leave the cell.
Cytoplasm	Supports the organelles. The site of many chemical reactions.
Nucleus	Controls the characteristics and functioning of the cell. Essential for cell division.
Mitochondrion	Where **aerobic respiration** occurs to release energy for the cell.
Endoplasmic reticulum	Transports substances throughout the cell.
Ribosome	Where proteins are synthesised (produced) from amino acids.
Vacuole	Stores food, cell secretions or cell waste. Supports plant cells when turgid.
Cell wall	Supports and protects the plant cell and gives it shape.
Chloroplast	Where **photosynthesis** occurs to produce food for the plant.

Table 1.2 *Plant and animal cells compared*

Animal cells	Plant cells
Do not have a cell wall.	Have a **cell wall** which is made of cellulose.
Do not have chloroplasts or chlorophyll.	Usually have **chloroplasts** which contain **chlorophyll**.
When present, the vacuoles are small and scattered throughout the cytoplasm and their contents vary.	Usually have one large, central **vacuole** which contains **cell sap**.
May contain **glycogen granules** as a food store.	May contain **starch grains** as a food store.
Can have a great variety of shapes.	Have a regular shape, usually round, square or rectangular.

Microbes

Microbes or **microorganisms** are extremely small organisms which include **viruses**, **bacteria**, **protozoa** and some **fungi**. Many microbes are **pathogens**, i.e. they cause disease (see Chapter 12, page 133).

- **Viruses** lack a cellular structure and are therefore considered to be **particles**, not cells; they can only reproduce inside other living cells.

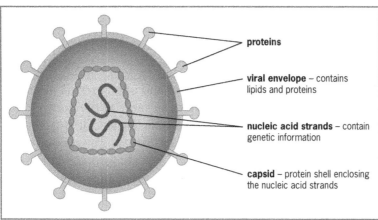

proteins

viral envelope – contains lipids and proteins

nucleic acid strands – contain genetic information

capsid – protein shell enclosing the nucleic acid strands

★ **Figure 1.3** *Structure of a typical virus particle*

- **Bacteria** are unicellular organisms. The cells of bacteria lack a true nucleus and other membrane-bound organelles. Their DNA exists in a region called the **nucleoid**, which lacks a nuclear membrane, and also in smaller regions called **plasmids**.

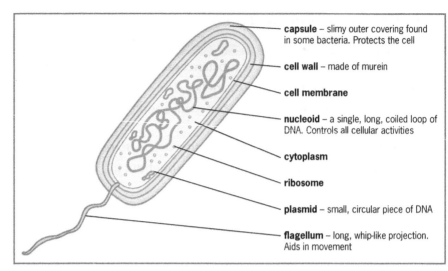

★ **Figure 1.4** *Structure of a generalised bacterial cell*

- Most **fungi** are multicellular, though **yeasts** are unicellular. Their cells contain true nuclei and other membrane-bound organelles except chloroplasts, and are surrounded by a cell wall made of **chitin**. In multicellular fungi the cells form thread-like branching filaments called **hyphae** (singular: hypha), and a network of hyphae, known as a **mycelium**, makes up the body of the fungus.

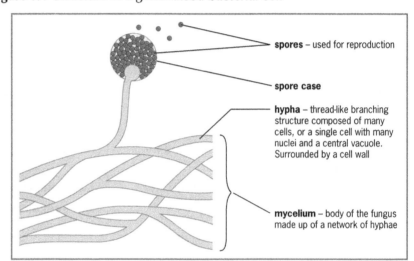

★ **Figure 1.5** *Structure of a typical fungus*

Cell specialisation and organisation in humans

The human body is composed of trillions of cells. These cells are of different types due to them becoming **specialised** or **differentiated** to carry out specific functions. This enables the cells to be **better able** to carry out their specific functions, which then enables humans to carry out all essential life processes as **efficiently** as possible.

Table 1.3 *Specialised cells, their distinguishing features and their functions*

Cell type	Distinguishing features	Function
Epithelial cells	Can be cuboidal, columnar or flattened in shape, and are arranged in sheets.	Cover and often protect inner and outer surfaces of the body.
Sperm cell or spermatozoon	Consists of a head containing the nucleus, a middle section containing many mitochondria and a tail.	**Male gamete** (sex cell); fuses with the female gamete during fertilisation to form a zygote.
Egg cell or ovum	Spherical in shape with cytoplasm containing yolk. Surrounded by a membrane, a layer of jelly and a layer of follicle cells.	**Female gamete**; fuses with the male gamete during fertilisation to form a zygote.
Nerve cells or neurones	Long, thin cells with a cell body that has one or two thin nerve fibres containing cytoplasm extending from it.	Transmit **impulses** throughout the body to control and coordinate the functioning of the body.

Cell type	Distinguishing features	Function
Muscle cells	May be narrow and spindle-shaped, each with a single nucleus, or long and cylindrical with cross bands and many nuclei (see page 67).	Groups of muscle cells, working together, contract to cause movement of parts of the body.
Connective tissue cells	May be of several different types. The most common are **fibroblasts**, which are elongated cells with projections from their ends.	Produce the **extracellular matrix** of connective tissue (see below).

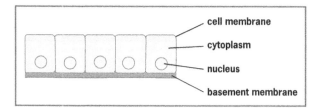

★ **Figure 1.6** *Epithelial cells*

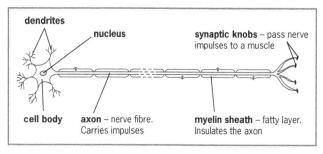

★ **Figure 1.7** *A sperm cell or spermatozoon*

★ **Figure 1.8** *An egg cell or ovum*

★ **Figure 1.9** *A motor neurone (nerve cell)*

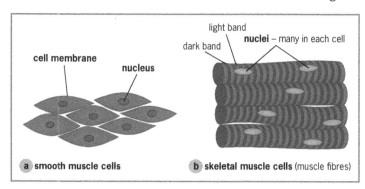

a smooth muscle cells   b skeletal muscle cells (muscle fibres)

★ **Figure 1.10** *Muscle cells*

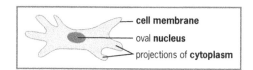

★ **Figure 1.11** *One type of connective tissue cell – a fibroblast*

Cells of the same type that are specialised to carry out a particular function then work together in groups called **tissues**. Tissues may contain one or, in some cases, more than one type of cell. **Four main types of tissue are found in the human body: epithelial tissue** composed of epithelial cells, **nervous tissue** composed of nerve cells, **muscle tissue** composed of muscle cells and **connective tissue** composed of different types of connective tissue cells surrounded by an **extracellular matrix**. This matrix is usually made up of a jelly-like **ground substance** that contains **fibres** made of protein. Examples of connective tissues include blood, cartilage, bone, adipose (fat) tissue and areolar (loose connective) tissue that surrounds organs.

Different tissues are then grouped together to form specialised **organs** which may perform one or more specific functions, e.g. the **stomach** is composed of epithelial, connective, muscle and nerve tissues. Organs work together in **organ systems** to carry out a major function. All organ systems then work together in an organised way to form an **organism**.

i.e. cells ⟶ tissues ⟶ organs ⟶ organ systems ⟶ organism

Table 1.4 *Examples of organ systems*

Organ system	Organs	Function
Digestive	Stomach, liver, pancreas, intestines	Digests and absorbs food.
Reproductive	Ovaries and uterus in females; testes and penis in males	Produces offspring.
Respiratory	Nose, larynx, trachea, bronchi, lungs	Exchanges oxygen and carbon dioxide.
Nervous	Brain, spinal cord, nerves	Detects and coordinates responses to stimuli.
Circulatory	Heart, blood vessels	Transports substances around the body.

Revision questions

1. Explain THREE ways in which a car can be considered similar to a living organism and THREE ways in which it is different from a living organism.

2. What is a cell?

3. Describe the structure and outline the function of EACH of the following cell structures:

   a a mitochondrion   **b** the endoplasmic reticulum   **c** a chloroplast

   d ribosomes   **e** the cell membrane

4. What would happen to a cell if its nucleus is removed?

5. Give FOUR differences and THREE similarities between the structure of a typical plant cell and a typical animal cell.

6. What features would enable a scientist to distinguish a bacterial cell from other cells when viewed under the microscope?

7. **a** Explain the need for cell specialisation in multicellular organisms.

   b Name THREE different types of cells found in the human body and give the distinguishing features and function of EACH.

8. Suggest a definition for EACH of the following:

   a a tissue   **b** an organ   **c** an organ system

Movement of substances into and out of cells

Substances can move into and out of cells, and from cell to cell by **three** different processes:

- **simple diffusion**   • **osmosis**   • **active transport**

Simple diffusion and osmosis are **passive** processes because they do not require energy released in respiration.

Simple diffusion

Simple diffusion is the net movement of particles from an area of higher concentration to an area of lower concentration until the particles are evenly distributed.

The particles, which can be **molecules** or **ions**, are said to move **down a concentration gradient**. Particles in gases, liquids and solutions are capable of diffusing. Diffusion is the way cells obtain many of their requirements and get rid of their waste products which, if not removed, would poison them.

Examples of the importance of diffusion in living organisms

- **Oxygen** for use in **aerobic respiration** moves into cells by diffusion, and **carbon dioxide** produced in aerobic respiration moves out of cells by diffusion.
- Some of the **glucose** and **amino acids** produced in digestion are absorbed through the cells in the ileum and capillary walls and into the blood by diffusion.
- **Carbon dioxide** for use in **photosynthesis** moves into leaves and plant cells by diffusion, and **oxygen** produced in photosynthesis moves out of plant cells and leaves by diffusion.
- **Neurotransmitters** (chemicals) pass across **synapses** (gaps) between adjacent neurones in the nervous system by diffusion.

Osmosis

*Osmosis is the movement of **water molecules** through a partially (differentially) permeable membrane from a solution containing a lot of water molecules; for example, a dilute solution (or water), to a solution containing fewer water molecules; for example, a concentrated solution.*

Osmosis is a special form of diffusion. Only **water molecules** move by osmosis, and they always move from a solution with a **higher water content** (a more dilute solution) to one with a **lower water content** (a more concentrated solution) through a **partially** or **differentially permeable membrane**.

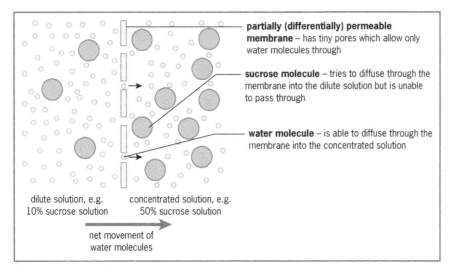

Figure 1.12 *Explanation of osmosis*

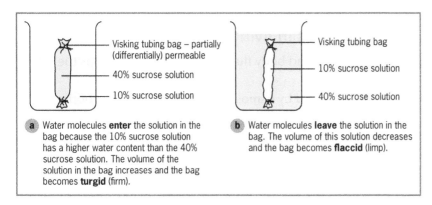

Figure 1.13 *Demonstrating osmosis*

In any **living cell**, the **cell membrane** is partially (differentially) permeable. There is always **cytoplasm**, a solution of protein and other substances in water, on the inside of the membrane, and usually a solution, such as tissue fluid, on the outside. **Water molecules**, therefore, move into and out of living cells by **osmosis**. It is important to note that osmosis does **not** occur in **dead** cells.

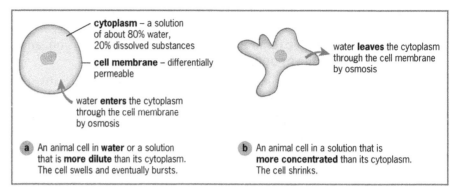

Figure 1.14 *The effect of different solutions on a single animal cell*

Plant cells are surrounded by a strong, freely permeable **cell wall**. Because of this they behave differently from animal cells when placed in different solutions.

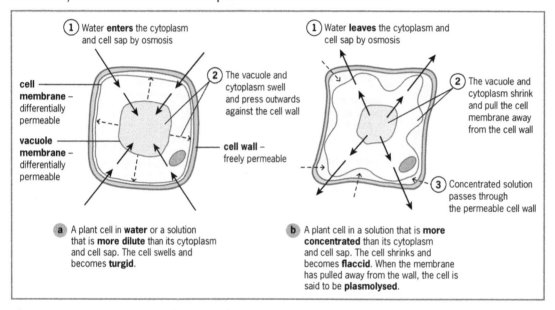

Figure 1.15 *The effect of different solutions on a single plant cell*

Examples of the importance of osmosis in living organisms

- **Water** moves into animal cells from blood plasma and body fluids by osmosis. This keeps the cells **hydrated**.
- **Water** is absorbed from the intestines into the blood by osmosis. This ensures that the body obtains the water it needs from food and drink consumed.
- **Water** is reabsorbed from the filtrate in the kidney tubules into the blood by osmosis. This prevents the body from losing too much water.
- **Water** is absorbed from the soil by the root hairs of plants and moves through the cells of roots and leaves by osmosis. This ensures that leaves get a constant supply of water for **photosynthesis**.
- **Water** moves into plant cells by osmosis. This keeps the cells **turgid**, which causes non-woody stems to stand upright and keeps leaves firm.

Active transport

Active transport is the movement of particles through cell membranes against a concentration gradient using energy released in respiration.

During active transport, **energy** released in respiration in the form of ATP (see page 48) is used to move the particles (molecules or ions) through cell membranes from areas of **lower** concentration to areas of **higher** concentration. Active transport allows cells to accumulate high concentrations of important substances, e.g. glucose, amino acids and ions.

Examples of the importance of active transport in living organisms

- Some of the **glucose** and **amino acids** produced in digestion are absorbed from the ileum into the blood by active transport.
- **Useful substances**, e.g. glucose, amino acids, hormones and vitamins, are reabsorbed from the filtrate in kidney tubules into the blood by active transport, which prevents the body losing these substances.
- **Mineral ions** move from the soil into plant roots by active transport.

Revision questions

9 Provide a definition for EACH of the following:

    a simple diffusion   **b** osmosis   **c** active transport

10 Give THREE reasons to support the fact that diffusion is important to living organisms.

11 Explain what happens to an animal cell if it is placed in a solution more dilute than its cytoplasm.

12 You place a plant cell in a solution that is more concentrated than its cell sap and cytoplasm. Draw a labelled diagram to show how the cell would appear when viewed under the microscope after being left for 15 minutes in the solution.

13 Give THREE reasons why osmosis is important to living organisms.

14 Why is the root of a plant unable to absorb mineral ions from the soil if it is given a poison that prevents respiration?

15 Construct a table to compare simple diffusion, osmosis and active transport by referring to their energy requirements, the particles that move, the direction of movement of the particles and their membrane requirements.

2 Photosynthesis, food chains and cycles

Green plants produce their own food by **photosynthesis**. All other living organisms depend either directly or indirectly on green plants for their food. This food is passed on from one living organism to the next through **food chains**.

Photosynthesis

Photosynthesis is the process by which green plants convert carbon dioxide and water into glucose by using energy from sunlight absorbed by chlorophyll in chloroplasts.

Oxygen is produced as a by-product. The process can be summarised by the following **equations**:

word equation:

$$\text{carbon dioxide} + \text{water} \xrightarrow[\text{by chlorophyll}]{\text{energy from sunlight absorbed}} \text{glucose} + \text{oxygen}$$

chemical equation:

$$6CO_2 + 6H_2O \xrightarrow[\text{by chlorophyll}]{\text{energy from sunlight absorbed}} C_6H_{12}O_6 + 6O_2$$

Photosynthesis occurs in any plant structure that contains **chlorophyll**, i.e. which is green; however, it mainly occurs in the **leaves**. Chlorophyll molecules in the **chloroplasts** of leaf cells absorb the energy from sunlight and use it to convert carbon dioxide, absorbed from the air, and water, absorbed from the soil, into **glucose** and **oxygen**.

Fate of the products of photosynthesis

The plant uses the **oxygen** and **glucose** produced during photosynthesis for various different functions.

Oxygen

The **oxygen** is used by the leaf cells in **respiration**. Excess oxygen diffuses out of the leaves into the air.

Glucose

The **glucose** can be used in a variety of ways:
* It can be used by the leaf cells in **respiration** to release energy.
* It can be converted to **starch** by the leaf cells and **stored**. The starch can then be converted back to glucose and used, e.g. during the night.
* It can be converted to other useful **organic substances** by leaf cells, e.g. amino acids and proteins which are used for growth, vitamins or chlorophyll.
* It can be converted to **sucrose** and **transported** to other parts of the plant such as growing parts and storage organs, where it can be converted to:
  * **Glucose**, and used in **respiration** to release energy.
  * **Starch**, and **stored** in seeds, e.g. wheat and rice; in fruits, e.g. breadfruit; and in tubers, e.g. English (Irish) potato and sweet potato.
  * **Amino acids** and **proteins**, by the addition of nitrogen from nitrates and sulfur from sulfates obtained from the soil. Proteins are then used for **growth**.
  * **Lipids**, and **stored**, mainly in seeds, e.g. peanuts and soya beans.

Food chains and webs

Food chains

Energy from sunlight enters living organisms through **photosynthesis** occurring in green plants, which are also known as **producers**. This energy is incorporated into the **organic food molecules** (carbohydrates, proteins and lipids) produced by the plants and is passed on to **consumers** through **food chains**. The organisms in a food chain are linked by **arrows** that show the direction in which the **food** and **energy** flow.

*A **food chain** is a diagram showing the flow of food and energy from one organism to the next in an ecosystem.*

A food chain includes:

* A **producer**, i.e. a green plant.
* A **primary consumer** that eats the producer.
* A **secondary consumer** that eats the primary consumer.
* A **tertiary consumer** that eats the secondary consumer.

Consumers can also be classified according to what they consume:

* **Herbivores** consume plants or plant material only, e.g. cows, grasshoppers, snails, slugs, parrot fish, sea urchins.
* **Carnivores** consume animals or animal material only, e.g. lizards, toads, spiders, centipedes, eagles, octopuses, sharks.
* **Omnivores** consume both plants and animals, or plant and animal material, e.g. hummingbirds, crickets, mice, humans and crayfish.

***Trophic level** refers to the position or level that an organism occupies in a food chain.*

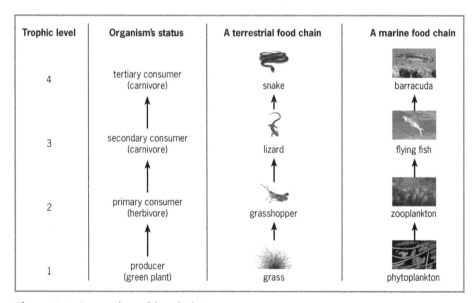

Trophic level	Organism's status	A terrestrial food chain	A marine food chain
4	tertiary consumer (carnivore)	snake	barracuda
3	secondary consumer (carnivore)	lizard	flying fish
2	primary consumer (herbivore)	grasshopper	zooplankton
1	producer (green plant)	grass	phytoplankton

Figure 2.1 *Examples of food chains*

Food chains can also be written horizontally, as in the following example from a **mangrove swamp**:

green algae ⟶ insect larvae ⟶ tilapia ⟶ egret

Food webs

Any ecosystem usually has more than one producer and most consumers have more than one source of food. Consequently, food chains are interconnected to form **food webs**.

*A **food web** is a diagram that links food chains together to show all the pathways along which food and energy flow between organisms in an ecosystem.*

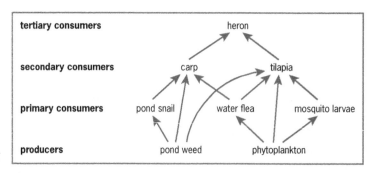

Figure 2.2 *An example of a food web from a freshwater lake*

Dependence of other living organisms on plants

All other living organisms, including **humans**, depend both directly and indirectly on plants for **food** since plants are the only living organisms capable of producing organic food molecules from simple inorganic molecules, i.e. carbon dioxide and water. When animals, including humans, eat any food of **plant origin**, e.g. fruits, vegetables, cereals and nuts, and microorganisms decompose dead plant matter, they are depending **directly** on plants. When animals eat other animals or humans eat any food of **animal origin**, e.g. meat or fish, and microorganisms decompose dead animal matter, they are depending **indirectly** on plants.

Energy transfer in food chains

Not all the **energy** incorporated into organic food molecules made by green plants during photosynthesis is passed along a food chain; some is **used** and some is **lost** at each trophic level.

Some of the food produced by **plants** is **used** by the plants in **respiration**. This releases energy that the plants use in **life processes**. The rest of the food is used by the plants for **growth** or is **stored**.

When plants are eaten by **herbivores**, some of the organic matter that contains energy is **lost** in **faeces** and some is lost in organic **excretory products**, e.g. urea. Some is used in **respiration** during which the stored energy is released and used in **life processes**, or is lost as **heat**. The remaining food that contains energy is used to **build body tissues** or is **stored**, and is then passed on to the next trophic level when the herbivores are consumed. This then continues at each trophic level in a food chain.

Organisms that are not consumed eventually **die**. These dead organisms, together with the organic matter in faeces and excretory products, are **decomposed** by decomposers (bacteria and fungi), and they release the stored energy during **respiration**. **Energy**, therefore, flows from producers to consumers and decomposers in **one direction** and is not recycled. In general, only about **1 to 2%** of the energy from sunlight is absorbed by plants and used in photosynthesis, and only about **10%** of the energy from one trophic level is transferred to the next level.

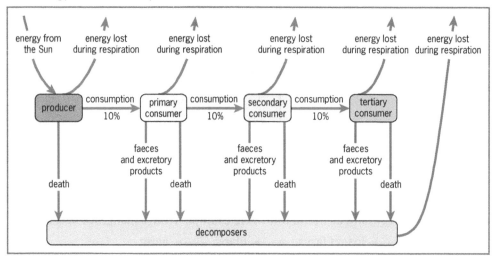

Figure 2.3 *Energy flow through a food chain*

Ecological pyramids

Because there is less energy and biomass (mass of biological matter) at each trophic level in a food chain, fewer organisms can be supported at each level. **Energy**, **biomass** and the **number of organisms** at successive levels can be represented by **ecological pyramids** in which the **width** of each bar is proportional to the quantity of the factor being measured. Due to the loss of energy and biomass at each level, food chains rarely have more than **four** or **five** trophic levels.

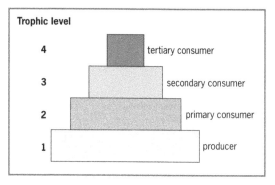

Figure 2.4 *Pyramid of energy, biomass or numbers*

Bioaccumulation and biomagnification, and their effects on human health

- **Bioaccumulation** refers to the process by which **toxic chemicals** or **toxins**, e.g. mercury, lead, arsenic, cyanide and various pesticides, gradually **build up** inside the tissues of living organisms, especially in **adipose (fat) tissue**, because they are not excreted or broken down by the body.

- **Biomagnification** refers to the process by which toxic chemicals **increase** in concentration in the tissues of organisms from one trophic level to the next **up food chains**. This is because, going up food chains, the organisms are likely to consume increasingly larger quantities of food through their lifetimes.

Bioaccumulation and **biomagnification**, working together, cause toxins to reach **harmful levels** in top consumers, including **humans** who eat meat and fish, especially large, long-living fish, e.g. tuna, marlin, shark and swordfish. Harmful effects include damage to the nervous and circulatory systems, liver and kidney damage, and reproductive and developmental problems. Some toxins may also cause cancer.

Recycling in nature

The different **chemical elements** which make up the bodies of all living organisms, e.g. carbon, oxygen and nitrogen, are continually **cycled** through these living organisms and their physical environment. Unlike the energy from the sun, these elements are present in nature in **finite** amounts; therefore, **recycling** is essential to prevent them from gradually running out.

Decomposers are essential for recycling. These are microorganisms, i.e. bacteria and fungi, which feed on dead and waste organic matter causing it to **decompose**. Decomposers are also known as **saprophytes**.

The carbon cycle

The cycling of **carbon (C) atoms** occurs by them being converted into different **carbon-containing compounds**, including **carbon dioxide (CO_2)** present in the **air**, and various **organic compounds**, mainly carbohydrates, proteins and lipids, present in **living organisms**. This cycling is **important** because it ensures plants have a continuous supply of carbon dioxide to make food by photosynthesis, and that animals and decomposers have a continuous supply of food.

- **Carbon dioxide** is **removed** from the air and converted to organic compounds by green plants during **photosynthesis.**

- **Carbon dioxide** is **returned** to the air by:
  - **Respiration** occurring in all living organisms including plants, animals and decomposers.
  - **Combustion**, mainly of **fossil fuels** such as coal, oil and natural gas, though all materials containing organic compounds release carbon dioxide when burned, e.g. wood and paper.

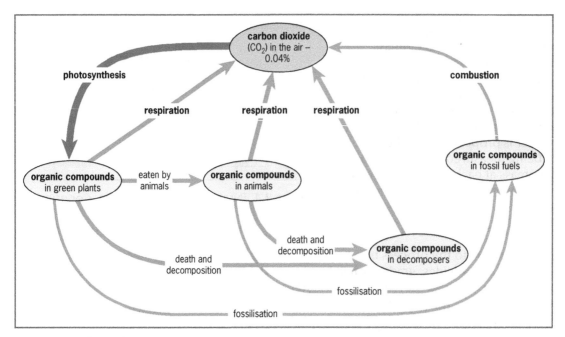

Figure 2.5 *The carbon cycle*

The greenhouse effect and global warming

Carbon dioxide, released during respiration and combustion, is known as a **greenhouse gas**. This, together with other greenhouse gases, e.g. methane, nitrous oxide (N_2O) and water vapour, which are present in the Earth's atmosphere, cause warming of the Earth known as the **greenhouse effect**.

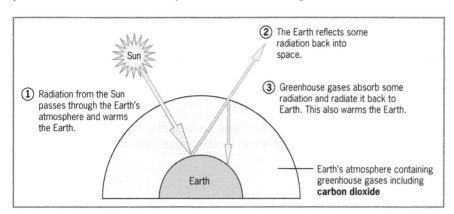

Figure 2.6 *The greenhouse effect*

An **increase** in **carbon dioxide**, caused by burning fossil fuels and deforestation, is **enhancing** the greenhouse effect and contributing to a gradual increase in the Earth's temperature. This warming is known as **global warming**, and it is leading to **global climate change**. Global warming is starting to cause glaciers and polar ice sheets to melt, to change global weather patterns, to cause more severe weather events and natural hazards, and to create changes in ecosystems. These effects are starting to have negative impacts on **human health** and **well-being**, including the following.

- An increase in the incidence of **vector-borne diseases**, e.g. dengue fever; **food-borne diseases**, e.g. gastroenteritis; and **water-borne diseases**, e.g. cholera.
- An increase in cases of **non-communicable diseases**, e.g. respiratory diseases and cardiovascular diseases, **allergic illnesses** and **heat-related conditions**, e.g. heat exhaustion and heatstroke.

- Shortages of fish and livestock, crop failures, decreased nutritional value of food and disruption of food distribution, all leading to **decreased food security** and **food shortages.**
- A decrease in quantity and quality of **water supplies.**
- Injury or loss of life, damage to property, a loss of assets, infrastructure and public services, environmental degradation, an increase in mental health and social issues, and an overall **decrease in well-being** associated with more extreme weather events and natural hazards.
- Increased **coastal erosion** and **flooding** of low-lying coastal areas and islands due to sea level rises caused by melting of polar ice sheets and glaciers, resulting in the loss of property and assets, damage to infrastructure and crops, and displacement of coastal and island communities.

Revision questions

1 Define the term 'photosynthesis' and give a word and a chemical equation to summarise the process.

2 Suggest FOUR ways that a plant can make use of the glucose produced in photosynthesis.

3 a What is a food chain?

  b Some aphids were observed on the tomato plants in a garden and ladybird beetles were seen feeding on the aphids. The ladybirds were, in turn, being eaten by dragonflies which were, themselves, being fed on by toads. Use this information to draw a food chain for the organisms in the garden.

4 From the organisms in item 3 b above, identify:

  a a carnivore   b a herbivore   c a producer

  d a primary consumer   e a secondary consumer

5 Why are all other living organisms dependent on plants for food?

6 When Jared eats a barracuda he only gets about 10% of the energy that the barracuda obtained from the flying fish it ate. Explain THREE reasons why so little energy is passed on to Jared.

7 What does an ecological pyramid show?

8 Distinguish between bioaccumulation and biomagnification and explain how they can affect human health.

9 a Outline how carbon is recycled in nature.

  b Explain the importance of recycling carbon in nature.

10 a Explain what is meant by the term 'global warming' and how it is caused.

  b Give THREE ways in which global warming is impacting on human health and well-being.

Exam-style questions – Chapters 1 to 2

Structured questions

1   **a)** Figure 1 shows a generalised animal cell.

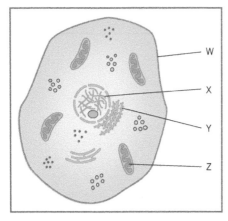

Figure 1 *A generalised animal cell*

   i)   Name the structures labelled W and X.   **(2 marks)**

   ii)   State ONE function of EACH organelle labelled Y and Z.   **(2 marks)**

   iii) In what way does the property of structure W differ from the cell wall
            in a plant cell?   **(2 marks)**

b) Figure 2 shows two different specialised cells found in the human body.

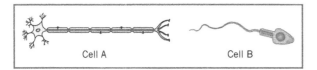

Figure 2 *Specialised cells found in the human body*

   i)   Identify cell A.   **(1 mark)**

   ii)   Explain TWO ways in which the structure of cell B makes it suitable for
            its function.   **(2 marks)**

   iii) Why is it important that the human body is made of specialised cells?   **(1 mark)**

c) **i)**   Anya thinks that a virus is a living organism. Do you agree with her?
                 Give ONE reason for your opinion.   **(1 mark)**

        ii)   Anton and Elijah are playing a game of tennis. Identify and explain
                 TWO characteristics of living organisms that they are displaying.   **(4 marks)**

                                                                                Total 15 marks

2 **a)** Figure 3 summarises the process of photosynthesis.

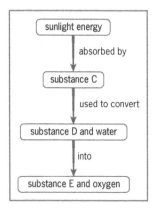

Figure 3 *The process of photosynthesis*

i) Identify substances C, D and E. (3 marks)

ii) Explain TWO ways in which the leaves of plants use substance E. (2 marks)

iii) Tasha tells Mia that they both depend directly and indirectly on plants to survive. Provide a suitable explanation to support what Tasha said. (2 marks)

b) Table 1 below shows the food sources of several organisms found in the ocean.

Table 1 *Food sources of some organisms found in the ocean*

Organism	Food source
zooplankton	phytoplankton
shrimp	phytoplankton
jellyfish	zooplankton and shrimp
crab	shrimp
sea turtle	crab and jellyfish

i) Using only the information contained in Table 1, construct a food web for the organisms. (2 marks)

ii) Which organism in the food web would you expect to be present in the LOWEST numbers? (1 mark)

iii) Outline the reason for your answer to **b) ii)** above. (3 marks)

c) In 2015, the Paris Climate Agreement to substantially reduce global greenhouse emissions in an effort to limit global temperature increase this century to 1.5 °C was adopted by nearly every nation in the world. Suggest TWO reasons why so many nations adopted the Agreement. (2 marks)

Total 15 marks

Structured essay question

3　**a)**　Jacinta set up the apparatus in Figure 4 below and observed that the level of the meniscus in the capillary tube gradually rose up the tube.

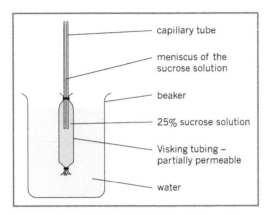

Figure 4 *Apparatus used to study the movement of particles*

　　i)　Give an account of why the meniscus gradually rose up the capillary tube.　　**(4 marks)**

　　ii)　Explain TWO differences between the process occurring in Jacinta's apparatus and the process of diffusion. At the beginning of your answer, name the process occurring in the apparatus.　　**(5 marks)**

b)　**i)**　Define the term 'active transport'.　　**(2 marks)**

　　ii)　By referring to TWO different places in your body where active transport occurs, explain its importance to you.　　**(4 marks)**

Total 15 marks

Section B – Life processes

3 Nutrition

Humans need a variety of **nutrients** to provide them with energy, to enable them to grow and develop, and to keep them healthy. These nutrients include carbohydrates, proteins, lipids, vitamins and minerals, and they are contained in the **food** we eat. After consumption, this food must be broken down in our alimentary canal into a form that is useful for our body's activities. This is carried out by a process known as **digestion**.

Nutrition is the process by which living organisms obtain or make food.

The human diet

The **food** an animal eats is called its **diet**. The human diet must contain the following:

- **Carbohydrates**, **proteins** and **lipids**, also known as **macronutrients**.
- **Vitamins** and **minerals**, also known as **micronutrients**.
- **Water** and **dietary fibre (roughage)**.

Macronutrients, their structures and properties

Macronutrients are chemical substances that provide the body with energy and are required in relatively large amounts in the diet.

Carbohydrates

Carbohydrates include **reducing sugars**, **non-reducing sugars** and **starch**. They are **molecules** composed of carbon, hydrogen and oxygen atoms. The ratio of hydrogen atoms to oxygen atoms is always 2:1. Based on their **chemical structure**, carbohydrates can be classified into **three** groups: **monosaccharides**, **disaccharides** and **polysaccharides**.

- **Monosaccharides** are the simplest carbohydrate molecules. Many have the formula $C_6H_{12}O_6$. All monosaccharides are reducing sugars (see Table 3.1, page 20).
- **Disaccharides** are formed by chemically joining two monosaccharide molecules together. They have the formula $C_{12}H_{22}O_{11}$. All disaccharides are reducing sugars except sucrose, which is a non-reducing sugar.
- **Polysaccharides** are formed by joining many monosaccharide molecules into straight or branched chains. Polysaccharides include starch, cellulose and glycogen (animal starch).

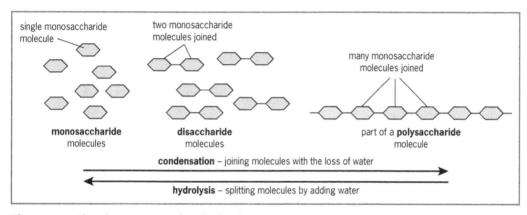

Figure 3.1 *The three types of carbohydrates*

Table 3.1 *Properties of different carbohydrates*

Carbohydrate	Physical and chemical properties	Examples
Reducing sugars	Have a **sweet** taste. **Soluble** in water. React with **Benedict's solution**.	Glucose (a monosaccharide) Fructose (a monosaccharide) Galactose (a monosaccharide) Maltose (a disaccharide) Lactose (a disaccharide)
Non-reducing sugars	Have a **sweet** taste. **Soluble** in water. Do not react with Benedict's solution.	Sucrose (a disaccharide)
Starch	Does not have a sweet taste. **Insoluble** in water. Reacts with **iodine solution**.	

Proteins

Proteins are **molecules** composed of carbon, hydrogen, oxygen, nitrogen, and sometimes sulfur and phosphorus atoms. These atoms form small molecules known as **amino acids**. There are 20 different common amino acids. Protein molecules are formed by joining hundreds or thousands of amino acid molecules together in long chains.

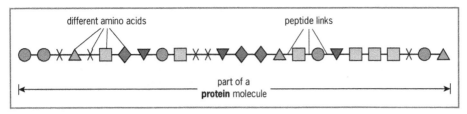

Figure 3.2 *Part of a protein molecule*

Proteins have the following **properties:**

- Their chemical structure can be changed by heat or certain other chemicals, i.e. they can be **denatured**.
- Some are **globular** in structure and are **soluble** in water, e.g. haemoglobin and albumen, others are **fibrous** and are **insoluble**, e.g. collagen and keratin.
- They react with **biuret reagent.**

Lipids

Lipids are fats and oils. They are **molecules** composed of carbon, hydrogen and oxygen atoms. Their molecules have fewer oxygen atoms than carbohydrate molecules, e.g. beef fat has the formula $C_{57}H_{110}O_6$. Each lipid molecule is made up of **four** smaller molecules joined together; three **fatty acid** molecules and one **glycerol** molecule.

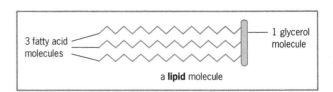

Figure 3.3 *A lipid molecule*

Lipids feel greasy, are **insoluble** in water and they leave a **grease spot** on paper.

Carbohydrates, proteins and lipids are organic compounds because they contain carbon, hydrogen and oxygen atoms in their molecules. They supply the body with energy and the materials for growth, to repair damaged tissues and to manufacture biologically important molecules.

Table 3.2 *Sources and functions of carbohydrates, proteins and lipids*

Class	Sources	Functions
Carbohydrates	**Sugars:** fruits, cakes, sweets, jams, sugar-sweetened beverages **Starch:** yams, potatoes, rice, pasta, bread	• To provide **energy** (16 kJ g^{-1}): energy is easily released when respired. • For **storage:** glycogen granules are stored in the cytoplasm of many cells.
Proteins	Fish, lean meat, milk, cheese, eggs, peas, beans, nuts	• To make **new cells** for growth and to repair damaged tissues. • To make **enzymes** that catalyse (speed up) reactions in the body. • To make **hormones** that control various processes in the body. • To make **antibodies** to fight disease. • To provide **energy** (17 kJ g^{-1}): used only when stored carbohydrates and lipids have been used up.
Lipids	Butter, vegetable oils, margarine, nuts, fatty meats	• To make **cell membranes** of newly formed cells. • To provide **energy** (38 kJ g^{-1}): used after carbohydrates because their metabolism is more complex and takes longer. • For **storage:** fat is stored under the skin and around organs. • For **insulation:** fat under the skin acts as an insulator.

Hidden sugars and natural sugars

Hidden sugars are refined sugars which are added to foods, including breakfast bars and cereals, yoghurt, fruit juices, sauces, dressings, condiments, baked goods, sugar-sweetened beverages and low-fat diet foods. Hidden or added sugars provide the body with energy, but they have no other nutritional benefits. Consuming more than the recommended 25 g of added sugar per day can cause a person to gain weight, leading to obesity and obesity-related conditions (see pages 27 and 142), and can speed up tooth decay. Sugar-sweetened beverages such as sodas, fruit drinks, sports drinks and sweetened waters contain some of the highest amounts of added sugars.

Certain foods, particularly fresh fruits and vegetables, contain natural sugars. These foods can provide the body with all the sugar it needs daily. They also have health benefits because the sugars are less concentrated, and fruits and vegetables are high in fibre and provide vitamins, minerals and water. Many Caribbean fruits and vegetables such as bananas, mangoes, pomegranates, sugar apples, pineapples, plantains, sweet potatoes, pumpkins, onions and carrots are good sources of natural sugars.

Recognising carbohydrates, proteins and lipids

Tests can be performed in the laboratory to identify carbohydrates, proteins and lipids. Apart from the tests for lipids, the tests are usually carried out on about 2 cm^3 of a solution of the test substance in a test tube.

Table 3.3 *Laboratory tests to identify carbohydrates, proteins and lipids*

Food substance	Test	Positive result
Reducing sugars	Add an equal volume of **Benedict's solution** and shake. Heat the mixture.	An **orange-red** precipitate forms.
Non-reducing sugars	Add a few drops of dilute **hydrochloric acid** and heat for 1 minute. Add **sodium hydrogencarbonate** until effervescence stops. Add an equal volume of Benedict's solution and shake. Heat the mixture.	An **orange-red** precipitate forms. *Explanation:* The acid splits the disaccharide molecules into monosaccharide molecules, which then react with the Benedict's solution.
Starch	Add a few drops of **iodine solution** and shake.	Solution turns **blue-black**.
Protein – the biuret test	Add an equal volume of **sodium hydroxide solution** and shake. Add drops of dilute **copper sulfate solution** and shake. Or add an equal volume of **biuret reagent** and shake.	Solution turns **purple**.
Lipid – the emulsion test	Place 4 cm³ of **ethanol** in a dry test tube. Add 1 drop of test substance and shake. Add an equal volume of **water** and shake.	A **milky-white** emulsion forms.
Lipid – the grease spot test	Rub a drop of test substance onto **absorbent paper**. Leave for 10 minutes.	A **translucent mark** (grease spot) remains.

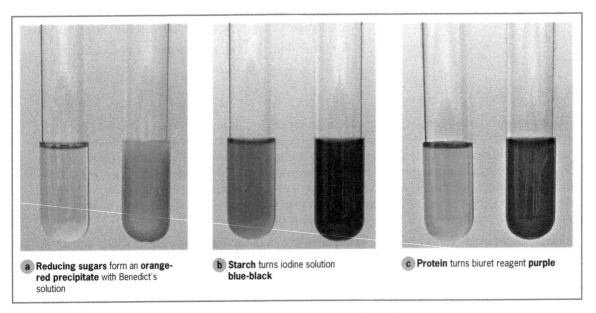

a **Reducing sugars** form an **orange-red precipitate** with Benedict's solution

b **Starch** turns iodine solution **blue-black**

c **Protein** turns biuret reagent **purple**

Figure 3.4 *Laboratory tests to identify reducing sugars, starch and protein*

Micronutrients

Micronutrients are chemical substances that are required in very small amounts in the diet.

Vitamins

Vitamins are **organic compounds** that are essential for **healthy growth** and **development**. Vitamins can be classified based on whether they dissolve in water or fat.

- **Group B vitamins** and **vitamin C** are **water-soluble**.
- **Vitamins A**, **D**, **E** and **K** are **fat-soluble**.

Table 3.4 *The sources and functions of some important vitamins required by the human body*

Vitamin	Sources	Functions
Vitamin A	Liver, cod liver oil, yellow and orange vegetables and fruits, e.g. carrots and pumpkin, green leafy vegetables, e.g. spinach	• Helps to keep the skin, cornea and mucous membranes healthy. • Helps vision in dim light (night vision). • Strengthens the immune system.
Vitamin B$_1$	Whole-grain cereals and bread, brown rice, peas, beans, nuts, yeast extract, lean pork	• Aids in respiration to produce energy. • Important for the proper functioning of the nervous system.
Vitamin C	West Indian cherries, citrus fruits, raw green vegetables	• Keeps tissues healthy, especially the skin and connective tissue. • Strengthens the immune system. • Helps the body absorb iron in the ileum.
Vitamin D	Oily fish, eggs, cod liver oil. Also made in the body by the action of sunlight on the skin	• Promotes the absorption of calcium and phosphorus in the ileum. • Helps build and maintain strong bones and teeth. • Strengthens the immune system.
Vitamin E	Nuts, seeds, vegetable oils, wheat germ, green leafy vegetables	• Acts as an antioxidant helping to protect cells from damage caused by chemicals called free radicals. • Strengthens the immune system. • Inhibits clot formation in arteries.
Vitamin K	Green leafy vegetables, liver	• Helps blood to clot at cuts.

Minerals

Minerals are **inorganic substances** that are essential for **healthy growth** and **development**.

Table 3.5 *The sources and functions of some important minerals required by the human body*

Mineral	Sources	Functions
Calcium (Ca)	Dairy products, e.g. milk, cheese and yoghurt; green vegetables, e.g. broccoli.	• To build and maintain healthy bones and teeth. • Helps blood to clot at cuts.
Iron (Fe)	Red meat, liver, eggs, beans, nuts, dark green leafy vegetables	• To make haemoglobin, the red pigment in red blood cells. Haemoglobin transports oxygen around the body for use in respiration.
Magnesium (Mg)	Nuts, green leafy vegetables, whole-grain cereals, peas and beans	• Helps enzymes to function in over 300 biochemical reactions in the body. • Helps maintain strong bones. • Helps maintain normal nerve and muscle function.
Iodine (I)	Seafood, e.g. fish, shellfish and seaweed; iodised table salt; milk; eggs	• Used by the thyroid gland to make the hormone thyroxine (see Table 8.5, page 91).
Phosphorous (P)	Whole grains, protein-rich foods, e.g. milk, cheese, meat, poultry, fish and nuts.	• To build and maintain healthy bones and teeth. • To make ATP, an energy-rich compound (see page 48).
Sodium (Na)	Table salt, cheese, cured meats, many packaged and processed foods	• Needed for the transmission of nerve impulses and muscle contraction. • Helps maintain the correct concentration of body fluids.
Fluorine (Fl)	Fluoridated tap water, fluoride toothpaste	• Strengthens tooth enamel, making it more resistant to decay.

Hidden salt

Most **packaged** and **processed foods** contain **hidden salt**, usually referred to as **sodium.** These foods include cured meats, sausages, cheeses, pickles, dressings, condiments, savoury snacks, cereals, breads, canned foods and sodas. Consuming more than the recommended 2.3 g of sodium daily can increase a person's risk of developing **hypertension** and **coronary heart disease**, and of suffering from a **heart attack** or **stroke.**

Vitamin and mineral deficiency diseases

A shortage or lack of any of the essential vitamins or minerals in the diet can lead to health problems and certain **deficiency diseases.**

Table 3.6 *Some vitamin and mineral deficiency diseases*

Disease	Cause	Symptoms	Treatment
Night blindness	Deficiency of vitamin A	• Poor vision in dim light. • Vision adapts slowly between bright and dim conditions.	• Increase the intake of foods rich in vitamin A. • Take vitamin A supplements.
Rickets (in children)	Deficiency of vitamin D and/or calcium	• Soft, weak, painful, deformed bones, especially limb bones. • Bow legs.	• Increase the intake of foods rich in vitamin D and calcium. • Take vitamin D and calcium supplements. • Increase exposure to sunlight.

Disease	Cause	Symptoms	Treatment
Iron-deficiency anaemia	Deficiency of iron	• A reduced number of red blood cells in the blood. • Pale complexion. • Tiredness. • Lack of energy.	• Increase the intake of foods rich in iron. • Take iron supplements. • Increase the intake of foods rich in vitamin C.
Goitre	Deficiency of iodine	• Swelling of the thyroid gland at the base of the neck. • Hoarseness and a cough. • Difficulty swallowing or breathing.	• Increase the intake of foods rich in iodine. • Take iodine supplements. • Use iodised table salt.

Other vitamin deficiency diseases include **beri-beri**, caused by a shortage of **vitamin B₁**, and **scurvy**, caused by a shortage of **vitamin C**.

Water

Water is essential in the diet since the human body is about **65% water**.

- Water acts as a **solvent** to **dissolve** chemicals in cells so that they can **react**.

- Water acts as a **solvent** to **dissolve** substances so that they can be **transported** around the body, e.g. products of digestion are dissolved in blood plasma.

- Water acts as a **solvent** to **dissolve** waste substances so that they can be **excreted** from the body, e.g. urine contains dissolved urea.

- Water acts as a **reactant**, e.g. in **hydrolysis** which occurs during digestion of food.

- Water acts as a **coolant**, removing heat from the body when it **evaporates** from sweat.

Figure 3.5 *A child with rickets*

Dietary fibre (roughage)

Dietary fibre is food that **cannot be digested**. It consists mainly of the cellulose of plant cell walls, lignin of plant xylem vessels, husks of brown rice and bran of wholegrain cereals. Fruits, vegetables and grains are excellent sources of dietary fibre.

Dietary fibre has several **health benefits**.

- It adds **bulk** to the food, which stimulates **peristalsis** (see page 36) so that food is kept moving through the digestive system. This helps prevent **constipation** and reduces the risk of **colorectal (bowel) cancer**.

- It helps make a person feel **full**. This **reduces overall** food intake, which helps reduce **obesity**. Insufficient fibre intake is linked with a greater risk of developing obesity.

Figure 3.6 *Fruit and cereals are rich in dietary fibre*

- It **lowers cholesterol**, reducing the risk of **cardiovascular disease**, and it reduces the risk of a person developing **type 2 diabetes**.

Constipation and diarrhoea

Constipation is a condition of the bowels (colon and rectum) in which the faeces are dry and hard, difficult and often painful to pass, and passed infrequently. **Diarrhoea** is a condition in which faeces are passed frequently and in a liquid form. It is usually a symptom of **gastroenteritis** (see page 137).

Table 3.7 *Common causes and effects of constipation and diarrhoea*

Condition	Causes	Effects
Constipation	• Not eating enough dietary fibre. • Not drinking enough water or other fluids. • Not exercising or being inactive. • A change in diet or daily routine. • Ignoring the urge to defaecate. • Stress, anxiety or depression, and certain medications.	• Bloating. • Abdominal pain. • Haemorrhoids (piles). • Faecal impaction, in which the faeces become stuck in the colon and rectum. • Colorectal (bowel) cancer.
Diarrhoea	• Being infected with certain viruses, e.g. norovirus. • Being infected with certain bacteria, e.g. *Salmonella, E. coli, Shigella*. • Being infected with an intestinal parasite, e.g. *Giardia*. • Conditions such as irritable bowel syndrome, colorectal cancer, coeliac or Crohn's disease.	• Dehydration. • Electrolyte imbalance. • Impaired kidney function (kidney failure). • Malnutrition in severe cases.

Proper hygiene in food preparation

Food poisoning, caused by eating contaminated food, is a common way of becoming infected with pathogens that cause **diarrhoea**. Chances of getting food poisoning can be reduced by practising **good food hygiene** when preparing food:

- **Wash** hands, utensils and food preparation surfaces regularly.
- **Wash** fruits and vegetables thoroughly in clean water before cooking or eating.
- Keep uncooked foods, especially meat, poultry and fish, **separate** from ready-to-eat foods.
- Keep **pests** that carry diseases away from food, especially flies, cockroaches and rodents.
- **Cook** food thoroughly, especially meat, poultry and fish.
- **Defrost** frozen food thoroughly and safely, before cooking. This should be done in a refrigerator.

A balanced diet

*A **balanced diet** is a **diet** that contains carbohydrates, proteins, lipids, vitamins, minerals, water and dietary fibre in the **correct proportions** to maintain **growth** and **good health**.*

Humans must consume a **balanced diet** each day for the following reasons.

- To supply the body with enough **energy** for daily activities.
- To supply the body with the correct materials for **growth**, **repair** and **development**, and to **manufacture** biologically important molecules.
- To keep the body in a **healthy state**.

A balanced diet should contain a **variety** of foods selected from each of the six different **Caribbean food groups** shown in Figure 3.7. Each group contains foods that supply similar nutrients in similar proportions. The **size** of each sector indicates the relative amount of each group that should be eaten daily.

Factors affecting dietary needs

The amount of **energy** required daily from the diet depends on a person's **age**, **occupation** and **sex**. If energy input exceeds energy output, a person will **gain weight**. If energy output exceeds energy input, a person will **lose weight**. In general, daily energy requirements:

- **Increase** as **age increases** up to adulthood. They then remain fairly constant up to old age when less energy is required daily.

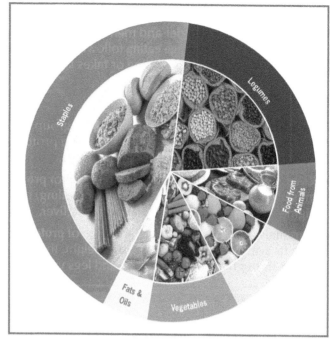

Figure 3.7 *The six Caribbean food groups*

- **Increase** as **activity increases**, e.g. a manual labourer requires more energy than a person working in an office.

- Are **higher** in **males** than in females of the same age and occupation.

- **Increase** in a female when she is **pregnant** or **breastfeeding**.

Malnutrition

Malnutrition is the result of eating a diet that does not contain the right amount of one or more nutrients.

Malnutrition can be caused in **two** ways.

- By eating a diet in which one or more nutrients are **lacking**, known as **undernutrition**.
- By eating a diet in which one or more nutrients are in **excess**, known as **overnutrition**.

Malnutrition can lead to several **serious conditions** outlined below.

Obesity

Obesity is characterised by an excessive accumulation and storage of **fat** in the body. It is generally caused by the excessive consumption of energy rich foods high in **carbohydrates**, particularly **sugar**, and/or **fat**, especially animal fat, and a lack of physical activity. Obesity increases a person's risk of developing **hypertension, coronary heart disease, type 2 diabetes, osteoarthritis** and some **cancers**, and suffering from a **heart attack** or **stroke** (see page 142). **Childhood obesity** is increasing in the Caribbean and poses serious problems since heavier children have an elevated risk of continued rapid increase in weight as they grow older.

Anorexia nervosa

Anorexia is an eating disorder and serious mental health condition where a person deliberately keeps their body weight as **low** as possible by eating very little, exercising excessively, and often taking laxatives or vomiting after eating. It mainly affects girls and young women, and can eventually lead to death.

Bulimia is an eating disorder and mental health condition where a person tries to **control** their weight by repeating a cycle of **binge eating** followed by **purging**. The person eats large quantities of food very quickly and then induces vomiting or takes laxatives to get rid of the food to avoid gaining weight.

Protein-energy malnutrition (PEM)

Protein-energy malnutrition (PEM) refers to a group of related disorders, including **kwashiorkor** and **marasmus**, which are caused by an inadequate protein and/or energy intake. Both disorders mainly affect young children in developing countries.

- **Kwashiorkor** is caused by a severe shortage of **protein** in the diet. Its symptoms include loss of muscle mass, failure to grow, oedema (swelling) of the abdomen and legs, changes in skin and hair pigmentation, and fat accumulation in the liver.

- **Marasmus** is caused by a severe shortage of **protein** and **energy rich foods** such as carbohydrates in the diet. Its symptoms include low body weight, thin face with sunken eyes, ribs and shoulders clearly visible through the skin, thin arms and legs with very little muscle and fat, dry skin and brittle hair.

Figure 3.8 *A child with kwashiorkor*

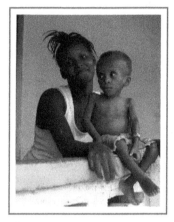

Figure 3.9 *A child with marasmus*

Body mass index (BMI) and waist circumference

Body mass index and **waist circumference** can be used as indicators of the amount of **body fat** a person has. **BMI** compares the **mass** of a person, measured in kilograms, to their **height**, measured in metres, using the following formula:

$$\text{body mass index (kg per m}^2) = \frac{\text{body mass (in kilograms)}}{\text{height (in metres)} \times \text{height (in metres)}}$$

Table 3.8 *Classification of adults based on their body mass index*

Body mass index in kg per m²	Condition
18.4 and below	Underweight
18.5 to 24.9	Healthy weight
25.0 to 29.9	Overweight
30.0 to 39.9	Obese
40.0 and above	Severely obese

A person with a BMI below 18.5 kg per m² may need to put on some weight and a person with a BMI greater than 30.0 kg per m² is at risk of developing **obesity-related** health conditions.

Waist circumference can also be used to assess a person's risk of developing **obesity-related** conditions. **Fat** accumulated in a person's abdominal region can increase the person's risk of developing **hypertension, coronary heart disease** and **type 2 diabetes**. This risk greatly increases in a non-pregnant **female** adult with a waist circumference greater than **89 cm** (35 inches) and a male adult with a waist circumference greater than **102 cm** (40 inches).

Revision questions

1 Construct a table to give TWO physical properties, TWO sources and TWO functions of EACH of the following macronutrients in the human diet: starch, proteins, lipids.

2 Distinguish between a reducing sugar and a non-reducing sugar and give a named example of EACH.

3 Outline the health risks associated with consuming 3 or 4 sodas daily.

4 You are given three solutions labelled X, Y and Z and told that they contain starch, glucose and gelatin (a protein), respectively. Describe THREE laboratory tests you could perform to confirm what you are told about X, Y and Z.

5 Classify vitamins based on their solubility in water or fat.

6 Construct a table to give ONE source and the major functions of the following micronutrients: vitamin B_1, vitamin C, vitamin E, iron, fluorine and magnesium.

7 Identify the cause, symptoms and treatment of EACH of the following:

  a night blindness   **b** rickets   **c** iron-deficiency anaemia

8 Identify THREE reasons why water is important in the diet.

9 Outline the consequences of Annette not consuming enough dietary fibre daily.

10 Food poisoning can result in a person suffering from diarrhoea. Suggest THREE consequences of diarrhoea and THREE ways a person can reduce their chances of food poisoning.

11 **a** What is a balanced diet?
  b Identify THREE factors that affect a person's daily energy requirements.

12 **a** What is malnutrition?
  b Name THREE serious conditions that can result from malnutrition.

13 **a** Keenan is 1.5 m tall and weighs 75 kg. Determine his body mass index (BMI).
  b What can you deduce about Keenan?
  c What other measurement could you take to confirm your deduction in **b**?

Digestion

*Digestion is the process by which food is **broken down** into a form that is useful for body activities.*

To be **useful**, large food molecules such as polysaccharides, disaccharides, proteins and lipids must be broken down into **simple**, **soluble food molecules**, namely monosaccharides, amino acids, fatty acids and glycerol. Digestion occurs in the **alimentary canal** which is a tube, 8 to 9 metres long with muscular walls, running from the **mouth** to the **anus**. The alimentary canal and its various associated organs including the liver, gall bladder and pancreas make up the **digestive system** (see Figure 3.16, page 35).

Digestion involves the following **two** processes.

- **Mechanical digestion** during which large **pieces** of food are broken down into smaller pieces. Mechanical digestion begins in the **mouth** where food is chewed by the **teeth**, and it continues in the **stomach** where contractions of the stomach walls churn the food.
- **Chemical digestion** during which large, usually insoluble **food molecules** are broken down into small, soluble food molecules by **enzymes** (see pages 32–36). Chemical digestion begins in the **mouth** and is completed in the **small intestine**.

Teeth and mechanical digestion

The importance of teeth in digestion

When food is **chewed** or **masticated**, the teeth break up **large pieces** of food into **smaller pieces**. This is important for the following reasons.

- It gives the pieces of food a **larger surface area** for digestive enzymes to act on, making chemical digestion quicker and easier.
- It makes food easier to **swallow**.

Types of teeth

Humans have **four** different types of teeth, **incisors**, **canines**, **premolars** and **molars**, and they have **two** sets of these teeth in their lifetime.

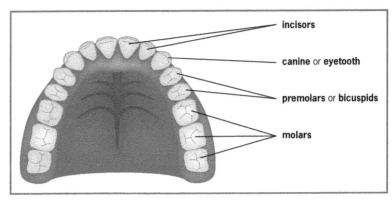

- **Milk teeth** start to appear from about 6 months and start falling out from about 6 years old. They consist of **8** incisors, **4** canines and **8** molars.

Figure 3.10 *Teeth of the upper jaw of an adult human*

- **Permanent teeth** replace the 20 lost milk teeth and an additional 12 develop. They consist of **8** incisors, **4** canines, **8** premolars and **12** molars.

Table 3.9 *The different types of teeth in humans*

Type	Position	Shape		Functions
Incisor	At the front of the jaw.	Chisel-shaped with sharp, thin edges.	crown / root	To cut food. To bite off pieces of food.
Canine (eye tooth)	Next to the incisors.	Cone-shaped and pointed.		To grip food. To tear off pieces of food.
Premolar	At the side of the jaw next to the canines.	Have a fairly broad surface with two pointed cusps.	cusp / root	To crush and grind food.
Molar	At the back of the jaw next to the premolars.	Have a broad surface with 4 or 5 pointed cusps.		To crush and grind food.

Tooth structure

A tooth is divided into **two** parts; the **crown**, which is the part above the jaw, and the **root**, which is the part embedded in the jawbone. The internal structure of all teeth is similar. The crown is covered with **enamel** and the root with a thin layer of **cement** and the **periodontal membrane**. The bulk of the tooth is composed of **dentine** and the **pulp cavity** occupies the centre. **Nerves** and **blood vessels** run throughout the pulp cavity.

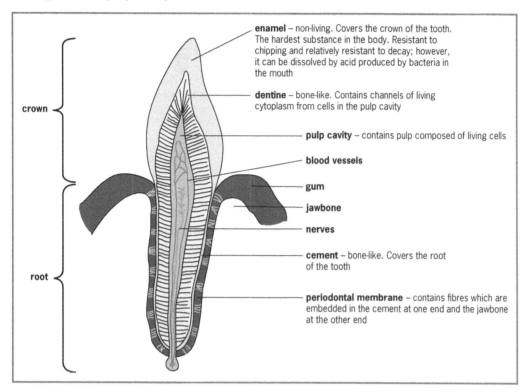

enamel – non-living. Covers the crown of the tooth. The hardest substance in the body. Resistant to chipping and relatively resistant to decay; however, it can be dissolved by acid produced by bacteria in the mouth

dentine – bone-like. Contains channels of living cytoplasm from cells in the pulp cavity

pulp cavity – contains pulp composed of living cells

blood vessels

gum

jawbone

nerves

cement – bone-like. Covers the root of the tooth

periodontal membrane – contains fibres which are embedded in the cement at one end and the jawbone at the other end

crown

root

★ **Figure 3.11** *Internal structure of a canine tooth*

Table 3.10 *Functions of the main parts of a tooth*

Structure	Functions
Enamel	Protects the tooth against decay. Insulates the tooth against hot and cold foods. Provides a hard surface for chewing.
Dentine	Forms the bulk of the tooth. Supports the enamel. Protects the pulp.
Pulp cavity	Blood vessels supply living cells of the tooth with food and oxygen, and remove carbon dioxide and other waste. Nerves are sensitive to pain, hot and cold.
Cement	Covers the dentine in the root of the tooth.
Periodontal membrane	Anchors the root of the tooth in the jawbone. Allows slight movement for shock absorption.

Tooth decay (dental caries)

Tooth decay occurs when bacteria, saliva and food particles in the mouth form a sticky layer on teeth and gums called **plaque**. **Bacteria** in the plaque feed on **sugars** in food and make **acid**, which eats away at teeth.

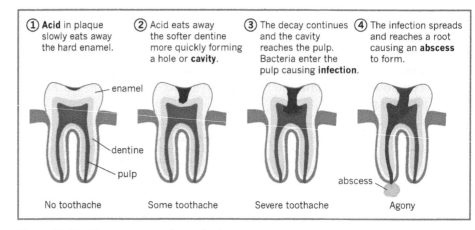

① **Acid** in plaque slowly eats away the hard enamel.

② Acid eats away the softer dentine more quickly forming a hole or **cavity**.

③ The decay continues and the cavity reaches the pulp. Bacteria enter the pulp causing **infection**.

④ The infection spreads and reaches a root causing an **abscess** to form.

enamel

dentine

pulp

abscess

No toothache   Some toothache   Severe toothache   Agony

Figure 3.12 *The process of tooth decay*

Causes of tooth decay

Tooth decay is made more likely by the following.

- Eating foods with a high **sugar** or **starch** content.
- Drinking **sugar-sweetened** and **carbonated beverages**, many of which are **acidic**. The acid attacks the tooth enamel directly and the sugar causes more acid to be produced in the mouth.
- **Poor oral hygiene** practices, e.g. not brushing properly, not brushing and flossing regularly, and not visiting the dentist regularly.
- **Eating disorders** such as anorexia and bulimia.
- Not getting enough **fluoride** to strengthen the enamel.
- **Grinding** the teeth.
- **Smoking**.

Guidelines for the care of teeth and gums

- **Brush** teeth and gums in the proper way, at least twice a day.
- Use a **fluoride toothpaste** and good quality **toothbrush** when brushing.
- Use **dental floss** and an **interdental brush** once a day.
- Use an antibacterial **mouthwash** after brushing and flossing.
- Eat plenty of **tooth-healthy foods** such as fresh fruits and raw vegetables, and drink water or unsweetened and non-carbonated beverages.
- **Avoid** eating sugary and starchy foods and drinking sugar-sweetened and carbonated beverages, especially between meals and before going to bed.
- Visit a **dentist** regularly for a checkup and have teeth **professionally cleaned** twice a year.

Enzymes and chemical digestion

During **chemical digestion** the large food molecules are broken down into small molecules by **hydrolysis**. During hydrolysis, the bonds within the large food molecules are broken down by the addition of water molecules. Chemical digestion is catalysed (speeded up) by **digestive enzymes** (see Table 3.11, page 34).

Enzymes

Enzymes are biological catalysts produced by all living cells. They speed up chemical reactions occurring in living organisms without being changed themselves.

Enzymes are **protein molecules** that living cells produce from amino acids obtained from the diet. Without enzymes, chemical reactions would occur too slowly to maintain life. The reactants acted on by enzymes are known as **substrates**.

Examples of enzymes

- **Amylase** catalyses the breakdown of **starch** into sugars, mainly the disaccharide **maltose**. It is present in saliva and pancreatic juice.

$$\text{starch} \xrightarrow{\text{amylase}} \text{maltose}$$

- **Catalase** catalyses the breakdown of hydrogen peroxide into water and oxygen:

$$\text{hydrogen peroxide} \xrightarrow{\text{catalase}} \text{water} + \text{oxygen}$$

Catalase is found in most cells. It prevents the build-up of harmful hydrogen peroxide, which is produced as a by-product of many chemical reactions occurring in cells.

Properties of enzymes

All enzymes have similar **properties.**

- Enzymes are **specific**, meaning each type of enzyme catalyses only **one** type of reaction. Each type of enzyme molecule has an **active site** which has a specific shape and only one type of substrate molecule fits into it, like a key fits into a lock (see Figure 3.14).

- Enzymes are affected by **temperature** and work best at a particular temperature, known as the **optimum temperature.** This is about 37 °C for human enzymes.

- High temperatures **denature** enzymes by causing the **shape** of the molecules, most importantly the active site, to change so that they are **inactivated.** Enzymes start to be denatured at about 40 °C to 45 °C.

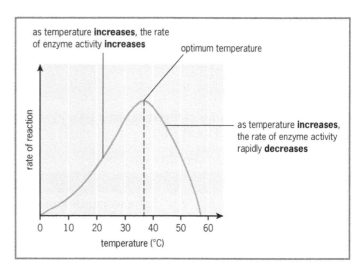

Figure 3.13 *The effect of temperature on the rate of a reaction catalysed by enzymes*

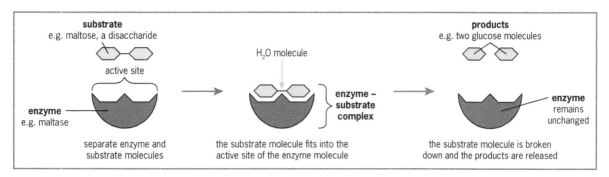

Figure 3.14 *Lock and key mechanism of enzyme action*

- Enzymes are affected by **pH** and work best at a particular pH known as the **optimum pH**. This is about pH 7 for most enzymes.

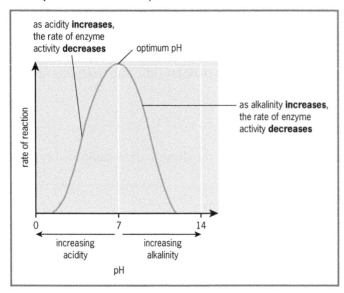

Figure 3.15 *The effect of pH on the rate of a reaction catalysed by enzymes*

- Extremes of acidity or alkalinity **denature** most enzymes by causing their shapes to change.
- The action of enzymes is **helped** by certain vitamins and minerals, e.g. vitamin B_1 helps the action of respiratory enzymes.
- The action of enzymes is **inhibited** by certain poisons, e.g. arsenic and cyanide.

Digestive enzymes

There are **three** categories of **digestive enzymes** and several different enzymes may belong to each category (see Tables 3.11 and 3.12).

Table 3.11 *Categories of digestive enzymes*

Category of digestive enzyme	Food molecules hydrolysed	Products of hydrolysis
Carbohydrases	Polysaccharides and disaccharides	Monosaccharides
Proteases	Proteins	Amino acids
Lipases	Lipids	Fatty acids and glycerol

The digestive system and chemical digestion

The process of **chemical digestion**, which begins in the **mouth** and is completed in the **small intestine**, is summarised in Table 3.12.

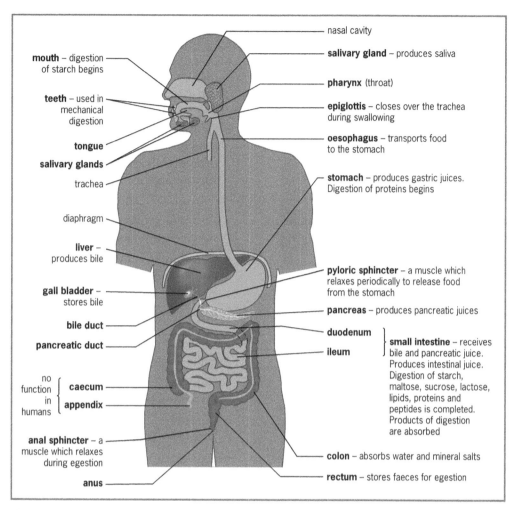

★ **Figure 3.16** *The structures of the human digestive system and their functions*

Table 3.12 *A summary of chemical digestion*

Organ	Digestive juice	Source	Main components	Functions of the components
Mouth	Saliva (pH 7–8)	Salivary glands.	• Water and mucus	• Moisten and lubricate the food allowing tasting and easy swallowing.
			• **Salivary amylase***	• Begins to digest: **starch ⟶ maltose** (a disaccharide)
Stomach	Gastric juice (pH 1–2)	Cells in the stomach wall.	• Hydrochloric acid	• Maintains an optimum pH of 1–2 for pepsin and rennin, and kills bacteria.
			• **Rennin***	• Produced in infants to clot soluble protein in milk so the protein is retained in the stomach.
			• **Pepsin***	• Begins to digest: **protein ⟶ peptides** (shorter chains of amino acids)

Organ	Digestive juice	Source	Main components	Functions of the components
Small intestine (duodenum and ileum)	Bile (pH 7–8)	Cells in the liver. It is stored in the gall bladder and enters the duodenum via the bile duct.	• Bile pigments, e.g. bilirubin • Organic bile salts	• Excretory products from the breakdown of haemoglobin in the liver. Have no function in digestion. • **Emulsify lipids**, i.e. break large lipid droplets into smaller droplets which increases their surface area for digestion.
	Pancreatic juice (pH 7–8)	Cells in the pancreas. It enters the duodenum via the pancreatic duct.	• **Pancreatic amylase*** • **Trypsin*** • **Pancreatic lipase***	• Continues to digest: **starch ⟶ maltose** • Continues to digest: **protein ⟶ peptides** • Digests: **lipids ⟶ fatty acids** and **glycerol**
	Intestinal juice (pH 7–8)	Cells in the walls of the small intestine.	• **Maltase*** • **Sucrase*** • **Lactase*** • **Peptidase*** (erepsin)	• Digests: **maltose ⟶ glucose** • Digests: **sucrose ⟶ glucose** and **fructose** • Digests: **lactose ⟶ glucose** and **galactose** • Digests: **peptides ⟶ amino acids**

* = digestive enzyme

⟶ = into

Movement of food through the alimentary canal

Food is moved through the oesophagus and the rest of the alimentary canal by a process known as **peristalsis**.

Absorption

Absorption is the process by which the soluble food molecules, produced in digestion, move into body fluids.

The **soluble food molecules** must move from inside the intestines into the **blood** and **lymph** to be transported to the body cells for use. Absorption occurs in the **small intestine** and **colon**.

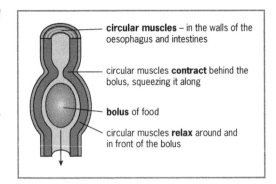

circular muscles – in the walls of the oesophagus and intestines

circular muscles **contract** behind the bolus, squeezing it along

bolus of food

circular muscles **relax** around and in front of the bolus

Figure 3.17 *The mechanism of peristalsis*

Absorption in the small intestine

The products of digestion are **absorbed** through the lining of the small intestine, mainly the ileum, and into the **blood capillaries** and **lacteals (lymph capillaries)** in its walls. Substances absorbed include monosaccharides, amino acids, fatty acids, glycerol, vitamins, minerals and water. Water is absorbed by **osmosis**; the other substances are absorbed by both **diffusion** and **active transport** (see pages 6–9).

The ileum is very **long**, about 5 m in an adult, and its inner surface has thousands of finger-like projections called **villi** (singular: villus); both features help to give it a very **large surface area** for absorption. The wall of each villus, known as the **epithelium**, is only one cell thick and the epithelial cells have tiny projections called **microvilli**. Each villus has a network of **blood capillaries** and a **lacteal (lymph capillary)** inside.

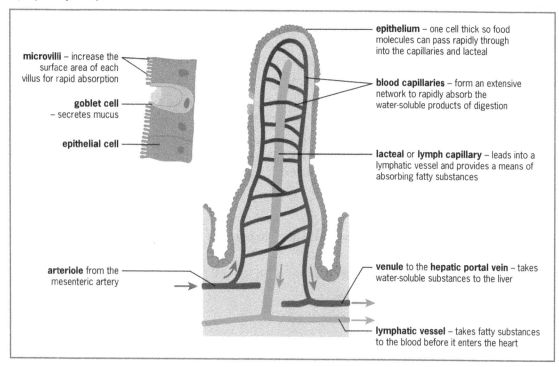

★ **Figure 3.18** *Structure of a villus showing its adaptations for absorption*

- **Water-soluble substances**, i.e. monosaccharides, amino acids, minerals, vitamins B and C, and some water are absorbed into the **blood** in the capillaries.
- **Fatty substances**, i.e. fatty acids, glycerol, and vitamins A, D, E and K are absorbed into the **lymph** in the lacteals.

Absorption in the colon

Any food that has not been digested in the small intestine passes into the **colon** where **water** and **mineral salts** are absorbed from it. As this undigested waste moves along the colon to the rectum it becomes progressively more solid as the water is absorbed.

Egestion

Egestion is the process by which undigested food material is removed from the body.

The almost solid material entering the rectum is called **faeces** and consists of undigested dietary fibre, dead bacteria and intestinal cells, mucus and bile pigments. Faeces are stored in the rectum and **egested** at intervals through the **anus** when the **anal sphincter** relaxes.

Egestion must not be confused with **excretion** which is the removal from the body, of waste and harmful substances produced by the body's metabolism. Other than the bile pigments, the components of faeces are not produced by the body's metabolism, so their removal cannot be classed as excretion.

Assimilation

Assimilation is the process by which the body uses the soluble food molecules absorbed after digestion.

Monosaccharides

Monosaccharides are taken by the blood to the **liver** in the **hepatic portal vein** and the liver converts any non-glucose monosaccharides to **glucose**. The glucose then enters the general circulation where:

- It is used by all body cells in **respiration** to release **energy**.
- Some of the excess is condensed to **glycogen** by cells in the **liver** and **muscles**. These cells then store the glycogen which can be converted back to glucose when needed.
- Some of the excess is converted to **fat** by cells in the **liver** and **adipose (fat) tissue** found under the skin and around organs. Fat made in adipose tissue is stored, and fat made in the liver is transported by the blood to adipose tissue and stored.

Amino acids

Amino acids are taken by the blood to the **liver** in the **hepatic portal vein**. They then enter the general circulation where:

- They are used by body cells to make **proteins** that are used for cell growth and repair.
- They are used by body cells to make **enzymes**.
- They are used by cells of endocrine glands to make **hormones**.
- They are used to make **antibodies**.
- Excess are **deaminated** by the **liver** because they cannot be stored. The nitrogen-containing amine groups (NH_2) are removed from the molecules and converted to **urea** ($CO(NH_2)_2$). The urea enters the blood and is transported to the **kidneys** where it is **excreted**. The remaining parts of the molecules are converted to **glucose** which is used in respiration, or are converted to **glycogen** or **fat** and stored.

Fatty acids and glycerol

Fatty acids and **glycerol** are carried by the **lymph** to the general circulation where:

- They are used to make **cell membranes** of newly forming cells.
- They are used by body cells in **respiration** under some circumstances.
- Excess are converted to **fat** and **stored** in adipose tissue under the skin and around organs.

Revision questions

14 Describe what happens during:

   a mechanical digestion   **b** chemical digestion.

15 Why are teeth important in the digestive process?

16 Joyann has FOUR types of teeth in her mouth. Identify these and state the function of EACH.

17 By means of a fully labelled and annotated diagram only, describe the internal structure of a canine tooth.

18 Matthew develops a cavity in one of his teeth. Outline how this cavity formed and suggest FOUR things he should do to prevent cavities forming in his other teeth.

19 What are enzymes?

20 a Outline the effect that temperature has on enzyme activity.

b Other than the effect of temperature on enzyme activity, give THREE other properties of enzymes.

21 State the function of EACH of the following parts of the digestive system in the digestive process.

a the salivary glands   b the oesophagus   c the pyloric sphincter

d the liver   e the colon   f the rectum

22 For lunch, Beth consumes a ham sandwich made with two slices of buttered bread and two slices of ham. Describe how this sandwich is digested as it passes through Beth's digestive system.

23 Explain how the structure of each villus in Beth's ileum is adapted to absorb the products of the digestion of her meal.

24 What use does the body make of any amino acids produced during digestion?

4 The respiratory system

All living organisms need **energy** to carry out life processes in order to survive. They obtain this energy from food when the food is **respired**. Humans respire **aerobically** and their **respiratory system** is responsible for taking in the oxygen they need to sustain this respiration and to constantly get rid of the carbon dioxide they produce. **Breathing movements** draw air containing the oxygen into the respiratory system and remove air containing the waste carbon dioxide.

Breathing

*Breathing refers to the **movements** that cause air to be moved into and out of the **lungs**.*

Breathing must not be confused with **respiration**, which is the process by which energy is released from food by all living cells (see page 48). Humans respire **aerobically**; therefore they require **oxygen** and produce waste **carbon dioxide.**

Humans have two **lungs**, which form part of the **respiratory system.** Air that is **inhaled** into the lungs contains the **oxygen** required for aerobic respiration. Some of this oxygen diffuses from the inhaled air into the blood in the lungs to be carried around the body, and **carbon dioxide**, produced in respiration, diffuses from the blood in the lungs into the air that is **exhaled**. This **diffusion** of gases between the air and the blood is known as **gaseous exchange** (see page 44).

Breathing is **essential** to humans for the following reasons.

* It ensures that humans have a **continual supply** of **oxygen** to meet the demands of aerobic respiration, which provides them with the **energy** they need to carry out all other life processes.
* It ensures that the **carbon dioxide** produced in aerobic respiration is **continually removed** from the body so that it does not build up and poison cells.

Structure of the human respiratory system

The **respiratory tract** forms the main part of the **respiratory system**. The tract begins in the **nasal cavities** and **mouth**, which join in the **pharynx**. The pharynx leads into the **larynx**, situated at the top of the **trachea**. The trachea leads downwards and branches into two **bronchi** (singular: bronchus), which lead into the two **lungs**. On entering the lungs, the bronchi divide repeatedly into **bronchioles** which branch throughout each lung. Each bronchiole ends in a cluster of pocket-shaped air sacs called **alveoli** (singular: alveolus). Each lung is composed of millions of bronchioles and alveoli.

Each lung receives blood from the heart via a **pulmonary artery**, and blood is carried back to the heart via a **pulmonary vein.** As a pulmonary artery enters a lung it branches repeatedly into capillaries and a **network** of these **capillaries** surrounds the outside of each alveolus.

The lungs are situated inside the **chest cavity** or **thorax** and are surrounded by the **ribs** which form the **rib cage.** The ribs have **intercostal muscles** between them, and a dome-shaped sheet of muscle, called the **diaphragm**, stretches across the floor of the thorax. Each lung is surrounded by two **pleural membranes** which have **pleural fluid** between them.

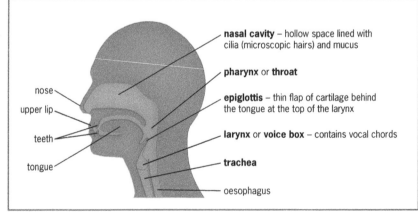

★ **Figure 4.1** *Structure of upper part of the human respiratory system*

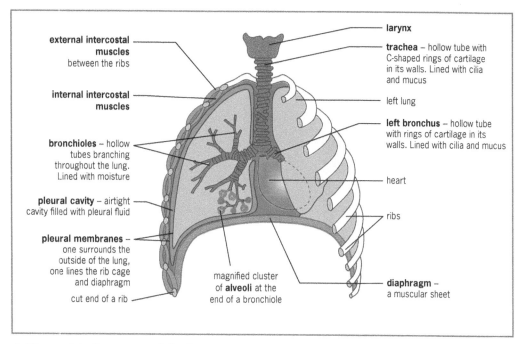

★ **Figure 4.2** *Structure of the human thorax*

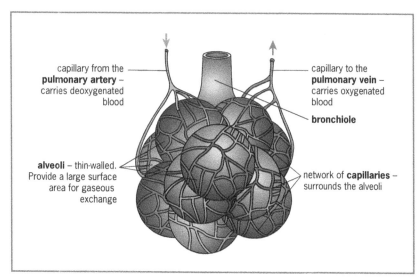

★ **Figure 4.3** *Surface view of a cluster of alveoli showing the blood supply*

Table 4.1 *Summary of the functions of the main parts of the respiratory system*

Structure	Functions
Nasal cavities	Warm the inhaled air. Mucus traps dust and pathogens in the inhaled air and moistens the air. Cilia move the mucus to the throat to be swallowed.
Epiglottis	Prevents food from entering the trachea when swallowing.
Larynx	Vocal cords produce the sounds of speech.
Trachea and bronchi	Allow air to flow into and out of the lungs. Rings of cartilage in their walls keep them open. Mucus traps dust and pathogens and cilia move the mucus upwards to the throat.
Bronchioles	Allow air to flow to and from the alveoli.
Alveoli	Exchange oxygen and carbon dioxide between inhaled air and blood in the capillaries.

Structure	Functions
Pleural membranes and pleural fluid	Form an airtight cavity between the lungs and the rib cage and diaphragm, which adheres (sticks) the lungs to the rib cage and diaphragm. Therefore, any changes in volume of the chest cavity causes the volume inside the lungs to change. Pleural fluid also acts as a lubricant during breathing.
Intercostal muscles and diaphragm	Contract and relax to change the volume inside the chest cavity and lungs, which causes air to move into and out of the lungs.

The mechanism of breathing

Breathing is brought about two sets of muscles, the **intercostal muscles** and the **diaphragm**.

Table 4.2 *The mechanism of breathing*

Features		Inhalation (inspiration)	Exhalation (expiration)
①	External intercostal muscles	Contract	Relax
	Internal intercostal muscles	Relax	Contract
	Ribs and sternum	Move upwards and outwards	Move downwards and inwards
②	Diaphragm muscles	Contract	Relax
	Diaphragm	Moves downwards or flattens	Domes upwards
③	Volume inside thorax and lungs	Increases	Decreases
	Pressure inside thorax and lungs	Decreases	Increases
④	Movement of air	Air is drawn into the lungs due to the decrease in pressure	Air is pushed out of the lungs due to the increase in pressure

As the air is drawn in during inhalation it is **warmed** in the nasal passages, and **cleaned** and **moistened** by mucus lining the nasal passages and trachea. The air passes through the bronchi and bronchioles and enters the alveoli where **gaseous exchange** occurs between the air and the blood in the capillaries surrounding the alveoli (see page 44).

Factors affecting the breathing rate

The **normal** breathing rate for a healthy adult at rest ranges from **12 to 16 breaths per minute**. The **medulla** of the **brain** (see page 83) controls the breathing rate by detecting the level of **carbon dioxide** in the blood and sending impulses to the intercostal and diaphragm muscles.

- Any factor that **increases** the **rate of respiration** in body cells will cause the level of carbon dioxide in the blood to increase. If carbon dioxide levels **increase**, breathing rate **increases** to remove the excess carbon dioxide. Factors that increase breathing rate include:
  - Carrying out **exercise**.
  - Taking **drugs** that are **stimulants**, e.g. caffeine, amphetamines, cocaine.
  - Smoking **cigarettes**.
  - Suffering from **anxiety** or **fear**.
  - Being exposed to certain **environmental factors**, e.g. being in a confined space or in polluted air.
  - Being at **high altitude**.
  - Being **overweight** or **obese**.
- Any factor that **decreases** the **rate of respiration** in body cells will cause the level of carbon dioxide in the blood to decrease. If carbon dioxide levels **decrease**, breathing rate **decreases**. Factors that decrease breathing rate include:
  - **Resting** or **sleeping**.
  - Taking **drugs** that are **depressants**, e.g. sedatives, sleeping pills, alcohol.
  - Being exposed to certain **environmental factors**, e.g. being in fresh, unpolluted air.

Vital capacity

Vital capacity is the maximum volume of air that can be exhaled from the lungs after inhaling as deeply as possible.

Measuring vital capacity can be used to indicate **lung function** and if a person is suffering from lung disease. **Vital capacity** depends on age, sex, body size and fitness. It can be **increased** by regular exercise and is **decreased** by smoking, obesity or respiratory disease. Other volumes and capacities associated with the lungs are shown in Figure 4.4.

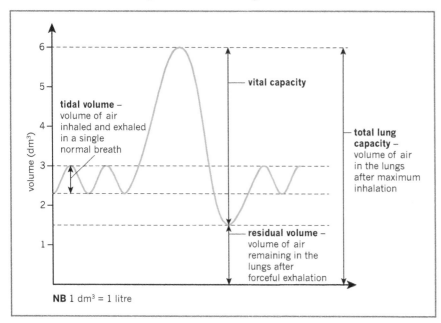

Figure 4.4 *Lung capacities and volumes*

Gaseous exchange

Gaseous exchange is the process by which oxygen diffuses into the blood and carbon dioxide diffuses out of the blood through a gaseous exchange surface.

In humans, the **walls** of the **alveoli** form the surface through which gaseous exchange occurs, known as the **gaseous exchange surface.**

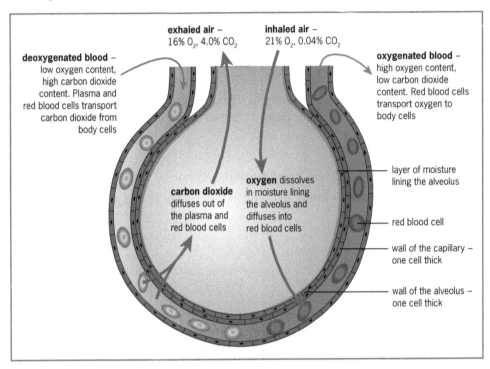

★ **Figure 4.5** *Gaseous exchange in an alveolus*

Table 4.3 *The composition of inhaled and exhaled air*

Component	Inhaled air (%)	Exhaled air (%)	Reason for the differences
Oxygen (O_2)	21	16	Oxygen is used by body cells in respiration.
Carbon dioxide (CO_2)	0.04	4	Carbon dioxide is produced by body cells during respiration and excreted by the lungs.
Nitrogen (N_2)	78	78	Nitrogen gas is not used by body cells.
Water vapour (H_2O)	Variable	Saturated	Moisture from the respiratory system evaporates into the air being exhaled.

Gaseous exchange surfaces

In organisms respiring aerobically, including humans, **gaseous exchange surfaces** have several **adaptations** which make the exchange of gases through them as **efficient** as possible.

- They have a **large surface area** so that large quantities of gases can be exchanged. In **humans**, each alveolus has a pocket-shaped wall, and humans have two lungs, each with over 350 million alveoli, which gives the walls a very large surface area of about 90 m^2.
- They are very **thin** so that gases can diffuse through them rapidly. In **humans**, the walls of the alveoli are only **one cell thick** making them very thin for rapid diffusion.

- They have a **rich blood supply** to quickly transport gases between the surface and the body cells. In **humans**, the walls of the alveoli are surrounded by **networks of capillaries** giving them a rich supply of blood.
- They are **moist** so that gases can dissolve before they diffuse through the surface. In **humans**, the walls of the alveoli are lined with **moisture** to dissolve gases.

Cardiopulmonary resuscitation (CPR)

CPR is an emergency procedure performed on a person whose heart has stopped beating (cardiac arrest) and/or who has stopped breathing (respiratory arrest). During CPR, the rescuer performs **chest compressions** to maintain circulation so that oxygen can be delivered to vital organs. **Rescue breathing** or **mouth-to-mouth resuscitation** can also be performed to deliver oxygen to the victim's lungs.

Hands-only CPR

Hands-only CPR involves performing chest compressions only, using the following steps:
- Lay the victim on their back.
- Kneel next to the victim's shoulders and place the heel of one hand on the breastbone in the centre of the victim's chest. Place your other hand on top of the first and interlock your fingers.
- With straight elbows, use your body weight to push straight downwards on the victim's chest so that it is compressed by approximately **5 cm.**
- Release the compression so the chest returns to its original position.
- Repeat these compressions at a rate of about **100** to **120 per minute** until the heart begins beating or medical help arrives.

CPR with rescue breathing

Rescue breaths can be given with chest compressions by persons who are **trained** to carry out CPR. By doing this, the rescuer forces their exhaled air containing about 16% oxygen into the victim's lungs, using the following steps:

- Perform **30 chest** compressions.
- Tilt the victim's head backwards and lift the chin to open the airways.
- Open the victim's mouth, remove any debris and pinch their nose.

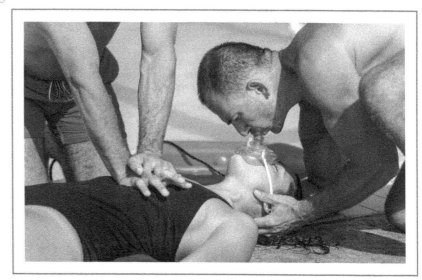

Figure 4.6 *Using a pocket mask to give mouth-to-mouth resuscitation*

- Inhale and seal your lips over the victim's open mouth. Exhale into the victim's mouth for **1 second.**
- If the victim's chest rises, exhale into the mouth a second time.
- Continue to alternate **30 chest compressions** at a rate of **100 to 120 per minute** with **2 rescue breaths** until the victim shows signs of recovery or medical help arrives.

Disposable barrier devices, such as a pocket mask, can be used when giving rescue breaths. These provide a **physical barrier** between the rescuer and the victim, which protects both individuals against any **contagious diseases** that might be transmitted between them.

Smoking

Smoking usually refers to the act of **inhaling smoke** produced by burning plant material in **cigarettes**, **cigars**, **pipes** and **hookahs**, or **vapour** produced by **electronic cigarettes** or **e-cigarettes**. The most commonly smoked plant materials are **tobacco** and **marijuana**.

The effects of smoking cigarettes

When smoking **cigarettes** made from **tobacco**, **smoke** containing over 7000 different chemicals, including **nicotine**, **carbon monoxide** and a black sticky material known as **tar**, is inhaled into the lungs. This smoke poses serious **health risks** outlined below.

Nicotine addiction

Nicotine is an **addictive** substance that causes smokers to continue to smoke and makes it extremely difficult for them to stop. Addicted smokers need enough nicotine during each day to 'feel normal'.

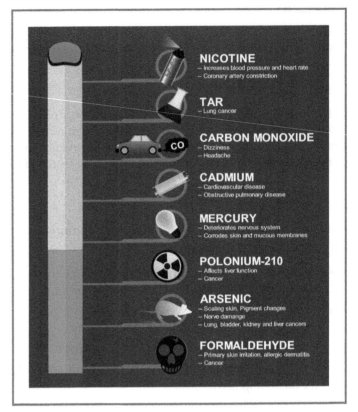

Figure 4.7 *Some components of cigarette smoke*

Reduced oxygen-carrying capacity of the blood

Carbon monoxide combines more readily with haemoglobin than oxygen does, and this reduces the amount of oxygen carried to body cells. This **reduces** respiration and the smoker's ability to exercise. In a pregnant woman, it deprives the foetus of oxygen, reducing its growth and development.

Lung damage

Cigarette smoke **damages** the lungs in a variety of ways.

* It causes **mucus** production to increase and it paralyses the **cilia**, which stops them from beating so the mucus is not removed. The person then develops a **persistent cough** to try and remove the mucus.

* It irritates and inflames the walls of the **bronchi** and **bronchioles**. This, together with the increased mucus production and paralysis of the cilia, causes the airways to become **obstructed**, making breathing difficult, and leads to **chronic bronchitis** (see page 136).

* It causes the walls of the **alveoli** to become less elastic and the walls between the alveoli to break down, which decreases their surface area. This reduces gaseous exchange, makes exhaling difficult and causes air to remain trapped in the lungs, a condition known as **emphysema**. The bronchioles often collapse when exhaling, **obstructing** the airways, making exhaling even harder. Other symptoms of emphysema include severe shortness of breath and fatigue.

Note: Chronic bronchitis and emphysema are two types of **chronic obstructive pulmonary disease** or **COPD**.

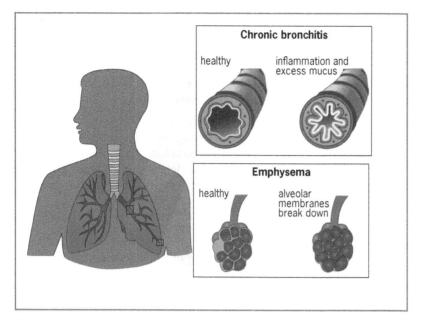

Figure 4.8 *Chronic obstructive pulmonary disease (COPD)*

Cancer of the mouth, throat, oesophagus or lungs

Many components of **tar** and some of the other chemicals in cigarette smoke are **carcinogenic**. They cause **mutations** in cells in different regions of the respiratory system, and this leads to the development of **cancerous tumours** which replace normal, healthy tissue in these regions.

Hypertension (high blood pressure) and heart disease

Nicotine and other chemicals in cigarette smoke can lead to the development of **hypertension** and **heart disease** by **hardening** artery walls and causing **atherosclerosis** (see page 60). Nicotine also increases heart rate and it can make blood more likely to **clot** inside arteries, which can lead to a **heart attack** or **stroke**.

Effects of smoking marijuana, hookah and e-cigarettes

Smoking marijuana

Marijuana is usually **smoked** and long-term use can lead to similar health problems to those experienced by tobacco smokers, mainly a **persistent cough** and **chronic bronchitis**, frequent acute **lung infections** due to marijuana reducing the body's ability to fight infection, **lung cancer** and **marijuana addiction**.

Hookah smoking and smoking e-cigarettes

A **hookah** or **water pipe** is usually used to smoke sweetened and flavoured **tobacco**. The tobacco is burned and the smoke is passed through a water chamber before being inhaled. Smoking **e-cigarettes**, known as **vaping**, involves heating nicotine, flavourings and a variety of other chemicals in the e-cigarette to create a **vapour** which is inhaled. Hookah smoking and vaping have many of the same **health risks** as smoking cigarettes.

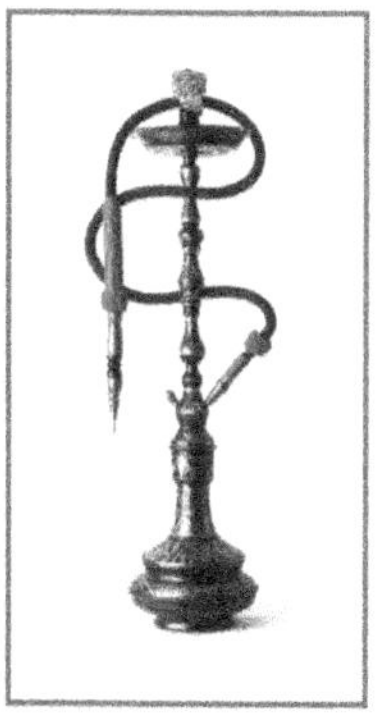

Figure 4.9 *A hookah*

Respiration

Respiration is the process by which energy is released from food by all living cells.

Respiration provides cells with a constant supply of **energy**. **Respiration** is catalysed by **enzymes** and occurs slowly in a large number of stages. The main food respired is **glucose**.

During respiration, about 60% of the energy is released as **heat energy** and this helps to maintain the body temperature at **37 °C**. The rest of the energy released at each stage is used to build **energy-carrying** molecules called **adenosine triphosphate** or **ATP**. An ATP molecule is formed by combining some of the **energy** released with an **adenosine diphosphate** or **ADP** molecule and a **phosphate** group present in the cell. The energy can then be re-released whenever and wherever it is needed in the cell by the reverse reaction:

$$ADP + phosphate + energy \rightleftharpoons ATP$$

ATP is known as the '**energy currency**' of cells. Cells earn ATP as a result of energy-producing reactions, and spend it on reactions requiring energy. Energy released by ATP is **used** by cells:

- To **manufacture** complex, biologically important molecules, e.g. proteins, DNA.
- For **cell growth** and **repair**.
- For **cell division**.
- In **active transport** to move molecules and ions into and out of the cells through their membranes.
- For **special functions** in specialised cells, e.g. contraction of muscle cells, transmission of impulses in nerve cells.

There are **two** types of respiration:

- **aerobic respiration**
- **anaerobic respiration**.

Aerobic respiration

Aerobic respiration is the process by which energy is released from food by living cells using oxygen.

Aerobic respiration occurs in most cells. It **uses oxygen** and takes place in the **mitochondria**. It always produces **carbon dioxide, water** and about **38 ATP molecules** per molecule of glucose.

$$glucose + oxygen \xrightarrow[\text{mitochondria}]{\text{enzymes in}} carbon\ dioxide + water + energy$$

or
$$C_6H_{12}O_6 + 6O_2 \xrightarrow[\text{mitochondria}]{\text{enzymes in}} 6CO_2 + 6H_2O + 38\ ATP$$

Anaerobic respiration

Anaerobic respiration is the process by which energy is released from food by living cells without the use of oxygen.

Anaerobic respiration occurs in some cells. It takes place **without oxygen** in the **cytoplasm** of the cells. The products of anaerobic respiration vary and it produces considerably **less energy** per molecule of glucose than aerobic respiration, usually **2 ATP molecules** per glucose molecule. Yeast cells, certain bacteria and muscle cells are capable of carrying out anaerobic respiration.

Industrial and domestic uses of anaerobic respiration

Making bread and alcoholic beverages

Yeast cells carry out anaerobic respiration known as **fermentation**. It produces **ethanol, carbon dioxide** and **2 ATP molecules** per molecule of glucose.

$$\text{glucose} \xrightarrow[\text{cytoplasm}]{\text{enzymes in}} \text{ethanol} + \text{carbon dioxide} + \text{energy}$$

or

$$C_6H_{12}O_6 \xrightarrow[\text{cytoplasm}]{\text{enzymes in}} 2C_2H_5OH + 2CO_2 + 2\,ATP$$

When **making bread**, the yeast ferments sugars present in dough. The **carbon dioxide** produced forms **bubbles** in the dough which cause it to rise. When baked, heat from the oven causes the bubbles to expand, kills the yeast and evaporates the ethanol.

When making **alcoholic beverages** such as beer, wine, rum and other spirits, the yeast ferments sugars present in grains, fruits or molasses. Fermentation stops when the **ethanol** concentration reaches about 14–16% because it kills yeast cells, so the ethanol content of beer and wine is always below about 16%. Spirits are made by **distillation** of the fermentation mixture.

Making yoghurt

Certain **bacteria**, e.g. *Lactobacillus*, ferment the lactose in milk forming **lactic acid**. The lactic acid makes the milk proteins curdle, which forms thick yoghurt and gives the yoghurt its sour taste.

Producing biogas

Certain **bacteria** are used to break down organic matter, e.g. manure and garden waste, anaerobically in an **anaerobic digester**. This produces **biogas** which is a mixture of approximately **60% methane (CH_4)**, **40% carbon dioxide** and traces of other gases, e.g. hydrogen sulfide (H_2S). Biogas can be used as a **fuel** for cooking, heating and to generate electricity.

Oxygen debt

Muscle cells can carry out anaerobic respiration during **strenuous exercise**. During this strenuous exercise, if oxygen cannot be delivered to the muscle cells quickly enough for the demands of aerobic respiration, the cells begin to respire **anaerobically**. This produces **lactic acid** and **2 ATP molecules** per molecule of glucose.

$$\text{glucose} \xrightarrow[\text{cytoplasm}]{\text{enzymes in}} \text{lactic acid} + \text{energy}$$

or

$$C_6H_{12}O_6 \xrightarrow[\text{cytoplasm}]{\text{enzymes in}} 2C_3H_6O_3 + 2\,ATP$$

Lactic acid builds up in the muscle cells and begins to harm them, causing fatigue and eventually collapse as they stop contracting. The muscle cells are said to have built up an **oxygen debt**. This debt must be **repaid** directly after exercise by resting and breathing deeply so that the lactic acid can be removed by respiring it **aerobically**.

1   What is meant by the term 'breathing' and why is breathing important to humans?

2   State the function of EACH of the following structures found in the respiratory system:

   a the nasal cavities   b the bronchi   c the bronchioles

3   Explain the mechanism by which air is drawn into the lungs.

4   Give FOUR factors that can increase the breathing rate and TWO factors that can decrease it.

5   a What is meant by the term 'vital capacity'?

   b Why is it important to measure a person's vital capacity?

6   Identify the gaseous exchange surface in a human and explain FOUR ways in which the surface is adapted to perform its function efficiently.

7   a What is CPR?

   b List the steps that a trained rescuer would take when giving CPR.

8   a Name the THREE main components of cigarette smoke.

   b Outline how smoking cigarettes damages the lungs.

9   What is ATP and what is its role in body cells?

10 Distinguish between aerobic and anaerobic respiration and write ONE word equation and ONE chemical equation to summarise EACH process.

11 Ché carried out strenuous exercise for an extended period of time and eventually collapsed and found he had to rest before resuming any exercise. Explain why he collapsed and why he had to rest before he could exercise again.

5 The circulatory system

Humans need to constantly exchange substances with their environment. They need to take in useful substances and get rid of waste. The **circulatory system** provides a means of **transporting** these substances between the surfaces where they are exchanged and the body cells. The circulatory system is composed of the **cardiovascular system** and the **lymphatic system**.

The need for a transport system in the human body

The absorption and transport of substances in humans is affected by **two** factors.

- The **limitations of simple diffusion**. Diffusion is a relatively slow process, therefore it is only effective over a short distance.
- The **surface area to volume ratio** of the human body. This limits the effectiveness of diffusion occurring through the surface of the body.

Humans have a very **small** surface area to volume ratio. Because of this, diffusion through their limited body surface is not adequate to supply all their body cells with their requirements and remove their waste. In addition, most of their body cells are too far from the surface for substances to move through them sufficiently quickly and efficiently by simple diffusion. Humans have, therefore, developed a **transport system** to carry **useful substances** from specialised organs that absorb them, e.g. the lungs and ileum, to body cells, and to carry **waste substances** from body cells to specialised organs that excrete them, e.g. the kidneys and lungs.

Materials transported around the human body

The following **materials** are transported around the human body.

- **Useful substances**: oxygen, water, products of digestion (mainly glucose, amino acids, vitamins and minerals), hormones, antibodies and plasma proteins. Heat is also carried.
- **Waste substances**: carbon dioxide and nitrogenous waste, mainly urea.

The cardiovascular system

The **cardiovascular system** consists of **three** basic components.

- **Blood**, which serves as the **medium** to transport substances around the body.
- **Blood vessels**, which are **tubes** through which the blood flows to and from all parts of the body.
- The **heart**, which **pumps** the blood through the blood vessels.

Blood

Blood is a **tissue** composed of **three** types of cells:

- **red blood cells**
- **white blood cells**
- **platelets**

These cells are suspended in a fluid called **plasma**. The cells make up about 45% by volume of the blood and the plasma makes up about 55%.

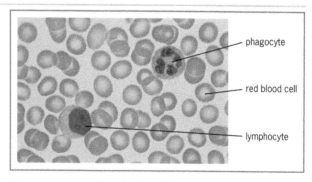

Figure 5.1 *Red and white blood cells under the microscope*

Composition of plasma

Plasma is a yellowish fluid composed of about 90% **water** and 10% **dissolved substances**. The dissolved substances include the following.

- **Products of digestion**, mainly glucose, amino acids, vitamins and minerals.
- **Waste products**, mainly dissolved carbon dioxide and urea.
- **Hormones**, e.g. insulin and thyroxine.
- **Plasma proteins**, e.g. fibrinogen, prothrombin, albumin and antibodies.

Functions of plasma

The main function of plasma is to **transport** the following around the body.

- **Products of digestion**, from the small intestine to the liver and the body cells.
- **Carbon dioxide**, from body cells to the lungs.
- **Urea**, from the liver to the kidneys.
- **Hormones**, from the glands that produce them (endocrine glands) to target organs.
- **Heat energy**, mainly from the liver and muscles to all parts of the body.

Serum

Serum is plasma without **fibrinogen** and other factors needed for the blood to clot (see page 54). Serum is the part of the blood that is left over after red and white blood cells, platelets and clotting factors have been removed. It still contains **antibodies**, therefore it can be used to make **antiserum**, which contains specific antibodies and is used to create vaccines to provide **passive immunity** to certain diseases (see page 156).

serum = plasma – clotting factors

Blood cells

Table 5.1 *Structure and functions of blood cells*

Cell type and structure	Formation of cells	Functions
Red blood cells (erythrocytes) *cell membrane* *cytoplasm rich in* **haemoglobin,** *an iron-containing protein* ★ - **Biconcave discs** with a thin centre and relatively large surface area to volume ratio so gases easily diffuse in and out. - Have **no nucleus**, therefore they only live for about 3 to 4 months. - Contain the red pigment **haemoglobin.** - Slightly **elastic** allowing them to squeeze through the narrowest capillaries.	- Formed in the red bone marrow found in flat bones, e.g. the pelvis, scapula, ribs, sternum, cranium and vertebrae; and in the ends of long bones, e.g. the humerus and femur. - Broken down mainly in the liver and spleen.	- Transport **oxygen** as **oxyhaemoglobin** from the lungs to body cells. - Transport small amounts of **carbon dioxide** from body cells to the lungs.

Cell type and structure	Formation of cells	Functions
White blood cells (leucocytes) Slightly larger than red blood cells and less numerous; approximately 1 white blood cell to 600 red blood cells. There are two main types; 25% are **lymphocytes** and 75% are **phagocytes**.		
Lymphocytes — cell membrane — large, round nucleus — non-granular cytoplasm ★ • Have a **rounded** shape. • Have a large, **round nucleus** that controls the production of antibodies. • Have only a small amount of cytoplasm.	• Develop from cells in the red bone marrow and mature in other organs, e.g. lymph nodes, spleen and thymus gland.	• Produce **antibodies** to destroy disease-causing bacteria and viruses (pathogens). • Produce **antitoxins** to neutralise toxins produced by pathogens.
Phagocytes — cell membrane — lobed nucleus — granular cytoplasm ★ • Have a **variable** shape. • Move by **pseudopodia** or **false feet**; can move out of capillaries through their walls and engulf pathogens using pseudopodia by a process known as **phagocytosis** (see Figure 5.2 below). • Have a **lobed nucleus**.	• Formed in the red bone marrow.	• Engulf and destroy pathogens. • Engulf pathogens destroyed by antibodies.
Platelets (thrombocytes) — cell membrane — cytoplasm • Cell **fragments**. • Have **no nucleus** and only live for about 10 days.	• Formed from cells in the red bone marrow.	• Help the blood to **clot** at a cut or wound (see page 54).

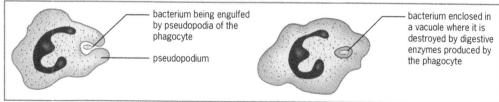

Figure 5.2 *A phagocyte destroying a pathogen by phagocytosis*

Blood clotting

When the skin is cut and bleeds, the blood quickly **clots**. The following events occur to form the **clot.**

- **Platelets** in the blood at the cut become spiky in shape, stick to each other and begin to plug the cut. They also release an enzyme called **thrombokinase** or **thromboplastin.**

- **Thrombokinase**, with the help of calcium ions (Ca^{2+}) and vitamin K in the blood, converts the inactive plasma protein, **prothrombin**, into active **thrombin.**

- **Thrombin** converts the soluble plasma protein, **fibrinogen**, into insoluble **fibrin** which forms fibres.

- The **fibrin fibres** form a network across the cut, which traps blood cells and forms a **clot.**

- The clot dries and develops into a **scab**. New skin forms below the scab and the scab drops off.

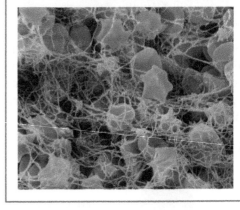

Figure 5.3 *Red blood cells and platelets trapped in a network of fibrin fibres*

Clotting is **important** because:
- The clot prevents further **blood loss.**
- The clot prevents **pathogens** from entering the body.

Blood groups

Blood can be classified into different **blood groups** based on chemicals present on the surface of red blood cells known as **antigens**. There are **two** grouping systems: the **ABO system** and the **Rhesus system.**

The ABO blood group system

The **ABO system** divides blood into **four** groups: group A, group B, group AB and group O. These are determined by the presence or absence of two **antigens** and also two **antibodies** in the plasma.

Table 5.2 *Antigens and antibodies of the ABO blood grouping system*

Blood group	Antigen on the surface of red blood cells	Antibody in the plasma
Group A	A	Anti-B
Group B	B	Anti-A
Group AB	Both A and B	No antibodies
Group O	No antigens	Both anti-A and anti-B

The antibodies in the plasma must be different from the antigens on the red blood cells. If they are the same, the antibodies bind to the antigens causing **agglutination** or **clumping** of the red blood cells.

The Rhesus (Rh) blood group system

The **Rhesus** or **Rh system** divides blood into **two** groups: Rh-positive and Rh-negative. These are determined by the presence or absence of an **antigen** known as the **Rh factor** or **RhD factor**. If the factor is present, the person has **Rh-positive** blood. If the factor is absent, the person has **Rh-negative** blood.

The **Rh factor** poses a risk to a woman with **Rh-negative** blood who wishes to have children. If she carries a **baby** with **Rh-positive** blood, a small amount of the baby's blood may enter her bloodstream, especially during labour, causing her to produce **anti-Rh antibodies**. During any **subsequent pregnancies** with Rh-positive babies, these antibodies can pass across the placenta and attack the baby's red blood cells causing anaemia, brain damage and even death. To **prevent** this, the mother is given an injection of a substance called **anti-D** immediately after delivery to stop her from making any anti-Rh antibodies.

Precautions for blood transfusions

During a **blood transfusion**, blood from a healthy person is given to a person who has lost blood. Certain **precautions** have to be followed when handling and transfusing blood.

- Persons handling blood for transfusion must avoid direct contact with the blood, e.g. by wearing medical gloves.

- Blood should **not** be taken from a person who is pregnant or has anaemia.

- Donated blood must be **screened** for pathogens such as HIV and hepatitis B and C.

- Blood from the donor must be **cross-matched** with the recipient's blood to ensure that their blood groups are **compatible**. This prevents **agglutination** of red blood cells in the **donated** blood. If agglutination occurs, blood vessels may become blocked and the agglutinated cells **disintegrate**, which can be fatal.

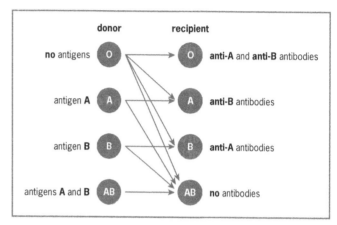

Figure 5.4 *ABO blood group system donors and recipients*

Type **O Rh-negative blood** or **O−** is known as the **universal donor** type because it has **no A, B or Rh antigens**, so it can be given to anybody. Type **AB Rh-positive blood** or **AB+** is known as the **universal recipient** type because it has **no A, B or Rh antibodies**, so a person with it can receive blood of any type.

Blood vessels

There are **three** main types of blood vessels:

- **arteries**
- **capillaries**
- **veins**

Arteries carry blood **away** from the heart. On entering an organ, an artery branches into smaller arteries called **arterioles** which then branch into a network of **capillaries** which run throughout the organ. Capillaries then join into small veins called **venules** which join to form a single **vein** which leads back from the organ **towards** the heart.

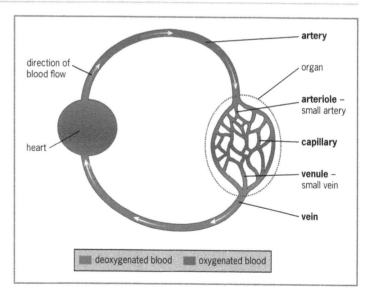

Figure 5.5 *The relationship between the different blood vessels*

Table 5.3 *Arteries, capillaries and veins compared*

Arteries	Capillaries	Veins
Transport blood **away** from the heart to body tissues and organs.	Transport blood **throughout** all body tissues and organs, linking arteries to veins.	Transport blood back **towards** the heart from body tissues and organs.
Blood flows through under **high pressure**.	Blood flows through under **low pressure**.	Blood flows through under **low pressure**.
Blood moves in **pulses** created as the ventricles contract.	Blood flows **smoothly**.	Blood flows **smoothly**.
Blood flows **rapidly**.	Blood flows **very slowly**.	Blood flows **slowly**.
Blood is **oxygenated** (high oxygen content, low carbon dioxide content), except in the pulmonary arteries.	Blood becomes **deoxygenated** as it travels through capillaries.	Blood is **deoxygenated** (low oxygen content, high carbon dioxide content), except in the pulmonary veins.
Most lie **deep** within the body so they are protected.	Run **throughout** all tissues and organs.	Many lie **close** to the body surface.
Do not possess valves, except the aorta and pulmonary artery as they leave the ventricles of the heart.	**Do not** possess valves.	Possess **valves** to prevent the low-pressure, slow-flowing blood from flowing backwards. free-flowing blood – **valve open** back-flowing blood – **valve closed**
Have walls composed of **three** layers. The walls are **thick** and **elastic** to withstand the high pressure of the blood. **fibrous layer** – fairly thick and elastic **muscle and elastic layer** – thick **endothelium** – one cell thick **lumen** – narrow	The walls are composed of a **single layer** of endothelial cells so substances pass easily between the blood and body cells. They are extremely narrow and branch repeatedly so that all body cells are close to capillaries. **endothelial cell** **lumen** – extremely narrow	Have walls composed of **three** layers. The walls are **thin** because they do not have to withstand high pressure. The lumen is wide so it does not resist the flow of low-pressure blood. **fibrous layer** – thin and elastic **muscle and elastic layer** – thin **endothelium** – one cell thick **lumen** – wide

The heart

The pumping action of the **heart** maintains a constant circulation of blood around the body. The walls of the heart are composed of **cardiac muscle** which contracts without nerve impulses, i.e. it is **myogenic**, and it does not get tired.

The heart is divided into **four** chambers. The two on the right contain **deoxygenated blood** and are completely separated from the two on the left, which contain **oxygenated blood**, by the **septum**.

- The top two chambers, called **atria**, have thin walls and they collect blood entering the heart from the **anterior vena cava**, the **posterior vena cava** and the **pulmonary veins**. Their walls are **thin** because they only have to pump blood a short distance into the ventricles.
- The bottom two chambers, called **ventricles**, have thick walls and they pump blood out of the heart via the **pulmonary artery** and **aorta**. Their walls are **thick** because they have to pump blood longer distances around the body and to the lungs. The wall of the **left ventricle** is **thicker** than the wall of the right ventricle because it has to pump blood longer distances; the left ventricle has to pump blood to all body cells, whereas the right ventricle only has to pump blood to the lungs, which are next to the heart.

Valves are present between each atrium and ventricle and in the pulmonary artery and aorta as they leave the ventricles to ensure that blood flows through the heart in **one direction**. The **coronary arteries** branch from the aorta as it leaves the heart and supply the heart muscle with oxygen.

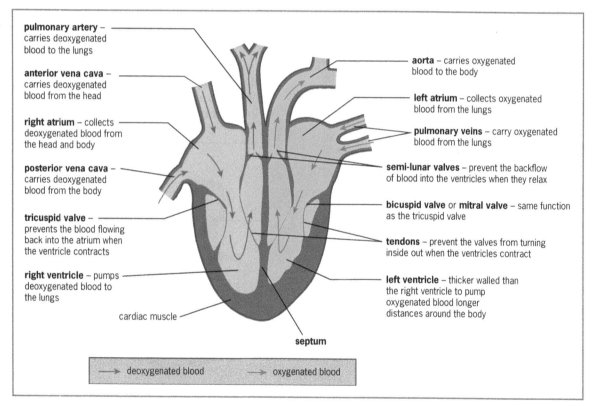

★ **Figure 5.6** *Longitudinal section through the human heart showing the function of the parts*

The heart's pacemaker (sinoatrial node)

A group of **specialised cells** in the wall of the **right atrium**, called the **pacemaker** or **sinoatrial node**, spontaneously produce electrical impulses which travel through the heart muscle causing it to contract about 75 times per minute. This rate can be **modified** by nerve impulses or the hormone adrenaline, e.g. the rate increases during exercise or when nervous.

An **artificial pacemaker** is a small, battery-operated device that generates **electrical impulses** to regulate heartbeat. It is implanted under the skin close to the heart and connected to the heart via tiny wires and may be used if the heartbeat is too slow, too fast or irregular.

Cardiac cycle

As the heart beats, the atria and ventricles at both sides contract and relax together. The **contraction** of a chamber is called **systole** and its **relaxation** is called **diastole**. One **cardiac cycle** or **heartbeat** involves the following:

- **Diastole** – the **atria** and **ventricles relax** together, the semi-lunar valves close, the atria fill up with blood from the anterior vena cava, posterior vena cava and pulmonary veins, and the blood flows into the ventricles. This takes 0.4 seconds.
- **Atrial systole** – the **atria contract** together forcing any remaining blood through the tricuspid and bicuspid valves into the ventricles. This takes 0.1 second.
- **Ventricular systole** – the **ventricles contract** together, the tricuspid and bicuspid valves close and blood is forced through the semi-lunar valves into the aorta and pulmonary arteries. This takes 0.3 seconds.

Circulation

During one complete circulation around the body, the blood flows through the heart **twice**, therefore, humans have a **double circulation.**

- In the **pulmonary circulation**, blood travels from the **right ventricle** through the **pulmonary arteries** to the **lungs** to pick up oxygen and lose carbon dioxide, i.e. it becomes **oxygenated**. It then travels back via the **pulmonary veins** to the **left atrium**.
- In the **systemic (body) circulation**, blood travels from the **left ventricle** through the **aorta** to the **body** where it gives up oxygen to the body cells and picks up carbon dioxide, i.e. it becomes **deoxygenated**. It then travels back via the **anterior** or **posterior vena cava** to the **right atrium**.

A **double circulation** is necessary because blood **loses pressure** when it passes through the lungs, so it goes back to the heart to be given enough pressure to reach body organs to supply them with oxygen and remove carbon dioxide. As it loses pressure passing through organs, the blood goes back to the heart again to be given enough pressure to reach the lungs to get rid of the waste carbon dioxide and pick up more oxygen.

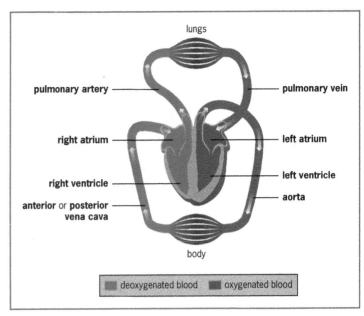

Figure 5.7 *Double circulation in the human body*

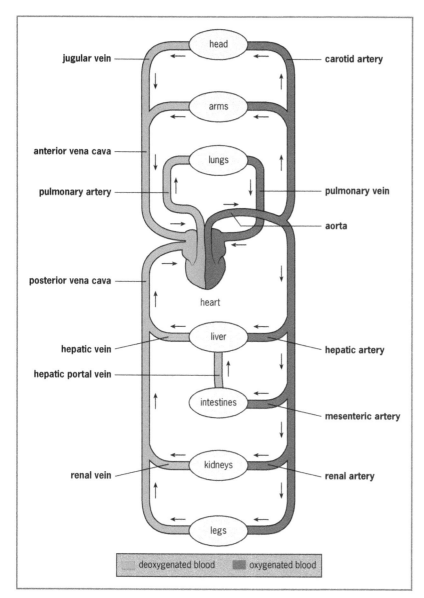

Figure 5.8 *The major blood vessels in the human body*

Blood pressure

Blood pressure is the pressure that circulating blood exerts on the walls of blood vessels.

Blood pressure is created by the pumping action of the heart and is determined by the·**volume** of blood being pumped and the amount of **resistance** to blood flow by the arteries. Blood pressure is usually measured in the brachial artery in the upper arm using a **blood pressure monitor**. The **units** usually used are **millimetres of mercury** or **mm Hg,** and it is expressed as **systolic pressure** over **diastolic pressure,** as follows:

$$\text{blood pressure (mm Hg)} = \frac{\textbf{systolic pressure (highest pressure when the heart contracts)}}{\textbf{diastolic pressure (lowest pressure when the heart relaxes)}}$$

Ideal blood pressure is between **90/60 mm Hg** and **120/80 mm Hg.**

High blood pressure or hypertension

High blood pressure or **hypertension** results if a person's blood pressure rises to **140/90 mm Hg** or **above**. Hypertension is known as the 'silent killer' because it usually has **no** obvious symptoms. However, it can lead to a variety of serious complications, including **angina** (chest pain), **coronary heart disease**, **heart attack**, **stroke**, **heart failure**, **kidney failure**, **impaired vision** and **dementia**.

A number of **factors** can put a person at risk of developing hypertension. Many of these are known as **modifiable risk factors** because they are factors that a person can **adjust** or **change** to help prevent or manage hypertension. These modifiable risk factors include the following.

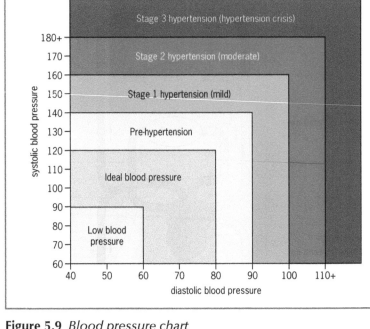

Figure 5.9 *Blood pressure chart*

- Being **overweight** or **obese**.
- Being **physically inactive**.
- Consuming too much **saturated fat** and **salt** in the diet.
- **Smoking**.
- Drinking too much **alcohol**.
- Being under **stress**.

Childhood obesity and hypertension

The number of **children** with hypertension is increasing in many Caribbean countries, and this can be linked to the **increase** in certain of these modifiable risk factors, particularly **childhood obesity**. The incidence of elevated blood pressure in children has been found to **increase** as **BMI increases** and this poses serious problems because high blood pressure in childhood usually continues into adulthood.

Causes and effects of heart disease

Heart disease refers to any condition that affects the **structure** or **function** of the **heart**.

- **Coronary heart disease** or **CHD** occurs when fatty deposits containing cholesterol, known as **atheromas** or **plaques**, build up on the inside of the walls of the **coronary arteries** that supply the heart muscle with oxygen. This process is known as **atherosclerosis**. The deposits cause the lumens of the arteries to narrow and their walls to harden and become less elastic, and the heart muscle to receive less oxygen (see page 144).

- **Heart attack** or **myocardial infarction** occurs when a **blood clot** or **thrombus** forms in one of the coronary arteries. The formation of a clot is referred to as **coronary thrombosis**. The clot partially or completely blocks the artery and oxygen cannot then reach the heart muscle supplied by the artery, so the muscle in that region starts to **die** and a heart attack occurs (see Figure 5.10, page 61). In some cases, the heart stops beating, known as **cardiac arrest**, and this can result in **death**.

- **Heart failure** occurs when the heart does not pump blood around the body **efficiently**. It is usually caused by **atherosclerosis** or **hypertension** weakening the heart muscle over time.

- **Arrhythmia** or **irregular heart rhythm** occurs when the electrical impulses that coordinate the heartbeat do not work properly. This makes the heart beat too **quickly**, too **slowly** or **erratically**.

- **Congenital heart disease** is a heart abnormality that is present at **birth** as a result of problems occurring during foetal development of the heart and can eventually lead to heart failure.

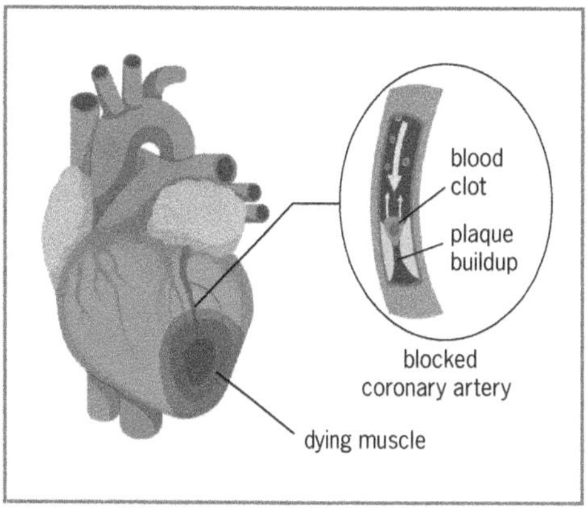

Common **symptoms** of **heart disease** include chest pain or discomfort known as **angina**, shortness of breath, fatigue, light-headedness, dizziness, irregular heartbeat or palpitations, and numbness or swelling in the arms and legs.

Figure 5.10 *Atherosclerosis and clot formation leading to a heart attack*

Causes of heart disease

The main **causes** of heart disease include the following.

- Having **high blood pressure** or **hypertension**.
- Having high levels of **cholesterol** in the blood.
- Having **diabetes**.
- Having a **family history** of heart disease.
- Being **overweight** or **obese**.
- Being **physically inactive**.
- Consuming a diet that is high in **saturated fat**, **salt** and **sugar**.
- **Smoking**.

The lymphatic system

Formation of tissue fluid and lymph

Body cells are surrounded by **tissue fluid** which forms from **blood plasma** that seeps out of blood capillaries. Some of this tissue fluid then returns to the blood in the capillaries and reforms plasma, and some enters **lymph capillaries** and forms **lymph**. The lymph eventually returns to the blood and reforms plasma. Lymph and lymph capillaries form part of the **lymphatic system**.

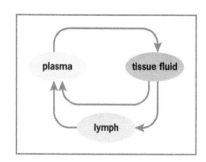

Figure 5.11 *The relationship between plasma, tissue fluid and lymph summarised*

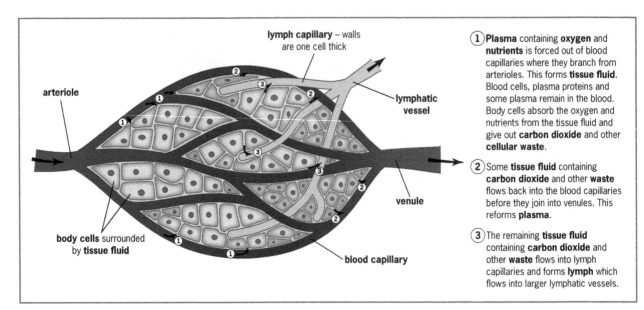

The diagram shows:

- lymph capillary – walls are one cell thick
- arteriole
- lymphatic vessel
- venule
- body cells surrounded by tissue fluid
- blood capillary

① **Plasma** containing **oxygen** and **nutrients** is forced out of blood capillaries where they branch from arterioles. This forms **tissue fluid**. Blood cells, plasma proteins and some plasma remain in the blood. Body cells absorb the oxygen and nutrients from the tissue fluid and give out **carbon dioxide** and other **cellular waste**.

② Some **tissue fluid** containing **carbon dioxide** and other **waste** flows back into the blood capillaries before they join into venules. This reforms **plasma**.

③ The remaining **tissue fluid** containing **carbon dioxide** and other **waste** flows into lymph capillaries and forms **lymph** which flows into larger lymphatic vessels.

★ **Figure 5.12** *The formation of tissue fluid and lymph*

Structure of the lymphatic system

The **lymphatic system** consists of **three** components: **lymph**, **lymphatic vessels** and **lymph nodes**.

Lymph

Lymph serves as the **transporting medium**. It is a colourless, watery fluid composed mainly of water and dissolved **carbon dioxide**, other **cellular waste** and **lymphocytes**. Lymph is formed in body tissues and flows in **one direction**, from tissues towards the heart.

Lymphatic vessels or lymph vessels

Lymphatic vessels are **tubes** through which lymph flows. They begin inside tissues. The smallest ones, known as **lymph capillaries**, have walls which are one cell thick. Larger lymphatic vessels have thin, muscular walls and **valves** to prevent the backflow of low-pressure lymph. Lymph travelling through these vessels rejoins plasma in the **subclavian veins** from the arms, which then lead into the anterior vena cava. The flow of lymph through lymphatic vessels is helped by the contraction of surrounding muscles, especially during **exercise**.

Lymph nodes or lymph glands

Lymph nodes are small, spherical or bean-shaped swellings found along the length of lymphatic vessels and they form clusters in various parts of the body, especially in the neck, armpits and groin. They contain large numbers of **lymphocytes** and **phagocytes**.

Functions of the lymphatic system

Functions of tissue fluid

- Tissue fluid supplies body cells with **oxygen** and **nutrients**.
- Tissue fluid removes **carbon dioxide** and other **cellular waste** from body cells.

Functions of lymph

- Lymph removes **carbon dioxide**, other **cellular waste** and **cell debris** from around body cells.
- Lymph drains **excess tissue fluid** from tissues, which helps prevent fluid from building up in them.

- Lymph helps maintain normal **blood volume** and **pressure**.
- **Lymphocytes** in lymph defend the body against **pathogens**.
- Lymph in the **lacteals** (lymph capillaries) in the ileum absorbs **fatty products** of digestion.

Functions of lymph nodes

- **Lymphocytes** and **phagocytes** in lymph nodes help destroy **pathogens** in lymph.
- Lymph nodes filter **dead cells** and **cancerous cells** out of lymph.
- Lymph nodes release **lymphocytes** into lymph during times of infection to help destroy **pathogens**.

Revision questions

1 **a** Explain why the human body needs a transport system.

   b Name FOUR materials transported around the human body.

2 Explain the relationship between plasma and serum.

3 **a** By means of TWO labelled and annotated diagrams only, give THREE differences between the structure of a red blood cell and a phagocyte.

   b State the function of EACH of the cells you have drawn in **a** above.

4 Explain how the loss of blood at a cut is prevented.

5 Name the TWO different blood grouping systems and explain why different blood groups exist.

6 Explain the potential risk to a woman with Rh-negative blood who wishes to have children, and what precaution she must take if she gives birth to a baby with Rh-positive blood.

7 State THREE differences between the structure of an artery and a vein and provide a reason for EACH difference.

8 Explain:

   a How blood flow through the heart is maintained in one direction.

   b Why the wall of the left ventricle of the heart is thicker than the wall of the right ventricle.

   c How the beating of the heart is controlled.

9 Distinguish between systole and diastole.

10 Explain to Naomi why humans need a double circulation.

11 Draw a simple flow diagram to show the pathway that a red blood cell takes as it journeys from the lungs around the body and back to the lungs.

12 **a** How is a person's blood pressure expressed and what is the ideal blood pressure?

   b Identify FOUR modifiable risk factors for elevated blood pressure.

13 Explain how coronary heart disease is caused and what can lead to a person having a heart attack.

14 Explain the relationship between blood plasma, tissue fluid and lymph.

15 Give FOUR functions of the lymphatic system.

6 The skeletal system

Humans need to be able to **move** their entire bodies from place to place as well as parts of their bodies. They also need to have a means of **supporting** and **protecting** the soft tissues and organs of their bodies. These functions are all carried out by the **skeletal system**.

The human skeleton

The **human skeleton** serves as a **framework** for the body and it can be divided into the **axial skeleton** and the **appendicular skeleton**. The skeleton of an adult is made of 206 bones which are held together at **joints** by **ligaments**.

The axial skeleton

The **axial skeleton** consists of the **skull**, **vertebral column**, **ribs** and **sternum**.

- The **skull** is made up of the **cranium** and **upper jaw** which are fused, and the **lower jaw** which articulates with the upper jaw. The skull encloses the brain and sense organs of the head.

- The **vertebral column** is composed of 33 bones known as **vertebrae** which have **intervertebral discs** of cartilage between them. The **spinal cord** runs through a hole in the centre of each vertebra. The column supports the body, provides points of attachment for the girdles and many muscles, and protects the spinal cord running through it. It also allows some movement.

- The **ribs** are attached to the vertebral column dorsally and the **sternum** ventrally. They form the **rib cage** around the heart and lungs; movement of the ribs is essential for breathing.

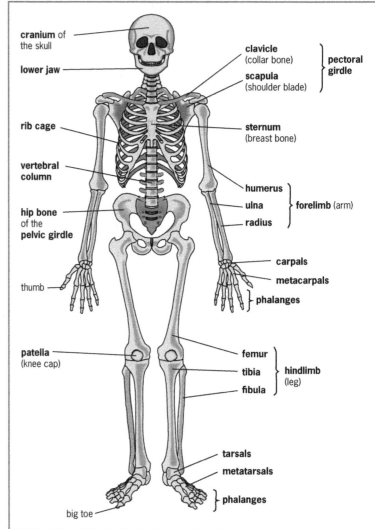

★ **Figure 6.1** *The human skeleton*

The appendicular skeleton

The **appendicular skeleton** is composed of the **pectoral girdle**, the **pelvic girdle**, the **arms** (forelimbs) and the **legs** (hindlimbs).

- The **girdles** connect the limbs to the axial skeleton and have broad flat surfaces for the attachment of muscles that move the limbs. The pelvic girdle is fused to the bottom of the vertebral column to provide **support** for the lower body and to transmit the **thrust** from the legs to the vertebral column which moves the body forwards.

- The **limbs** are composed of long bones which have **joints** between to allow for easy **movement**. Being long, the bones provide a large surface area for the **attachment** of muscles and permit long **strides** to be taken.

Both the arms and the legs are built on the same basic pattern known as the **pentadactyl limb**.

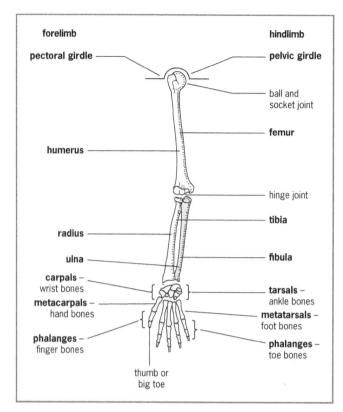

Figure 6.2 *The pentadactyl limb*

Structure of a typical long bone

The **long bones** of the limbs all have a similar structure which makes the bones suited to their functions.

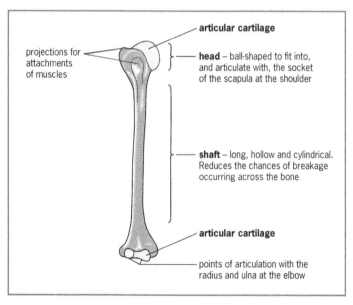

★ **Figure 6.3** *External view of a typical long bone – the humerus*

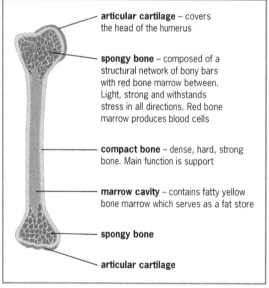

★ **Figure 6.4** *Internal structure of a typical long bone – the humerus*

Functions of the skeleton

The human skeleton has **six** main functions.

- **Movement.** The skeleton is jointed and muscles work across these joints to bring about movement. Most movement is brought about by the **legs** and **arms** while the **vertebral column** allows some movement.

- **Protection** for the internal organs. The **skull** protects the brain and sense organs of the head, i.e. the eyes, ears, nasal cavities and tongue. The **vertebral column** protects the spinal cord. The **rib cage** and **sternum** protect the lungs, heart and major blood vessels. The **pelvic girdle** protects the internal reproductive organs, bladder and lower part of the digestive system.

- **Support** for the soft parts of the body. This is mainly carried out by the **vertebral column, pelvic girdle** and **legs**.

- **Breathing.** Alternate contractions of the internal and external intercostal muscles between the ribs bring about movements of the **rib cage**, which cause air to be drawn into the lungs and expelled from the lungs (see page 42).

- **Production of blood cells.** Red blood cells, most white blood cells and platelets are produced in the red bone marrow found in the spongy bone inside **flat bones**, mainly the pelvis, scapula, ribs, sternum, cranium and vertebrae, and in the **ends** of long bones, mainly the humerus and femur.

- **Storage of minerals.** The bones of the skeleton are composed mainly of **calcium phosphate** **(Ca$_3$(PO$_4$)$_2$)** and they act as a reservoir for **calcium** and **phosphorus**, releasing calcium (Ca^{2+}) and phosphate (PO$_4^{3-}$) ions into the blood when needed.

Bone and cartilage

The human skeleton is made mainly from two types of connective tissue, **bone** and **cartilage**.

- **Bone** makes up the bulk of the skeleton. It is composed of **living cells** embedded in a hard, non-living **matrix** made up of **calcium salts**, mainly calcium phosphate, together with some tough, rubbery **collagen** (protein) fibres. Bone is **hard** and has **blood vessels** running throughout. **Two** types of bone are found in the skeleton: **compact bone** which is strong and dense, and s**pongy bone** which is less dense and lighter in weight (see Figure 6.4, page 65).

- **Cartilage** is composed of **living cells** surrounded by a non-living **matrix** made up mainly of **collagen** fibres. Cartilage is **elastic, rubbery** and **flexible**, and does **not** have blood vessels running through it. Cartilage is **important** because:

  - It covers the ends of bones at **joints** where it **protects** the ends from wearing away, it acts as a **shock absorber** and it helps to **reduce friction** in the joints.

  - It forms the **skeleton** of certain fleshy appendages which maintains their **shape**, e.g. the nose and outer ear.

  - It makes up the **intervertebral discs** between the vertebrae which enables the discs to act as **shock absorbers**.

Tendons and ligaments

Tendons and **ligaments** are both made of connective tissue with different compositions because of their different functions.

- **Tendons** attach the ends of **muscles** to the **bones** of the skeleton. They are made mainly of tough, fibrous **collagen**. This makes them strong and **non-elastic**, so that when a muscle contracts they do not stretch and the force is transmitted directly to the bone, causing the bone to move.

- **Ligaments** attach **bones** together at **joints**. They are made mainly of **collagen** with some **elastin**, which is more elastic. This makes them strong but **elastic** so they hold the bones together firmly and prevent dislocation, but can stretch slightly to allow movement at the joints.

Movement

Movement is a change in position of parts of an organism or the whole organism.

Movement in humans is brought about by **skeletal muscles** working across **joints.**

Muscles

Muscles are composed of **muscle tissue** which is made of specialised **muscle cells** that have the ability to **contract** when supplied with energy in the form of ATP. When muscles contract, they get shorter and bring about movement. **Three** types of muscle tissue are found in the human body.

- **Skeletal muscle** or **voluntary muscle tissue** is composed of long, cylindrical muscle fibres. Each fibre has dark and light cross bands called **striations** and **many nuclei** (see Figure 1.10, page 5). Skeletal muscle is under **voluntary** control. **Skeletal muscles** themselves consist of **bundles** of skeletal muscle fibres surrounded by connective tissue. **Tendons** attach these muscles to the bones of the skeleton.

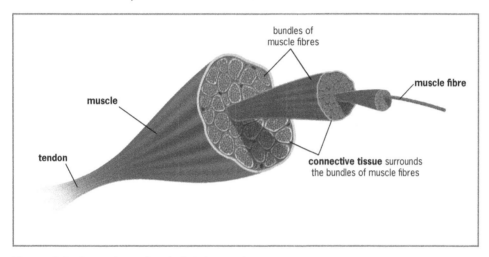

Figure 6.5 *A portion of a skeletal muscle*

- **Cardiac muscle** or **heart muscle tissue** is found only in the walls of the **heart**. It never gets tired and contracts **involuntarily**. Specialised **pacemaker cells** in the heart's natural pacemaker (see page 57) produce electrical impulses which cause the muscle cells to contract in a coordinated way to force blood out of the heart during systole.

- **Smooth muscle** or **involuntary muscle tissue** is composed of narrow, spindle-shaped cells with **single nuclei**. Smooth muscle contracts **involuntarily** and is found in the walls of hollow organs, e.g. the alimentary canal, arteries and veins, the bladder, the uterus and the trachea, bronchi and bronchioles of the lungs, and also in the iris of the eye and the hair erector muscles of the skin.

Joints

A joint is formed where two bones meet.

Most joints allow the rigid skeleton to **move**. There are **three** types of joints in the human body.

- **Fixed joints** or **fibrous joints**. The bones are joined firmly together by **fibrous connective tissue** which allows no movement, e.g. the cranium is made of eight bones joined by fixed joints and each hip bone of the pelvic girdle is made of three bones joined by fixed joints.

- **Partially movable joints** or **cartilaginous joints**. The bones are separated by **cartilage pads** which allow slight movement, e.g. the vertebrae are separated by intervertebral discs of cartilage.

- **Movable joints** or **synovial joints**. The articulating surfaces of the bones are covered with **articular cartilage** and **synovial fluid** fills the joint cavity between the bones. The bones are held together by **ligaments**. There are **two** types of movable joints:

  - **Hinge joints** are formed where the **ends** of the bones meet. They allow movement in **one plane** (direction) only. This limited movement provides **strength** and the joints are capable of bearing heavy loads, e.g. the elbow, knee, finger and toe joints.

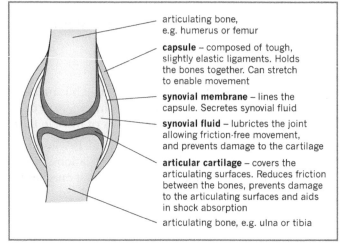

articulating bone, e.g. humerus or femur

capsule – composed of tough, slightly elastic ligaments. Holds the bones together. Can stretch to enable movement

synovial membrane – lines the capsule. Secretes synovial fluid

synovial fluid – lubricates the joint allowing friction-free movement, and prevents damage to the cartilage

articular cartilage – covers the articulating surfaces. Reduces friction between the bones, prevents damage to the articulating surfaces and aids in shock absorption

articulating bone, e.g. ulna or tibia

★ **Figure 6.6** *Structure and functions of the parts of a generalised hinge joint*

  - **Ball and socket joints** are formed where a **ball** at the end of one bone fits into a **socket** in the other bone. They allow rotational movement in **all planes**. The free range of movement provides less support and makes the joints more susceptible to dislocation than a hinge joint, e.g. the shoulder and hip joints.

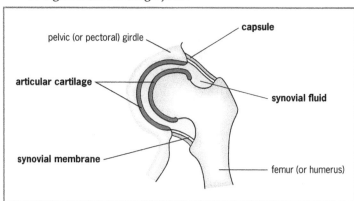

pelvic (or pectoral) girdle

capsule

articular cartilage

synovial fluid

synovial membrane

femur (or humerus)

★ **Figure 6.7** *Structure of the parts of a ball and socket joint*

Movement at a movable joint

When a muscle contracts it **shortens** and exerts a **pull**, but it cannot exert a push when it relaxes. Therefore, **two** muscles, known as an **antagonistic pair**, are always needed to produce movement at a movable joint.

- The **flexor muscle** is the muscle that brings about **flexion** when it contracts. **Flexion** refers to **bending** of a hinge joint or moving the arm or leg **forwards** at the shoulder or hip.
- The **extensor muscle** is the muscle that brings about **extension** when it contracts. **Extension** refers to **straightening** of a hinge joint or moving the arm or leg **backwards** at the shoulder or hip.

Both muscles are attached by **tendons** at one of their ends to a bone that does not move and at the other end to a bone that does move.

*The **origin** of a muscle is the attachment point of the end of the muscle to a bone that **does not move** during contraction.*

*The **insertion** of a muscle is the attachment point of the end of the muscle to the bone that **moves** during contraction.*

The **origin** is usually as **far** away from the joint as possible and the **insertion** is usually very **close** to the joint.

Movement of the elbow joint

The **biceps** and **triceps** muscles move the radius and ulna causing the elbow joint to bend or straighten.

- The **biceps** is the **flexor** muscle. Its origin is on the scapula which does not move, and its insertion is on the radius close to the elbow joint.
- The **triceps** is the **extensor** muscle. Its origin is on the scapula and top of the humerus which do not move, and its insertion is on the ulna close to the elbow joint.

To **bend** the elbow joint, the **biceps contracts** and the triceps relaxes. To **straighten** the elbow joint, the **triceps contracts** and the biceps relaxes.

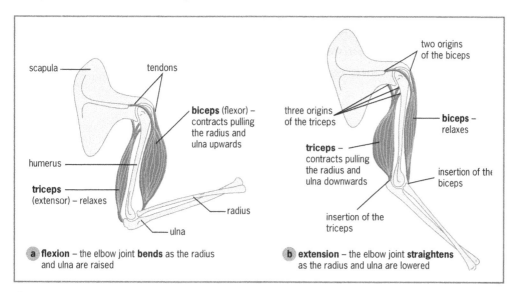

★ **Figure 6.8** *Movement of the elbow joint*

Muscle tone

Muscle tone is the unconscious low-level contraction of muscles while they are at rest.

Good muscle tone is important for several reasons.

- It keeps muscles in an **active state** so that they are ready for rapid, coordinated action.
- It helps to maintain **balance** and a **good, upright posture** when sitting, standing and walking.
- It helps to keep body movements **smooth** and **coordinated**.
- It helps to hold bones **firmly in place** at joints if antagonistic pairs of muscles have good muscle tone.

Regular exercise is important to **improve** muscle tone. It increases the number of **capillaries** within muscles, which increases blood flow to the muscles, it increases the number of **mitochondria** within muscle cells, and it improves the **efficiency** with which muscles use oxygen and glucose, which delays the onset of fatigue.

Factors which adversely affect the skeletal system

Poor posture

Posture refers to the relative position of the different parts of the body. A **poor posture** strains muscles and causes them to need more energy to keep the body upright, which leads to **muscle tightness**, **fatigue**, **backache** and **headaches**. It also changes the curvature of the spine, which leads to **back, neck** and **shoulder pain**, puts stress on certain joints leading to **joint pain** and wears down the intervertebral discs in the spine causing a **decrease in height**.

Poor posture also causes **major organs** to become **compressed** and to function less efficiently. Compression of the **lungs** and **airways** makes breathing less efficient, compression of the **digestive system** makes it harder to digest food, and compression of **blood vessels** makes it harder for blood to circulate properly.

Inappropriate foot-wear

Wearing the **incorrect foot-wear** for an activity can adversely affect the skeletal system.

- Wearing shoes with **high heels** causes the body weight to shift forwards to the ball of the foot leading to **painful arches** and **foot pain**, and a change in the curvature of the spine which leads to bad posture and **lower back pain**. High heels also cause calf muscles to **shorten** and **bulge**, and places excess pressure on **knee** and **hip joints**.
- Wearing **flat shoes** can lead to **knee**, **hip** and **back pain** and can also cause **painful heels**.
- Wearing **badly fitting shoes**, **high heels** or **narrow**, **pointed shoes** can lead to **toe deformities**.
- Wearing the **incorrect sports shoes** can increase the chances of **foot** and **ankle injuries**.

Lifting heavy objects

Using incorrect lifting techniques or attempting to lift a load that is too heavy can **sprain ligaments** and **strain muscles** and **tendons**, especially those of the lower back, which can then lead to **back pain.** It can also cause a **slipped disc**, especially in the lower part of the spine.

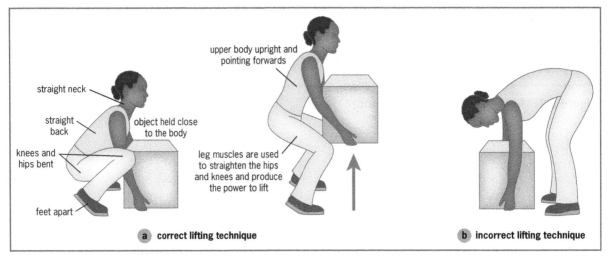

Figure 6.9 *Correct and incorrect lifting techniques*

Obesity

Extra weight puts strain on the skeleton, especially the **joints**. This causes cartilage to wear down and leads to **arthritis**, where joints become swollen and painful, and movement is restricted.

An unbalanced diet

A diet deficient in **vitamin D** leads to **rickets** in children (see page 24) and **osteomalacia** in adults. A diet deficient in **calcium** leads to **rickets** in children and **osteoporosis** in adults. A diet deficient in **protein** can cause a decrease in **bone density** and **muscle mass**.

The importance of locomotion to humans

Many human activities involve **locomotion**, which is movement of an entire organism from one place to another. Locomotion is essential for **work** and **recreation**, to find **food**, to find a partner for **reproduction**, to **escape** from danger, to avoid being **overcrowded** and for **exercise** to keep the body healthy. Walking on their two legs means humans can use their **arms** and **hands** for other activities, e.g. manipulating tools and writing.

Revision questions

1. Distinguish between the axial and appendicular skeleton and list the bones that make up the axial skeleton and those that make up the appendicular skeleton.

2. Describe the structure of a typical long bone and relate this structure to its functions.

3. By referring to the different parts of the human skeleton, discuss THREE of its functions.

4. Distinguish between:

   a bone and cartilage

   b a tendon and a ligament

5. Name the THREE types of muscles found in the human body and state ONE function of EACH type.

6. a What is a joint?

   b How does movement at a hinge joint differ from movement at a ball and socket joint?

   c Identify TWO places in the human body where you would find EACH type of joint named in **b** above.

7. Describe the structure of a ball and socket joint.

8. a Why are two muscles needed to bring about movement of a hinge joint?

   b Explain how muscles of the leg bring about bending and straightening of the knee joint.

9. What is the difference between the insertion and the origin of a muscle?

10. Name the muscle that bends Jaden's elbow joint and the muscle that straightens it.

11. What is meant by 'muscle tone' and why is good muscle tone important?

12. Outline the adverse effects that poor posture and inappropriate foot-wear have on the skeleton.

7 Excretion and homeostasis

Chemical reactions occurring in the human body constantly produce **waste** and **harmful** substances which must be got rid of from the body. **Excretion** is responsible for getting rid of these substances. It is also essential that the body's **internal environment** is kept constant. The mechanisms of **homeostasis** are responsible for keeping conditions surrounding cells constant.

Excretion

Excretion is the process by which waste and harmful substances, produced by the body's metabolism, are removed from the body.

The **body's metabolism** refers to all the **chemical reactions** occurring within the body. Excretion is **important** for the following reasons.

- It prevents **toxic** metabolic waste substances from building up in the body and damaging or killing cells.
- It helps to keep the environment within the body **constant** (see page 75).

Excretion must not be confused with **egestion**, which is the removal of undigested dietary fibre and other materials from the body as **faeces**. This dietary fibre is not produced in the body's metabolism, so its removal cannot be classed as excretion.

Metabolic waste excreted by humans

Humans produce the following **waste substances** during metabolism.

- **Carbon dioxide** is produced in respiration.
- **Water** is produced in respiration.
- **Urea (nitrogenous waste)** is produced by the **deamination** of amino acids in the liver (see page 38).
- **Bile pigments**, e.g. bilirubin, are produced by the breakdown of haemoglobin from red blood cells in the liver.
- **Heat** is produced in general metabolism, especially respiration.

Excretory organs

Humans have several **organs** that excrete waste products.

- The **kidneys** excrete water, urea and salts as **urine**.
- The **lungs** excrete carbon dioxide and water vapour during exhalation (see page 44).
- The **skin** excretes water, urea and salts as **sweat** (see Figure 7.4, page 75). It also excretes heat.
- The **liver** excretes bile pigments. It also makes urea.

The kidneys and excretion

Humans have two **kidneys** which form part of the **urinary system** (see Figure 7.1, page 73). Kidneys have **two** main functions.

- They **excrete** metabolic waste, mainly urea, from the body.
- They **regulate** the volume and concentration of blood plasma and body fluids by regulating the amount of water they contain, a process known as **osmoregulation** (see page 77).

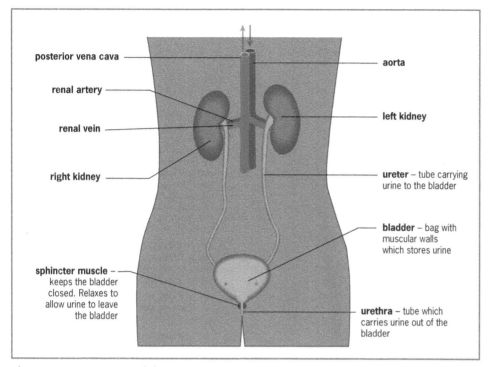

Figure 7.1 *Structure of the urinary system in a human*

Kidney structure and urine formation

Each kidney is divided into **three** regions: an outer region called the **cortex**, an inner region called the **medulla** and a central hollow region called the **pelvis** which leads into the top of the ureter. Each kidney is composed of about 1 million **kidney tubules** or **nephrons** that produce urine. A **renal artery** carries oxygenated blood containing urea from the aorta to each kidney and a **renal vein** carries deoxygenated blood lacking urea back to the posterior vena cava.

Each nephron begins with a cup-shaped **Bowman's capsule** in the cortex which surrounds an intertwined cluster of capillaries called a **glomerulus**. After the Bowman's capsule, each nephron is divided into **three** sections:

- The **first convoluted (coiled) tubule** or **proximal convoluted tubule** in the cortex.

- The **loop of Henle** in the medulla.

- The **second convoluted (coiled) tubule** or **distal convoluted tubule** in the cortex.

An **arteriole**, which branches from the renal artery, leads into each glomerulus. A capillary leads out of each glomerulus and branches to form a **network of capillaries** which wrap around each nephron and then join into a venule, which leads into the

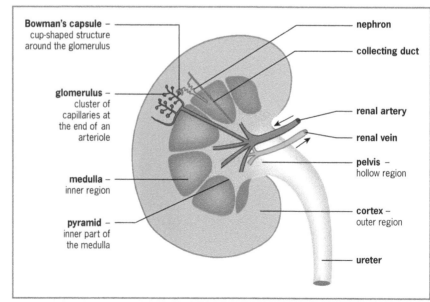

★ **Figure 7.2** *A longitudinal section through a kidney showing the position of a nephron*

renal vein. Nephrons join into **collecting ducts** in the cortex and these ducts lead through the medulla and out into the pelvis.

Urine is produced in the nephrons by **two** processes:

- **Ultra-filtration** or **pressure filtration**
- **Selective reabsorption**

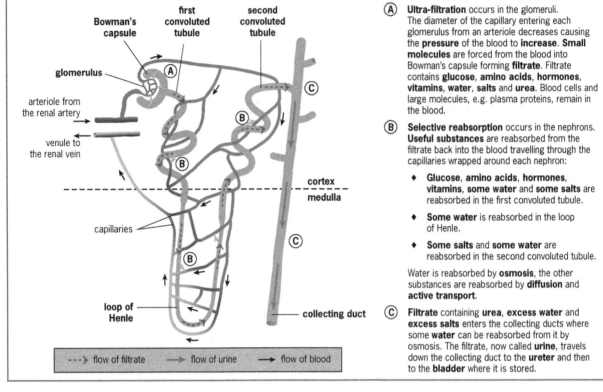

(A) **Ultra-filtration** occurs in the glomeruli. The diameter of the capillary entering each glomerulus from an arteriole decreases causing the **pressure** of the blood to **increase**. **Small molecules** are forced from the blood into Bowman's capsule forming **filtrate**. Filtrate contains **glucose, amino acids, hormones, vitamins, water, salts** and **urea**. Blood cells and large molecules, e.g. plasma proteins, remain in the blood.

(B) **Selective reabsorption** occurs in the nephrons. **Useful substances** are reabsorbed from the filtrate back into the blood travelling through the capillaries wrapped around each nephron:

- **Glucose, amino acids, hormones, vitamins, some water** and **some salts** are reabsorbed in the first convoluted tubule.

- **Some water** is reabsorbed in the loop of Henle.

- **Some salts** and **some water** are reabsorbed in the second convoluted tubule.

Water is reabsorbed by **osmosis**, the other substances are reabsorbed by **diffusion** and **active transport**.

(C) **Filtrate** containing **urea, excess water** and **excess salts** enters the collecting ducts where some **water** can be reabsorbed from it by osmosis. The filtrate, now called **urine**, travels down the collecting duct to the **ureter** and then to the **bladder** where it is stored.

★ **Figure 7.3** *Detailed structure of a nephron showing how urine is formed*

Renal dialysis

When nephrons stop functioning properly, **kidney failure** occurs, and the kidneys are unable to remove waste from the blood and regulate the volume and composition of blood plasma and body fluids. Harmful waste, especially urea, builds up in the blood and can reach toxic levels resulting in death. Kidney failure can be treated by a **kidney transplant** or **renal dialysis**.

During **dialysis,** blood from a blood vessel (usually in the arm) flows through a **dialysis machine** and is then returned to the body. In the machine, the blood is separated from **dialysis fluid** by a partially permeable membrane. **Waste products**, mainly **urea**, together with **excess water** and **salts**, pass from the blood into the dialysis fluid. In this way, waste is removed from the blood, and the volume and composition of the blood plasma and body fluids are regulated. Dialysis must occur at regular intervals; most people require three sessions per week, each lasting four hours.

The skin

The **skin** is the largest organ in the human body. It is made up of **three** layers.

- The **epidermis** is the outermost layer. It is waterproof and made of **three** layers (see Figure 7.4, page 75).
- The **dermis** is below the epidermis. It is made mainly of **connective tissue**.
- The **subcutaneous layer** is the bottom layer. It is made of **adipose tissue** composed mainly of **fat cells**.

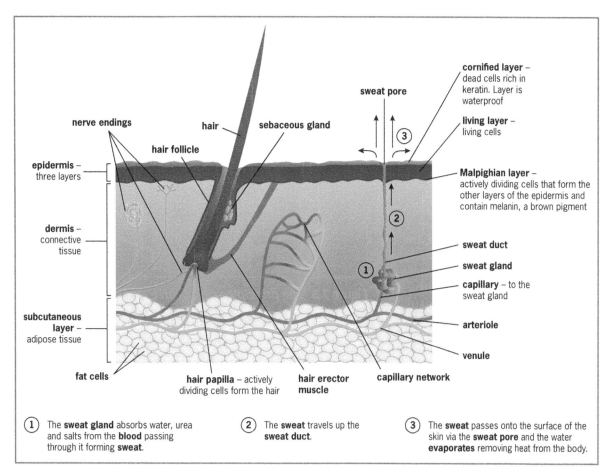

The sweat gland absorbs water, urea and salts from the **blood** passing through it forming **sweat**.

The sweat travels up the **sweat duct**.

The **sweat** passes onto the surface of the skin via the **sweat pore** and the water **evaporates** removing heat from the body.

★ **Figure 7.4** *A section through the human skin showing its structure and mechanism of sweat formation*

Table 7.1 *Functions of the structures of the skin*

Structure	Function
Epidermis	**Protects** the body against pathogens, the loss of water, the sun's harmful ultraviolet rays and harmful chemicals in the environment.
Sebaceous glands	Secrete **sebum**, an oily substance, which helps to keep the skin soft, supple and waterproof, and inhibits the growth of bacteria.
Nerve endings	**Detect** various stimuli, including touch, pressure, pain, temperature and hair movement.
Hairs and hair erector muscles	Muscles contract causing hairs to stand upright. This causes 'goose bumps' in humans, but traps a layer of air next to the skin which acts as **insulation** to prevent heat loss in hairy mammals.
Arterioles and capillary networks	Help regulate the **body temperature** (see page 78).
Sweat glands	**Produce sweat** to **cool** the body if it is too hot (see Figure 7.4).
Subcutaneous layer	**Protects** the body against heat loss in low environmental temperatures and against physical damage by acting as 'padding', and serves as a means of storing fat.

Homeostasis

Homeostasis is maintaining a constant internal environment.

Conditions surrounding cells must be very **carefully controlled** so they are at their **optimum** for enzyme action and for cells to function properly. Conditions controlled by **homeostasis** include: blood sugar levels, the water content of blood plasma and body fluids, the body temperature and the level of carbon dioxide in the blood.

Feedback mechanisms and homeostasis

Negative feedback

Homeostasis is achieved by using **negative feedback mechanisms** that involve both the **nervous system** and **hormones**. If the level of a particular factor in the body changes, **receptors** detect the change and send messages to the appropriate **effectors** causing them to respond and return the level to normal, i.e. the effectors exert an opposite or **negative** effect.

If the corrective mechanism **fails**, the level cannot be returned to normal and will continue to increase or decrease. This can result in a person's health being impaired, and may even result in death, e.g. diabetes mellitus, heat stroke and hypothermia.

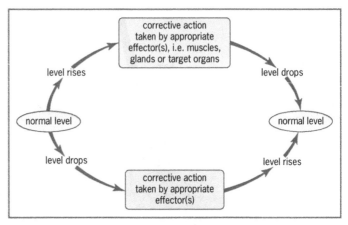

Figure 7.5 *The principles of negative feedback mechanisms*

Positive feedback

Positive feedback mechanisms intensify conditions rather than reverse them. They are not very common, occurring only when there is a definite **end point**, e.g. **childbirth** and **blood clotting**.

- During **childbirth**, the hormone **oxytocin** is released by the pituitary gland and stimulates contractions of the uterus wall (see page 99). These contractions push the baby's head against the cervix and start to **stretch** it, and this causes nerve impulses to be sent to the brain stimulating **more** oxytocin to be released. The increased oxytocin **intensifies** and **speeds up** contractions and the cycle continues until the cervix is fully stretched (dilated) and the **baby is born.**

- During **blood clotting**, as one clotting factor is activated, it activates the next factor in sequence until fibrin fibres form and a **clot develops** (see page 54).

Regulation of blood sugar (glucose) levels

The normal concentration of glucose in the blood is approximately **80 mg per 100 cm³ of blood**. The **pancreas** constantly monitors the level of glucose in the blood and secretes two **hormones** directly into the blood to keep the level constant.

- If the blood glucose level **rises**, e.g. after a meal rich in carbohydrates, the pancreas secretes **insulin**. Insulin stimulates body cells to absorb glucose for **respiration** and the liver cells to convert excess glucose to **glycogen**, which it stores.

- If the blood glucose level **falls**, e.g. between meals, or during exercise or sleep, the pancreas secretes **glucagon**. Glucagon stimulates liver cells to convert stored glycogen to **glucose**, which enters the blood.

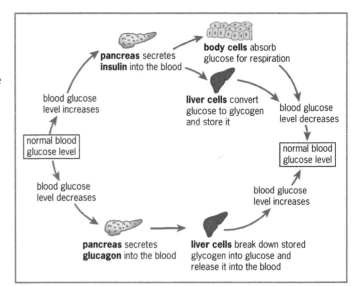

Figure 7.6 *Control of blood glucose levels*

Diabetes mellitus occurs when a person is unable to regulate their blood glucose levels such that they remain **too high** (see page 142).

Osmoregulation

Osmoregulation is the regulation of the water content of blood plasma and body fluids.

The water content of blood plasma and body fluids must be kept constant to prevent water moving into and out of body cells unnecessarily.

- If body fluids contain **too much water** (become too dilute), water will **enter** body cells by osmosis. The cells will swell and may burst. Drinking a lot of liquid or sweating very little because of being in cold weather can cause body fluids to become **too dilute**.

- If body fluids contain **too little water** (become too concentrated), water will **leave** body cells by osmosis. The cells will shrink and the body will become **dehydrated**. If too much water leaves cells, metabolic reactions cannot take place and cells will die. Not drinking enough, excessive sweating or eating a lot of salty foods can cause body fluids to become **too concentrated**.

The **kidneys** regulate the water content of body fluids by controlling how much **water** is reabsorbed into the blood plasma during **selective reabsorption**. This determines how much water is lost in urine. Control involves the following.

- The **hypothalamus** of the brain, which detects changes in the concentration of blood plasma.

- **Antidiuretic hormone (ADH)**, which is produced by the **pituitary gland** at the base of the brain in response to messages from the hypothalamus. ADH is carried by the blood to the kidneys where it controls the **permeability** of the walls of the second convoluted tubules and collecting ducts to water.

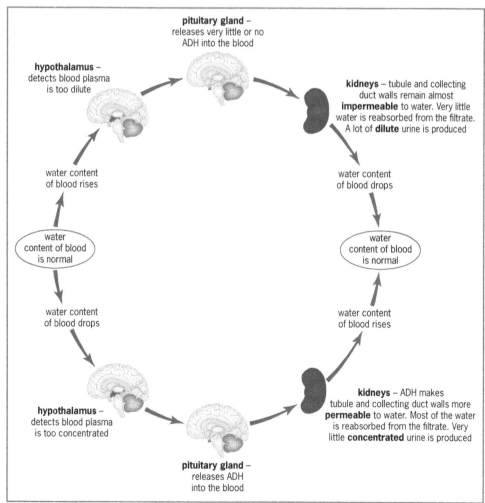

Figure 7.7 *Osmoregulation*

Regulation of body temperature

Humans must maintain a constant internal body temperature of **37 °C** for **enzymes** to function correctly. Most heat is **gained** from **metabolic processes**, mainly respiration, and the blood carries this heat around the body. Heat is **lost** mainly by conduction, convection and radiation through the skin, and also by evaporation of water during exhaling and sweating. The **hypothalamus** of the brain detects changes in temperature of the blood and sends messages to appropriate effectors, mainly in the **skin**, which respond.

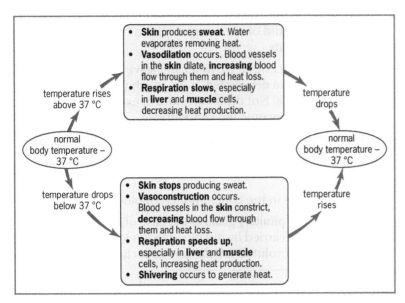

Figure 7.8 *Control of body temperature*

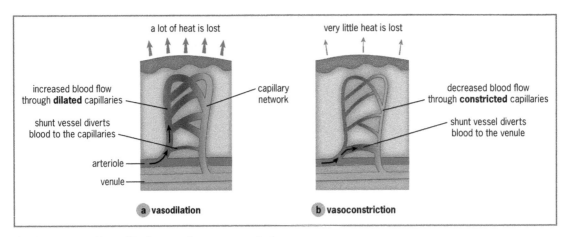

★ **Figure 7.9** *Vasodilation and vasoconstriction*

Note that heat and temperature are not the same.

- **Heat** is the total amount of **energy** an object contains. It is measured in **joules** or **J**.
- **Temperature** is a measure of how **hot** or how **cold** an object is. It is measured in **degrees Celsius** or **°C**.

Revision questions

1.   a Define 'excretion'.

     b Explain why egestion is not considered to be excretion.

2.   Explain what will happen to an organism if excretion does not occur.

3.   Construct a table to show the different excretory organs in the human body and what EACH excretes.

4.   Distinguish between the renal artery and the renal vein.

5.   Outline how urine is produced in Marissa's kidneys.

6.   A person suffering from kidney failure can be treated using dialysis. Explain why this treatment must occur at regular intervals.

7.   State the function of EACH of the following structures of the skin:

     a the epidermis   b the subcutaneous layer   c the hair erector muscles

8.   a What is meant by the term 'homeostasis'?

     b Distinguish between positive and negative feedback mechanisms and explain why negative feedback mechanisms are important in homeostasis.

9.   After a meal rich in carbohydrates, the blood glucose level rises. How does the body function to return the level to normal?

10. a Name the process by which the water content of body fluids is regulated.

     b Tyler plays tennis all day in the hot sun and drinks very little. What effect will his behaviour have on the quantity and concentration of his urine? Explain your answer.

11. a Distinguish between heat and temperature.

     b Explain the changes that occur in a person's skin if their body temperature rises above 37 °C.

8 Coordination and control

Humans must constantly monitor both their external environment and their internal environment and **respond** appropriately to any changes in these environments to help them survive. To do this, two systems are involved: the **nervous system** and the **endocrine** or **hormonal system**.

Some important definitions

*A **stimulus** is a change in the internal or external environment of an organism that initiates a response.*

*A **response** is a change in an organism or part of an organism which is brought about by a stimulus.*

*A **receptor** is the part of the organism that **detects** the stimulus.*

*An **effector** is the part of an organism that **responds** to the stimulus.*

Control by the nervous and endocrine systems compared

Coordination and **control** are brought about by **receptors** detecting **stimuli**, both internal and external, and passing messages on to the appropriate **effectors** causing them to **respond**. In humans, receptors are the **sense organs**, which contain specialised receptor cells, and effectors are **muscles**, **glands** and **target organs**. The **nervous** and **endocrine systems** are responsible for coordination and control.

Table 8.1 *Control by the nervous and endocrine systems compared*

Control by the nervous system	Control by the endocrine system
Messages are carried as **electrical impulses** along **nerves**.	Messages are carried by **chemicals** known as **hormones** in the **blood**.
Messages are transmitted **rapidly**.	Messages are usually transmitted **slowly**.
Messages are carried to **precise** places in the body.	Messages are carried to **generalised** regions of the body.
Messages have an **immediate** effect on the body.	Messages usually have a **slow** effect on the body.
Messages have a **short-lasting** effect on the body which is usually **temporary** and **reversible**.	Messages usually have a **long-lasting** effect on the body which is usually **permanent**.
Effectors are **muscles** and **glands**.	Effectors are **target organs**.

The nervous system

The human nervous system is composed of **neurones** or **nerve cells** and is divided into **two** parts.

- The **central nervous system (CNS)** consists of the **brain** and the **spinal cord**.
- The **peripheral nervous system (PNS)** consists of **cranial** and **spinal nerves** that connect the central nervous system to all parts of the body. The PNS is divided into the **voluntary** or **somatic nervous system** and the **autonomic nervous system**.

Neurones

Neurones are specialised cells that conduct nerve impulses throughout the nervous system.

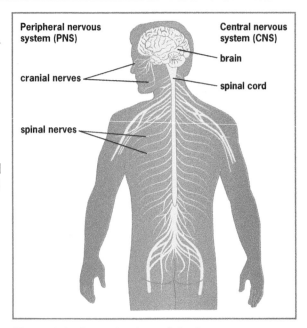

Figure 8.1 *Organisation of the human nervous system*

All **neurones** have a **cell body** with thin fibres of cytoplasm extending from it called **nerve fibres**. Nerve fibres that carry impulses **towards** the cell body are called **dendrites**. Nerve fibres that carry impulses **away from** the cell body are called **axons**; each neurone has only one axon. There are **three** types of neurones.

- **Sensory neurones** transmit impulses from **receptors** to the **CNS**.
- **Motor neurones** transmit impulses from the **CNS** to **effectors**.
- **Relay** or **intermediate neurones** transmit impulses throughout the **CNS**. They link sensory and motor neurones.

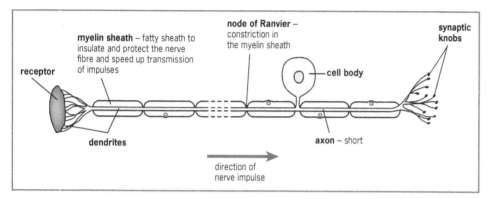

★ **Figure 8.2** *Structure of a sensory neurone*

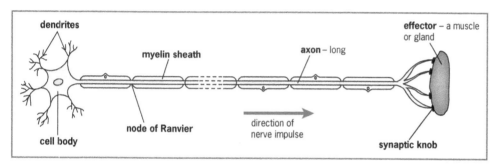

★ **Figure 8.3** *Structure of a motor neurone*

When a **receptor** is stimulated, impulses pass from the receptor along **sensory neurones** to the CNS, where they pass into **relay neurones**. The impulses then pass into **motor neurones** which carry them out of the CNS to **effectors**.

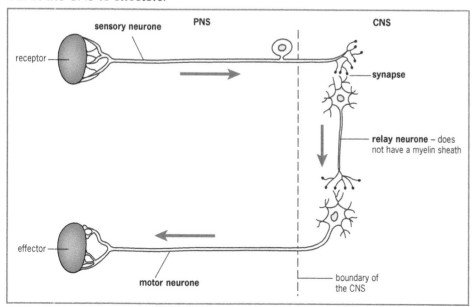

Figure 8.4 *The connection between a receptor and an effector*

Neurones have **two** major **properties:**

- **Irritability.** They can **convert** a stimulus into an electrical (nerve) impulse.
- **Conductivity.** They can **transmit** nerve impulses to other neurones, muscles or glands.

Synapses

*A **synapse** is the site of transmission of nerve impulses between adjacent neurones or between a neurone and an effector cell.*

Adjacent neurones do not touch. There are tiny gaps called **synaptic clefts** between the synaptic knobs at the ends of axons and the dendrites or cell bodies of adjacent neurones (see Figure 8.4). When a nerve impulse arrives at a synaptic knob, it causes **chemicals** called **neurotransmitters** to be released into the gap. These neurotransmitter molecules diffuse across the gap and cause an impulse to be set up in the adjacent neurone. This ensures that impulses travel in **one direction** only and allows **many** neurones to interconnect. **Synapses** are also found between synaptic knobs and **effector cells.**

Over 100 different chemicals can act as **neurotransmitters** and these can be either **excitatory neurotransmitters** which increase the likelihood of a response or **inhibitory neurotransmitters** which decrease the likelihood of a response.

Table 8.2 *The main neurotransmitters and their functions*

Neurotransmitter	Functions
Noradrenaline or **norepinephrine**	Increases heart rate, improves attention and improves the speed at which the body responds.
Dopamine	Associated with feelings of pleasure and satisfaction, and with addiction and motivation.
Serotonin	Contributes to feelings of well-being and happiness, and regulates the sleep cycle, appetite and mood.
GABA or **gamma-aminobutyric acid**	The main inhibitory neurotransmitter. It helps control anxiety and improves focus and relaxation.
Glutamate	The main excitatory neurotransmitter. It is involved in learning and helps form memories.
Acetylcholine	Involved in activating muscle contraction, learning and memory, and is associated with attention and awakening.
Endorphins	Released during exercise, excitement, pain and sexual activity. They give feelings of well-being and euphoria, and reduce pain.

Nerves

***Nerves** are cordlike bundles of nerve fibres of neurones surrounded by connective tissue through which impulses pass between the CNS and the rest of the body.*

Nerves can be classified into **three** types based on their **composition.**

- **Sensory nerves (afferent nerves)** are composed of the nerve fibres of **sensory neurones** only. They carry impulses from **receptors** to the **CNS.**
- **Motor nerves (efferent nerves)** are composed of nerve fibres of **motor neurones** only. They carry impulses from the **CNS** to **effectors.**
- **Mixed nerves** are composed of nerve fibres of both **sensory** and **motor neurones.** They carry impulses in both directions, from **receptors** to the **CNS** and from the **CNS** to **effectors.** Most nerves are mixed nerves.

Nerves can be classified into **two** types based on where they **connect to the CNS.**

- **Cranial nerves** connect to the **brain.**
- **Spinal nerves** connect to the **spinal cord.**

The brain

The **human brain** is an extremely complex organ composed of millions of interconnected **neurones**. It has **five** main regions, each concerned with different functions.

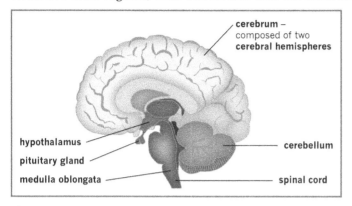

Figure 8.5 *The main parts of the human brain as seen in longitudinal section*

Table 8.3 *Functions of the main parts of the brain*

Part of the brain	Functions
Cerebrum	• Controls conscious thought, problem solving, decision making, planning and emotions. • Responsible for intelligence, memory, learning, speech and language. • Processes visual, auditory and other external information. • Coordinates voluntary actions.
Cerebellum	• Controls balance and posture. • Coordinates muscular activity and movement.
Medulla oblongata	• Controls automatic, involuntary actions, e.g. heart rate, breathing rate, blood pressure, peristalsis.
Hypothalamus	• Regulates body temperature. • Regulates the concentration of body fluids by controlling the release of ADH by the pituitary gland (see page 77). • Controls reproduction by controlling the release of FSH and LH by the pituitary gland (see pages 96–97).
Pituitary gland	• Secretes a variety of hormones, e.g. ADH, GH, FSH, LH (see Table 8.5, page 91).

Voluntary actions

*A **voluntary action** is an action that is consciously controlled by the brain.*

The **cerebrum** of the brain initiates voluntary actions in one of two ways, both of which involve **conscious thought**.

- It can receive **incoming information** from sensory neurones, **process** this information and then initiate an action.
- It can **spontaneously** initiate an action without receiving any incoming information.

To **initiate** the action in both cases, impulses are sent from the cerebrum along **relay neurones** in the brain and spinal cord to **motor neurones**. These motor neurones then carry these impulses to **skeletal muscles (effectors)** initiating a **conscious response**, e.g. talking, writing, running.

Voluntary actions:

- are **learned**
- are relatively **slow**
- are **complex** because a variety of **different responses** can result from **one stimulus**.

Involuntary actions

*An **involuntary action** is an action that occurs without conscious thought.*

Involuntary actions:

- are **not learned**
- are **rapid**
- are **simple** because the **same response** always results from the **same stimulus**.

There are **two** types of involuntary actions:

- Actions controlled by the **autonomic nervous system**.
- **Reflex actions**.

Actions controlled by the autonomic nervous system

The **autonomic nervous system** regulates the functioning of **internal organs**, e.g. it controls breathing rate, heart rate, digestion, peristalsis and blood pressure. Information from **internal receptors** passes to the **medulla oblongata** of the brain which sends impulses out along **motor neurones** in cranial and spinal nerves to the effectors. The autonomic nervous system is important in **homeostasis** (see pages 75–78).

Reflex actions

*A **reflex action** is a rapid, automatic, involuntary response to a stimulus by a muscle or gland.*

A **reflex action** is always initiated by an **external stimulus**. There are **two** types of reflex actions: **simple reflex actions** and **conditioned reflex actions**.

Simple reflex actions

Most **simple reflexes** are present from **birth** and they are **fixed**, i.e. when a particular receptor is stimulated, it always results in the same response. The **pathway** between receptor and effector is known as a **reflex arc**, and it involves the following.

- A **receptor** that detects the stimulus.
- A **sensory neurone** that carries the impulse to the central nervous system.
- A **relay neurone** in the central nervous system that carries the impulse to a motor neurone.
- A **motor neurone** that carries the impulse away from the central nervous system.
- An **effector** that responds to the stimulus.

Simple reflexes are classified as **cranial reflexes** or **spinal reflexes**.

In **cranial reflexes**, impulses pass through **cranial nerves** and the **brain**, e.g. the pupil reflex, blinking, sneezing, coughing and saliva production.

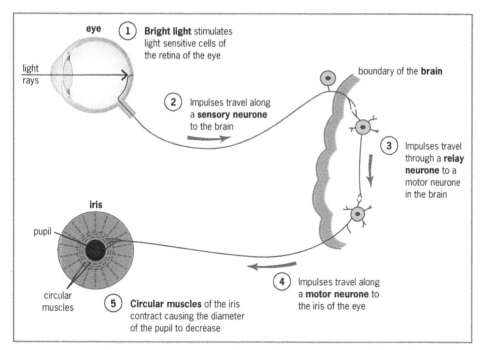

Figure 8.6 *The pupil reflex*

Spinal reflexes

In **spinal reflexes**, impulses pass through **spinal nerves** and the **spinal cord**. Spinal reflexes include the knee jerk reflex which lacks a relay neurone, and the withdrawal reflex in response to **pain**, e.g. when the finger is pricked, pain receptors are stimulated and the hand is rapidly withdrawn from the source of the pain.

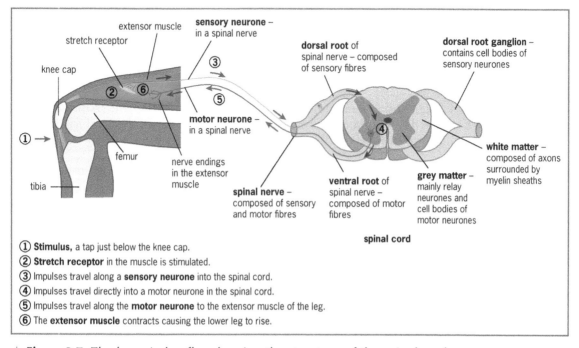

① **Stimulus**, a tap just below the knee cap.
② **Stretch receptor** in the muscle is stimulated.
③ Impulses travel along a **sensory neurone** into the spinal cord.
④ Impulses travel directly into a motor neurone in the spinal cord.
⑤ Impulses travel along the **motor neurone** to the extensor muscle of the leg.
⑥ The **extensor muscle** contracts causing the lower leg to rise.

★ **Figure 8.7** *The knee jerk reflex showing the structure of the spinal cord*

Conditioned reflex actions

*A **conditioned reflex** is a reflex action that is acquired through learning or through experiencing a stimulus which originally failed to bring about a response.*

Conditioned reflexes occur when the pattern of a simple reflex is changed by a period of **conditioning** or **learning**. For example, a dog produces saliva when presented with food due to a simple reflex, but it does not produce saliva when a bell is rung. However, if a bell is rung each time the dog is given food, after several days the dog produces saliva at the sound of the bell alone. The dog has become **conditioned**, or has **learnt**, to **associate** the bell with food.

Most **learning** is by conditioning, e.g. learning to write, use a knife and fork, ride a bicycle or play tennis. This learning usually needs to be **reinforced** periodically and it helps a person to acquire new skills.

Revision questions

1. Give THREE differences between coordination and control by the nervous system and coordination and control by the endocrine system.

2. Describe the main divisions of the nervous system.

3. a Distinguish between a neurone and a nerve.
   b Name the THREE types of neurones found in the nervous system and indicate the function of EACH.
   c Identify the TWO major properties of all neurones.

4. a What is a synapse and why are synapses important in the nervous system?
   b Name THREE different neurotransmitters and give the functions of EACH.

5. Give TWO functions of EACH of the following regions of the brain:
   a the medulla oblongata   b the cerebellum   c the cerebrum

6. Give THREE differences between a voluntary action and an involuntary action and give TWO examples of EACH.

7. What is the autonomic nervous system and what does it control?

8. What is a reflex action?

9. Jan pricked her finger and immediately withdrew her hand from the source of the pain. Draw a simple flow diagram to show the pathway along which the impulses passed in Jan's body to bring about her response.

10. What is a conditioned reflex action and of what importance are conditioned reflexes to humans?

Sense organs

Sense organs contain specialised receptor cells that **detect** changes in the environment, i.e. **stimuli.** The cells turn these stimuli into **electrical impulses** which travel along **sensory neurones** to the CNS. The **cerebrum** of the brain then interprets these impulses as **sensations** of seeing, hearing, smelling, tasting and touching.

Table 8.4 *Sense organs in the human body*

Sense organ	Specialised receptor cells	Stimuli detected
Eyes	Rods and cones (photoreceptors) in the retina.	Light.
Ears	Mechanoreceptor cells in the inner ear.	Sound waves and the position of the head.
Nose	Olfactory cells (chemoreceptors) in the top of the nasal cavities.	Chemicals in the air.
Tongue	Taste receptor cells (chemoreceptors) in the taste buds.	Chemicals in food. Five tastes are detected; sweet, sour, salty, bitter and umami (savoury).
Skin	Touch receptor cells.	Touch and texture.
	Pressure receptor cells.	Pressure.
	Pain receptor cells.	Pain and itching.
	Temperature receptor cells.	Hot and cold.

The eye

The **eye** detects **light** that has been reflected from an object and converts it into **electrical impulses**. The impulses are transmitted along the **optic nerve** to the brain, which translates them into a precise picture of the object.

The eyes are situated in bony sockets of the skull called **orbits** and have muscles attached to move them. The orbits protect the back of each eye from damage, and the **eyelids** and **eyelashes** protect the front from foreign particles. **Tears**, produced by tear glands above each eye, keep the eyes moist, wash away foreign particles and contain an enzyme that destroys microorganisms.

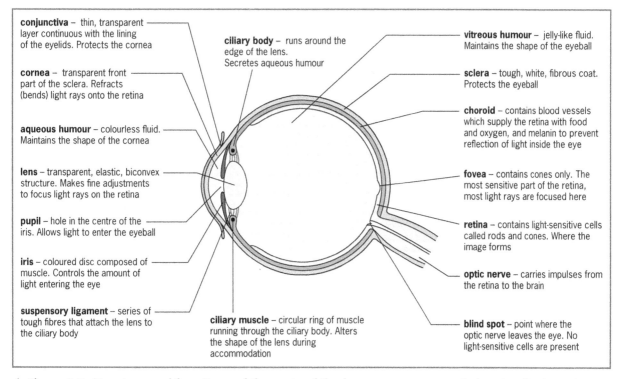

★ **Figure 8.8** *Structure and functions of the parts of the human eye, as seen in longitudinal section*

Image formation

In order to see, light rays from an object must be **refracted** (bent) as they enter the eye so that they form a clear **image** of the object on the receptor cells of the retina. Being **convex** in shape, both the **cornea** and the **lens** refract the light rays; the cornea refracts them to the greatest extent and the lens makes fine adjustments to focus them onto the retina.

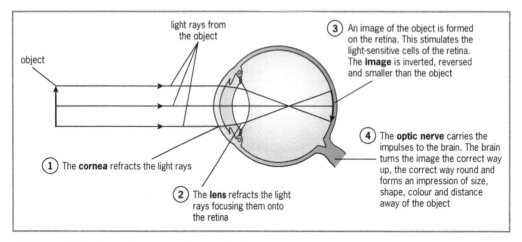

light rays from the object

object

3 An image of the object is formed on the retina. This stimulates the light-sensitive cells of the retina. The **image** is inverted, reversed and smaller than the object

4 The **optic nerve** carries the impulses to the brain. The brain turns the image the correct way up, the correct way round and forms an impression of size, shape, colour and distance away of the object

1 The **cornea** refracts the light rays

2 The **lens** refracts the light rays focusing them onto the retina

★ **Figure 8.9** *Formation of an image in the eye*

Detection of light intensity and colour by the eye

The **retina** is composed of **two** types of specialised **light-sensitive cells** or **photoreceptors**.

- **Rods** function in **low light intensities**. They are responsible for detecting the **brightness** of light and are mainly located around the sides of the retina. Images falling on the rods are seen in **shades** of black and white only.

- **Cones** function in **high light intensities**. They are responsible for detecting **colour** and **fine detail**, and are mainly located around the back of the retina. The **fovea** is composed entirely of cones which are packed closely together. Light rays focusing on the fovea produce the **sharpest** image. There are three types of cones which detect either the red, green or blue wavelengths of light.

Control of the amount of light entering the eye

The size of the **pupil** controls the amount of light entering the eye. Muscles of the **iris** control the pupil size.

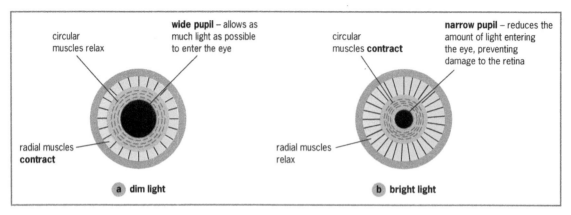

circular muscles relax

wide pupil – allows as much light as possible to enter the eye

circular muscles **contract**

narrow pupil – reduces the amount of light entering the eye, preventing damage to the retina

radial muscles **contract**

radial muscles relax

a dim light

b bright light

Figure 8.10 *Controlling the amount of light entering the eye*

Focusing light onto the retina – accommodation

Accommodation is the process by which the shape of the lens is changed to focus light coming from different distances onto the retina.

By its **shape** changing, the **lens** makes fine adjustments to focus light rays onto the retina. This is brought about by the **ciliary muscle** in the ciliary body and the **elasticity** of the **lens**.

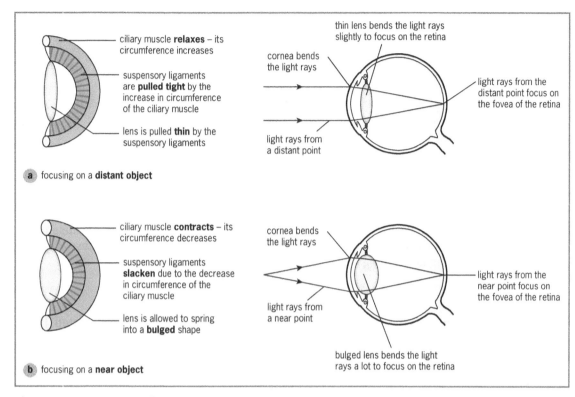

Figure 8.11 *Accommodation*

Sight defects and diseases, and their corrections

Short-sightedness (myopia)

A person with **short sight** can see **near** objects clearly, but distant objects are out of focus. Light rays from near objects focus on the retina; light rays from **distant** objects focus **in front** of the retina. It is caused by the eyeball being too **long** from front to back or the lens being too **curved** (thick). It is corrected by wearing **diverging (concave) lenses** as spectacles or contact lenses.

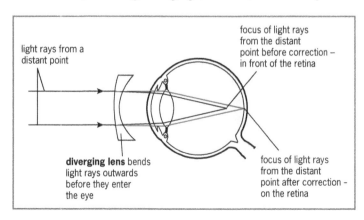

★ **Figure 8.12** *The cause and correction of short sight*

Long-sightedness (hyperopia or hypermetropia)

A person with **long sight** can see **distant** objects clearly, but near objects are out of focus. Light rays from distant objects focus on the retina; light rays from **near** objects focus **behind** the retina. It is caused by the eyeball being too **short** from front to back or the lens being too **flat** (thin). It is corrected by wearing **converging (convex) lenses** as spectacles or contact lenses.

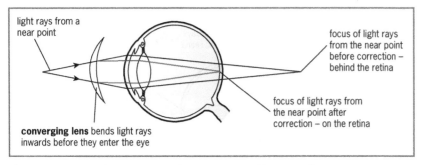

light rays from a near point

focus of light rays from the near point before correction – behind the retina

focus of light rays from the near point after correction – on the retina

converging lens bends light rays inwards before they enter the eye

★ **Figure 8.13** *The cause and correction of long sight*

Old sightedness (presbyopia)

A person with **old sight** finds it increasingly difficult to see **near** objects clearly. It occurs because the lens loses its elasticity as a person ages and the ciliary muscles weaken so that the lens is less able to curve. It is corrected by wearing **converging lenses** to look at near objects.

Astigmatism

A person who has **astigmatism** finds that both near and distant objects appear **blurry** or **distorted**. It occurs if the cornea or lens is **unevenly curved** so not all light rays are equally refracted and not all focus on the retina. It is corrected by wearing **unevenly curved lenses** that counteract the uneven curvature of the cornea or lens.

Glaucoma

Glaucoma is a condition in which the **pressure** of the fluid within the eye increases due to the drainage channels that allow aqueous humour to flow from the eye being blocked. If left untreated, the optic nerve becomes damaged and it can lead to **blindness**. The most common type develops slowly and causes a gradual loss of peripheral (side) vision. Glaucoma is treated with **eye drops** to reduce fluid production or improve the flow of fluid from the eye, or by **laser treatment** or **surgery** to open the drainage channels.

Cataract

A **cataract** is a **cloudy** area that forms in the lens. It develops slowly and, as it increases in size, it leads to cloudy or blurred vision, halos forming around lights, colours appearing faded, and difficulty seeing in bright light and at night. It is usually caused by **ageing** and is usually corrected by **surgery** to remove the clouded lens and to replace it with an **artificial lens**.

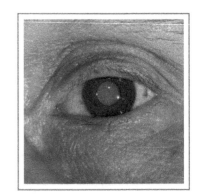

Figure 8.14 *An eye with a cataract*

Effects of diabetes on eyesight

High blood sugar levels experienced by a person with **diabetes** can damage the person's eyes and lead to **diabetic eye disease**, a group of conditions that includes **diabetic retinopathy, glaucoma** and **cataracts**. All these conditions can lead to poor vision and blindness. The most common is **diabetic retinopathy**, which is caused by high blood sugar levels damaging the small blood vessels in the **retina**. Symptoms include blurry or patchy vision, blank spots, impaired colour vision, dark floating shapes in the visual field and loss of vision.

The endocrine system

The **endocrine system** is composed of **endocrine glands** or **ductless glands** which secrete **hormones** directly into the **blood**. Some hormones have an effect on specific **target organs**, e.g. antidiuretic hormone (ADH), while others have an effect on cells and tissues throughout the body, e.g. thyroxine.

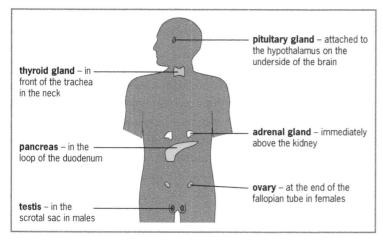

★ **Figure 8.15** *The position of the main endocrine glands*

Table 8.5 *Hormones of the main endocrine glands and their functions*

Endocrine gland	Hormone(s)	Function(s)
Pituitary gland	Antidiuretic hormone (ADH)	Controls the **water content** of blood plasma and body fluids by controlling water reabsorption in the **kidneys** (see page 77).
	Growth hormone (GH)	• In **children**: stimulates **growth** by stimulating protein synthesis in cells and bone growth. • In **adults**: helps maintain healthy **bone** and **muscle** masses.
	Follicle stimulating hormone (FSH)	• In **females**: helps regulate the **menstrual cycle** by stimulating the development and maturation of the **ova** and **Graafian follicles** in the ovaries, and stimulating the Graafian follicles to produce **oestrogen** (see page 96). • In **males**: helps control production of **sperm** in the testes.
	Luteinising hormone (LH)	• In **females**: helps regulate the **menstrual cycle** by stimulating **ovulation** and the development of the **corpus luteum** in the ovaries, and stimulating the corpus luteum to produce **progesterone** (see page 97). • In **males**: stimulates the production of **testosterone** by the testes.
Thyroid gland	Thyroxine	Controls the **rate of metabolism** and energy production in cells, and physical **growth** and **mental development**, especially in children.
Adrenal glands	Adrenaline (flight, fright or fight hormone)	Released in large amounts when frightened, excited or anxious. Speeds up **metabolism**, mainly respiration, and increases blood sugar levels, heartbeat, breathing rate and blood supply to muscles, i.e. it triggers the **fight-or-flight response** and gives the feeling of **fear**.
Pancreas	**Insulin** and **glucagon**	Regulate **blood glucose** levels (see page 76).

Endocrine gland	Hormone(s)	Function(s)
Ovaries	**Oestrogen** (produced by the Graafian follicle)	Controls the development of female **secondary sexual characteristics** at puberty, i.e. development of breasts, pubic and underarm hair, and a broad pelvis. Helps regulate the **menstrual cycle** by stimulating the **uterus lining** or **endometrium** to thicken each month after menstruation (see page 96).
	Progesterone (produced by the corpus luteum)	Helps regulate the **menstrual cycle** by maintaining a thickened **uterus lining** after ovulation each month (see page 97).
Placenta during pregnancy	**Progesterone**	Maintains a thickened **uterus lining** during pregnancy, which prevents menstruation. Stimulates the growth of **milk-producing glands** in the breasts during pregnancy.
Testes	**Testosterone**	Controls the development of male **reproductive organs** and **secondary sexual characteristics** at puberty, i.e. development of a deep voice, facial and body hair, muscles and broad shoulders. Controls **sperm** production in the testes.

Revision questions

11 Make a list of the different sense organs in the human body and indicate the stimulus or stimuli detected by EACH.

12 Construct a table to show the function of EACH of the following parts of the eye: the conjunctiva, the sclera, the pupil, the choroid, the optic nerve and the vitreous humour.

13 Explain how an image is formed in Omari's eye.

14 Explain how Samara's eyes adjust when she:

a walks from a dimly lit room into the bright sunshine

b looks at a book in her hand after watching an aeroplane in the sky.

15 Malik has his eyes tested and is told that he is long sighted. Explain the possible cause of his sight defect and how it can be corrected.

16 What is glaucoma and how can it be treated?

17 Solana, a diabetic, notices that she is starting to see dark, floating shapes and blank spots in her visual field. Suggest a possible reason for Solana's symptoms and what she should do to try and prevent them from worsening.

18 Suggest why the pituitary gland is often referred to as the 'master gland'.

19 For EACH of the following endocrine glands, identify where the gland is located in the body, name the hormone it produces and outline the functions of the hormone:

a the thyroid gland   b the adrenal glands   c the testes

9 The reproductive system

All living organisms must **produce offspring** in order for their species to survive. There are two types of reproduction: **asexual reproduction** and **sexual reproduction**. Humans reproduce sexually, and the male and female **reproductive systems** function to produce their offspring.

Reproduction is the process by which living organisms generate new individuals of the same kind as themselves.

Asexual and sexual reproduction compared

Asexual reproduction

Asexual reproduction involves only **one** parent and offspring are produced by **mitosis** (see pages 114–115). All offspring produced asexually from one parent are **genetically identical**, i.e. they do not show variation, and are collectively called a **clone**. The process is **rapid** because it does not involve gamete production, finding a mate, fertilisation and embryo development. Asexual reproduction occurs in unicellular organisms such as bacteria and protozoans, e.g. an amoeba. It also occurs in some fungi, some plants and a few animals.

Sexual reproduction

Sexual reproduction involves **two** parents. **Gametes**, or sex cells, are produced in reproductive organs by **meiosis** (see page 116). A male and a female gamete fuse during **fertilisation** to form a single cell called a **zygote**. The zygote divides by **mitosis** to form an **embryo** and ultimately an **adult**. Offspring produced sexually receive genes from both parents, therefore they possess characteristics of both parents, i.e. they show **variation**. The process is **slow** because it involves gamete production, finding a mate, fertilisation and embryo development. Sexual reproduction occurs in most plants and animals.

The female and male reproductive systems

The female reproductive system

The **female gametes** are called **ova** and they are produced in two **ovaries** which form part of the female reproductive system.

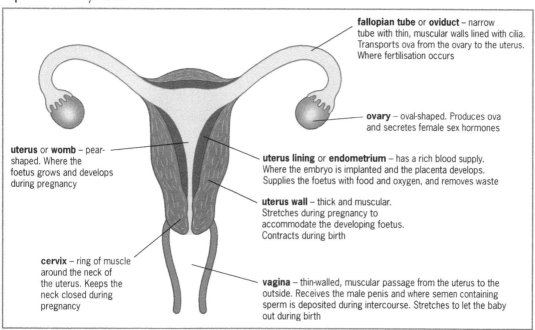

fallopian tube or **oviduct** – narrow tube with thin, muscular walls lined with cilia. Transports ova from the ovary to the uterus. Where fertilisation occurs

ovary – oval-shaped. Produces ova and secretes female sex hormones

uterus or **womb** – pear-shaped. Where the foetus grows and develops during pregnancy

uterus lining or **endometrium** – has a rich blood supply. Where the embryo is implanted and the placenta develops. Supplies the foetus with food and oxygen, and removes waste

uterus wall – thick and muscular. Stretches during pregnancy to accommodate the developing foetus. Contracts during birth

cervix – ring of muscle around the neck of the uterus. Keeps the neck closed during pregnancy

vagina – thin-walled, muscular passage from the uterus to the outside. Receives the male penis and where semen containing sperm is deposited during intercourse. Stretches to let the baby out during birth

★ **Figure 9.1** *Structure and function of the parts of the female reproductive system*

The male reproductive system

The male gametes are called **sperm** or **spermatozoa** and they are produced in the **testes** which form part of the male reproductive system.

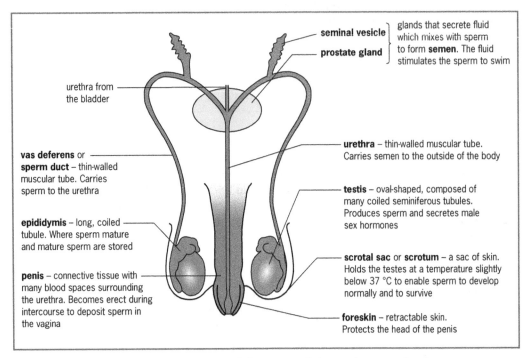

★ **Figure 9.2** *Structure and function of the parts of the male reproductive system*

Production and structure of ova and sperm

At birth, each female ovary contains many thousand **immature ova.** Each is surrounded by a fluid-filled space that forms a **primary follicle**. Each month between **puberty** at about 11 to 13 years old, and **menopause** at about 45 to 55 years old, one immature ovum develops into a **mature ovum**. About 450 immature ova will mature in a woman's lifetime. To produce a mature ovum, the immature ovum undergoes **meiosis** (see page 116). One of the four cells produced develops into a mature ovum which is released during **ovulation.**

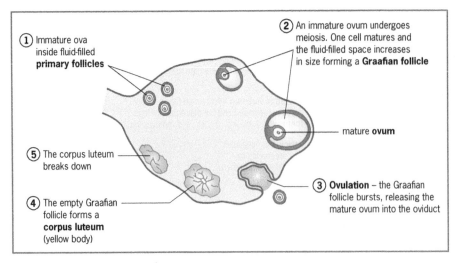

Figure 9.3 *Production of an ovum in an ovary*

Sperm cells are produced continuously from **puberty** in the **seminiferous tubules** of the **testes**. Cells in the tubule walls undergo **meiosis** and **all** the cells produced develop into sperm. These mature in the **epididymis** where they are stored until ejaculation.

Table 9.1 *Ova and sperm cells compared*

	Ova	Sperm cells
Structure	 layer of follicle cells – act as protection membrane nucleus layer of jelly cytoplasm containing yolk	 middle piece – contains mitochondria to release energy for swimming tail – for swimming nucleus head small amount of cytoplasm **acrosome** – contains enzymes to dissolve a passage into the ovum
Production	One is produced each month from puberty to menopause.	Thousands are produced continuously from puberty.
Movement	Are moved down an oviduct after ovulation by muscular contractions of the oviduct walls and beating of the cilia.	Swim actively using their tails when mixed with secretions from the seminal vesicles and prostate gland during ejaculation.
Life span	Live for about 24 hours after ovulation.	Can live for about 2 to 3 days in the female body after ejaculation.

Disorders and diseases of the reproductive systems

Cancer is the main disease of the reproductive systems. It results from abnormal cells developing and dividing in an uncontrolled way. These cells replace normal cells and usually produce a **tumour** or **cancerous lump** (see page 145). Cancer can be treated by **surgery** to remove the tumour or the entire organ containing the tumour, **radiotherapy** or **chemotherapy**. Cancer can affect various parts of the reproductive systems.

Table 9.2 *Cancers of the reproductive systems*

Type of cancer	Organ affected	Notes
Ovarian	Ovary	Symptoms include abdominal pain and lower back pain.
Cervical	Cervix	Usually caused by the **human papilloma virus (HPV)** passed on through sexual contact and can be detected by a cervical smear test (Pap smear test). Early stages are free of symptoms. Vaginal bleeding, pain during sexual intercourse and vaginal discharge are symptoms of the later stages.
Uterine	Uterus	The most common symptom is abnormal bleeding from the vagina.
Breast	Breast	A tumour in a breast can be detected by hand or by a **mammogram** (X-ray). Breast reconstruction often follows surgery when the entire breast is removed.
Prostate	Prostate gland	A tumour forms in the gland, which starts to block the urethra causing frequent but slow urination. It can be diagnosed using a prostate specific antigen (PSA) blood test or a digital rectal examination (DRE).
Testicular	Testis	A tumour in a testis can be detected by hand. Symptoms may include testicular discomfort.

Other disorders of the reproductive systems include **endometriosis**, which occurs when tissue similar to that of the endometrium grows outside the uterus, usually on other organs in the abdominal cavity, **uterine fibroids**, which are non-cancerous tumours that develop in the uterus, and **erectile dysfunction** or **impotence**, which occurs when a male is unable to get and keep an erection firm enough to have sexual intercourse.

The menstrual cycle

The **menstrual cycle** is a cycle of about 28 days which prepares the uterus lining each month to receive the embryo if fertilisation occurs. The cycle contains **two** main events: **ovulation** and **menstruation.**

- **Ovulation** is the release of an **ovum** from an ovary.
- **Menstruation** is the loss of the **uterus lining** from the body. This starts to occur about 14 days after ovulation if fertilisation has not occurred.

The **start** of each cycle is taken from the **first day** of menstruation.

Table 9.3 *A summary of the events occurring in an ovary and the uterus during the menstrual cycle*

Time	Events in an ovary	Events in the uterus
Day 1 to day 14	An immature ovum undergoes meiosis and one cell matures. The Graafian follicle develops around the ovum as it matures.	**Day 1 to day 5** – the uterus lining breaks down and is lost from the body. **Day 6 to day 14** – the uterus lining thickens.
Day 14	The mature ovum is released and the Graafian follicle forms the corpus luteum.	
Day 14 to day 25	The corpus luteum remains.	The uterus lining continues to thicken slightly and remains thick.
Day 26 to day 28	The corpus luteum breaks down.	The uterus lining begins to break down.

The cycle is controlled by **four hormones** which synchronise the production of an ovum with the uterus lining being ready to receive the embryo if the ovum is fertilised.

- **Follicle stimulating hormone (FSH)** is secreted by the **pituitary gland** at the **beginning** of the cycle.
  - FSH stimulates a Graafian follicle to develop in an ovary and an ovum to mature inside the follicle.
  - FSH stimulates the follicle to produce **oestrogen**.
- **Oestrogen** is produced by the **Graafian follicle** mainly during the **second week** of the cycle.
  - Oestrogen stimulates the uterus lining to thicken and its blood supply to increase after menstruation.
  - Oestrogen causes the pituitary gland to stop secreting FSH and to secrete **luteinising hormone (LH)**.

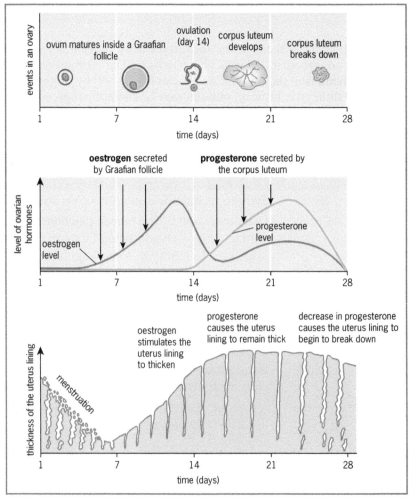

Figure 9.4 *A summary of the events occurring during the menstrual cycl*

- **Luteinising hormone (LH)** is secreted by the **pituitary gland** in the **middle** of the cycle.
  - A sudden rise in LH causes ovulation to take place.
  - LH stimulates the corpus luteum to develop in the ovary after ovulation and to secrete **progesterone**.
- **Progesterone** is produced by the **corpus luteum** during the **third week** of the cycle.
  - Progesterone causes the uterus lining to increase slightly in thickness and remain thick.
  - If fertilisation does not occur, the corpus luteum degenerates during the fourth week and reduces secretion of progesterone. The decrease in progesterone causes the uterus lining to begin to break down, and the pituitary gland to secrete **FSH** at the end of the fourth week.

Fertilisation, implantation and development

Bringing sperm and ova together

When a male becomes sexually excited, blood spaces in the penis fill with blood. The penis becomes **erect** and is placed into the female vagina. **Semen**, composed of sperm and secretions from the seminal vesicles and prostate gland, is **ejaculated** into the top of the vagina by muscular contractions of the tubules of the epididymis and sperm ducts. The **sperm** swim through the cervix and uterus and into the fallopian tubes.

Fertilisation

If an **ovum** is present in one of the fallopian tubes, one **sperm** enters using enzymes produced by the acrosome to digest a pathway. Its tail is left outside. A **fertilisation membrane** immediately develops around the ovum to prevent other sperm from entering, and the nuclei of the ovum and sperm fuse to form a **zygote**.

Implantation

The zygote divides repeatedly by **mitosis** using **yolk** stored in the original ovum as a source of nourishment. This forms a ball of cells called the **embryo**, which moves down the oviduct and sinks into the uterus lining, a process called **implantation**. Food and oxygen diffuse from the mother's blood in the lining into the embryo, and carbon dioxide and waste diffuse back into the mother's blood.

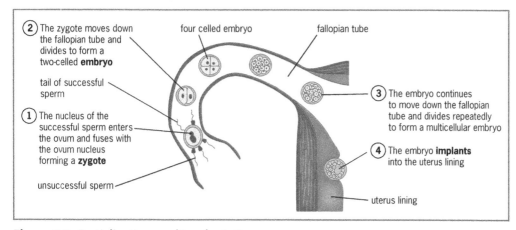

Figure 9.5 *Fertislisation and implantation*

Pregnancy and development

The cells of the embryo continue to divide and some of the cells develop into the **placenta**. The placenta is a disc of tissue with finger-like projections called **villi** which project into the uterus lining and give the placenta a large surface area. Capillaries run throughout the placenta, including inside the villi. The embryo is joined to the placenta by the **umbilical cord**, which has an **umbilical artery** and **umbilical vein** running through. These connect the capillaries in the embryo with those in the placenta.

The **placenta** allows exchange of materials between the mother's blood and the embryo's blood, but prevents mixing of the two bloods, which may be of different types. It also prevents certain unwanted substances entering the embryo's blood from the mother's blood, e.g. bacteria, viruses and harmful chemicals. However, some viruses and chemicals can pass across, e.g. the HIV virus, nicotine and heroin.

The embryo is surrounded by a thin, tough membrane called the **amnion**, which forms a sac containing **amniotic fluid** to support and protect the embryo as it develops.

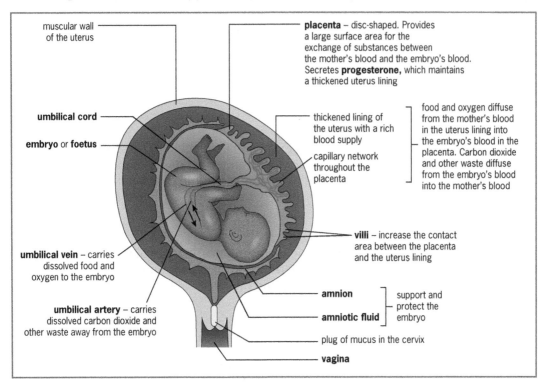

★ **Figure 9.6** *The developing human embryo/foetus in the uterus*

Table 9.4 *The development of a human embryo/foetus*

Time after fertilisation	Characteristics
7 to 10 days	A hollow ball of cells, which is implanted in the uterus lining.
4 weeks	The brain, eyes and ears are developing along with the nervous, digestive and respiratory systems. Limb buds are forming and the heart is beginning to beat.
8 weeks	The embryo has a distinctly human appearance. All the vital organs have been formed and limbs with fingers and toes are developed.
10 weeks	The embryo is now known as a **foetus**. External genitals are beginning to appear, fingernails and toenails form and the kidneys start to function.
11 to 38 weeks	The foetus continues to grow and the organs continue to develop and mature.
38 weeks	Birth occurs.

Note: The **gestation period (pregnancy)** is considered to last for 40 weeks or 280 days since it is calculated from the first day of the last menstrual cycle and not from the time of fertilisation.

The birthing process

Towards the end of the pregnancy, the baby turns to lie head down and as it continues to grow, it stretches the uterus wall to a point where **stretch receptors** are stimulated. This inhibits secretion of progesterone by the placenta and stimulates the **pituitary gland** to secrete the hormone **oxytocin**. Oxytocin then begins the **birthing process**, which is divided into **three** stages.

Stage 1: Dilation of the cervix

Oxytocin stimulates the muscles in the walls of the uterus to start **contracting**, i.e. **labour** begins. At some point, the amnion bursts and the amniotic fluid is released; this is referred to as **water breaking** or **waters breaking**. The contractions gradually strengthen, causing the **cervix** to gradually **dilate (widen)**, and they push the baby towards the cervix. Stage 1 ends when the cervix has fully dilated to **10 cm**.

Stage 2: Expulsion of the baby or birth

Pressure of the baby's head on the **cervix** gives the mother the urge to **push**. She aims to push with each contraction, and this pushes the baby, head-first, through the cervix into the vagina. **Crowning** occurs as the top of the baby's head emerges through the opening of the vagina and is visible. The rest of the baby's head then emerges, followed by its body. Once outside, the baby starts to **breathe** and the **umbilical cord** is clamped and cut.

Stage 3: Expulsion of the placenta

After the baby is born, the **placenta** detaches from the uterus lining and is expelled from the mother's body as the **afterbirth** by further **contractions** of the uterus wall.

The effect of pregnancy on the menstrual cycle

If fertilisation takes place, the **corpus luteum** remains in the ovary and it secretes increasing amounts of **progesterone**. This causes the uterus lining to increase in thickness and it prevents menstruation. As the **placenta** develops, it takes over secreting progesterone, which keeps the uterus lining thick and inhibits ovulation and menstruation throughout pregnancy.

Prenatal and postnatal care

Prenatal or antenatal care

Prenatal care, or care before birth, is essential to ensure the foetus **grows** and **develops normally** and **healthily**, and that the mother **remains healthy** throughout her pregnancy. During pregnancy the mother should:

- Attend regular **prenatal checkups** with her doctor or clinic to monitor her health and the development of her baby.
- Have two **ultrasound scans** if possible at about 6 to 8 weeks and at about 18 to 20 weeks to monitor the baby's growth and development, and to detect any abnormalities.
- Eat a **balanced diet** that contains adequate quantities of protein, carbohydrates, vitamins and minerals, especially calcium and iron, to ensure the foetus obtains all the nutrients it needs to grow and develop.
- Not use unprescribed **drugs** of any kind, especially alcohol, cigarettes and illegal drugs, which can harm the developing foetus.
- Protect herself against harmful **X-rays** and **infectious diseases**.
- **Exercise** regularly to maintain fitness.
- Prepare her body for the birth by attending **prenatal classes**, which teach correct exercises and breathing rhythms as well as how to care for her baby after the birth.

Conditions associated with drug use during pregnancy

Any **drug** taken by a woman during pregnancy may cross the placenta and reach the developing foetus, and cause **harm** by interfering with normal foetal development. In general, consuming **alcohol**, **smoking** and using **illegal drugs** increases the risk of miscarriages, stillbirths, and babies being born with low birth weights and birth defects. The children then often have deficiencies in physical growth, and in intellectual and behavioural development.

Frequent and heavy consumption of **alcohol** can lead to babies being born with **foetal alcohol syndrome**, characterised by intellectual impairment, and babies of **heroin addicts** often become addicts in the womb and suffer **withdrawal symptoms** when born.

Postnatal care

Postnatal care, or care after birth, is essential to ensure the baby **grows** and **develops healthily**, and that the mother remains both physically and emotionally **healthy**.

* The **newborn baby** should be **breastfed**, if possible for a minimum of 6 months, because:
  * Breast milk contains all the **nutrients** the baby needs in the correct proportions.
  * Breast milk contains **antibodies**, which protect the baby against bacterial and viral diseases.
  * Breast milk is **sterile** so reduces the risk of infection, is at the correct **temperature** and is **available** whenever needed.
  * Breastfeeding lowers the baby's risk of developing **asthma**, **allergies** and other **non-communicable diseases** as it grows older.
  * Breastfeeding creates a strong **emotional bond** between mother and baby.
* The **newborn baby** must be kept **warm** and **clean**, have plenty of **interaction** with both parents and its surroundings, and be taken for regular **checkups** with the doctor. As the baby grows, it must be **weaned** onto semi-solid and solid food, **cared for** physically and emotionally, and given continual **teaching**.
* The **baby** must be **vaccinated** to **immunise** it against various infectious diseases, following a vaccination or immunisation programme.
* The **mother** must continue to eat a **balanced diet**, not use unprescribed **drugs** of any kind, **exercise** regularly and be given both physical and emotional **support**.

Birth control and family planning

Methods of birth control (contraception)

Birth control is used to **prevent unintended pregnancies**. A variety of methods are available that are designed to **prevent fertilisation** or to **prevent implantation**, and they can be **natural**, **barrier**, **hormonal** or **surgical**. Two methods, **abstinence** and the **condom**, also protect against the spread of sexually transmitted infections (STIs), e.g. HIV/AIDS. When choosing a method, its reliability, availability, side effects and whether both partners are comfortable using it, must be considered.

Table 9.5 *Methods of birth control*

Method	How the method works	Advantages	Disadvantages
Abstinence	• Refraining from sexual intercourse.	• Completely effective. • Protects against sexually transmitted infections.	• Relies on self-control from both partners.
Withdrawal	• Penis is withdrawn before ejaculation.	• No artificial device needs to be used or pills taken, i.e. it is **natural**, therefore is acceptable to all religious groups.	• Very unreliable since some semen is released before ejaculation. • Relies on self-control.

Method	How the method works	Advantages	Disadvantages
Rhythm method	• Intercourse is restricted to times when ova should be absent from the oviducts.	• No artificial device needs to be used or pills taken, i.e. it is **natural**, therefore is acceptable to all religious groups.	• Unreliable since the time of ovulation can vary. • Restricts the time when intercourse can occur. • Unsuitable for women with an irregular menstrual cycle.
Spermicides	• Creams, jellies or foams inserted into the vagina before intercourse. • Act as a **barrier** by killing sperm, which prevents them from entering the uterus.	• Easy to use. • Readily available.	• Not reliable if used alone, should be used with a condom or diaphragm. • May cause irritation or an allergic reaction.
Condom	• A latex rubber or polyurethane sheath placed over the erect penis or into the female vagina before intercourse. • Acts as a **barrier** to prevent sperm entering the female body.	• Very reliable if used correctly. • Easy to use. • Readily available. • Protects against sexually transmitted infections.	• May reduce sensitivity so interferes with enjoyment. • Condoms can tear allowing sperm to enter the vagina. • Latex may cause an allergic reaction.
Diaphragm	• A dome-shaped latex rubber disc inserted over the cervix before intercourse. Should be used with a spermicide. • Acts as a **barrier** to prevent sperm entering the uterus.	• Fairly reliable if used correctly. • Not felt, therefore, does not interfere with enjoyment. • Easy to use once the female is taught.	• Must be left in place for 6 hours after intercourse, but no longer than 24 hours. • Latex may cause an allergic reaction. • May slip out of place if not fitted properly.
Intra-uterine device (IUD or coil)	• A T-shaped plastic device, usually containing copper or progesterone, inserted into the uterus by a doctor. • Prevents sperm reaching the ova or prevents implantation.	• Very reliable. • Once fitted, no further action is required except an annual checkup. • No need to think further about contraception. • Few, if any, side effects.	• Must be inserted by a medical practitioner. • May cause menstruation to be heavier, longer or more painful.
Contraceptive pill	• A **hormone** pill, taken daily, which contains oestrogen and progesterone, or progesterone only. • Prevents ovulation. • Makes cervical mucus thicker and more difficult for sperm to swim through.	• Almost totally reliable if taken daily. • Menstruation is lighter, shorter and less painful.	• Ceases to be effective if one pill is missed. • May cause side effects in some women, especially those who smoke.

Method	How the method works	Advantages	Disadvantages
Surgical sterilisation (**vasectomy** in males, **tubal ligation** in females)	• The sperm ducts or oviducts are **surgically** cut and tied off. • Prevents sperm leaving the male body or ova passing down the oviducts.	• Totally reliable. • No need to think further about contraception. • No artificial device needs to be used or pills taken.	• Usually irreversible.

Note: One **disadvantage** of all methods, except abstinence and condoms, is that they do not protect against sexually transmitted infections.

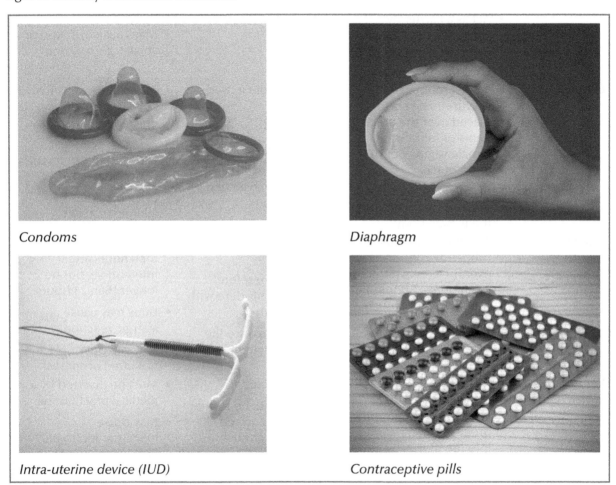

Condoms

Diaphragm

Intra-uterine device (IUD)

Contraceptive pills

Figure 9.7 *Methods of birth control*

The importance of family planning

Family planning involves making decisions about the **number** of children in a family and the **time** between their births. Contraception plays a major role in family planning. Family planning is important for a variety of reasons.

• It enables parents to **restrict the size** of their family. If the family is small, parents have more **time** to spend with each child, so each child receives greater emotional and physical care, and a better education from their parents. It is also **less expensive** to have a small family.

- It enables parents to decide at what **age** they wish to have a family, i.e. when they are young or later in life after pursuing their careers.
- It decreases **health risks** to women and **maternal deaths** caused by unintended pregnancies and unsafe abortions.
- It enables women to complete their **education** before having a family.
- It enables women to participate fully in **society** and advance in the **workplace** by allowing them to plan when they have a family.

From a **global** perspective, the human population is growing rapidly and predictions are that this will cause **shortages** of food, water, land and other natural resources, will **increase** pollution, the destruction of the environment, unemployment and the spread of disease, and will **decrease** living standards. Family planning can **reduce population growth** which should help maintain a healthy, productive environment without shortages, and should improve living standards.

Issues related to abortion

Abortion is the termination of a pregnancy. It can occur **naturally**, known as a **spontaneous abortion** or **miscarriage**, or it can be **induced**.

Spontaneous abortion

A **miscarriage** can occur for various reasons:
- The foetus has a **chromosomal abnormality**.
- The mother has a **uterine abnormality** so the embryo cannot implant properly in the lining, or she has a **weak cervix** that cannot hold the foetus in the uterus as it grows.
- The mother suffers from certain **medical conditions**, such as diabetes or thyroid disease, that can make conditions in the uterus difficult for the embryo to survive.
- The mother has an **immune system disorder** causing the foetus not to be accepted by her body.
- The mother **smokes** very heavily, drinks too much **alcohol** or overdoses on **illegal drugs** during pregnancy.

Induced abortion

Abortion can be **induced** by the mother taking an **abortion pill** containing hormones or undergoing a **surgical procedure**. Induced abortion is a very controversial topic and is illegal in many parts of the world.

Arguments for the use of induced abortion

The following could be put forward as reasons in **support** of carrying out **induced abortions**.
- If the **health** of the mother or of the foetus is at risk.
- If the foetus has a severe **genetic abnormality** which would adversely affect the quality of life after birth and put a strain on other family members.
- If the pregnancy is the result of **rape** and giving birth to an unwanted child would be a constant reminder to the mother of the traumatic event.
- If the parents are unable to support a child or the child was conceived as a result of contraceptive failure or the child is not wanted for other reasons, abortions prevent **unwanted children** from being brought into the world.

Arguments against the use of induced abortion

The following could be put forward as reasons **against** carrying out **induced abortions**.

- They can be used as a form of **contraception** and lead to irresponsible behaviour.
- They can give rise to **medical complications**, e.g. excessive blood loss, infection and damage to the uterus, and can lead to **infertility**, especially if carried out illegally by unqualified persons (back street abortions).
- They can have a serious impact on a woman's **mental state**, causing depression and other psychological problems, sometimes years after the abortion.
- They are considered to be **murder** by persons who believe that life begins at conception, and many religions believe that abortion is **morally wrong.**

Revision questions

1 Distinguish between sexual and asexual reproduction and suggest ONE possible advantage and ONE possible disadvantage of EACH.

2 By means of a labelled and annotated diagram, indicate the function of EACH of the different parts of the female reproductive system.

3 State the function of EACH of the following parts of the male reproductive system:
  a the epididymis   **b** the sperm ducts   **c** the prostate gland
  d the penis   **e** the testes   **f** the scrotal sac

4 **a** What happens in a person's body to cause cancer to develop?
  b Identify TWO parts of the female reproductive system and TWO parts of the male reproductive system where cancer may develop.

5 **a** What happens during ovulation and menstruation?
  b Explain the role of oestrogen and progesterone in the menstrual cycle.

6 Outline how ova and sperm are brought together for fertilisation to occur.

7 What role does the placenta play in the development of a human embryo?

8 Outline the stages involved in the birthing process.

9 **a** Sabrina is 3 months pregnant. Outline some of the steps she should take to ensure the health of her developing baby.
  b After Sabrina gives birth, she is strongly advised to breastfeed her baby for a minimum of 6 months. Give FOUR reasons to support this advice.

10 Explain why a pregnant woman should not consume alcohol or take illegal drugs during her pregnancy.

11 Construct a table which explains how EACH of the following methods of birth control prevents pregnancy, and gives ONE advantage and ONE disadvantage of EACH method: the contraceptive pill, surgical sterilisation, the rhythm method and the condom.

12 Suggest THREE reasons why family planning is important.

13 **a** What is the difference between a spontaneous abortion and an induced abortion?
  b Identify THREE possible causes of a spontaneous abortion.

Exam-style questions – Chapters 3 to 9

Structured questions

1   **a)** Figure 1 is a diagram of the human digestive system.

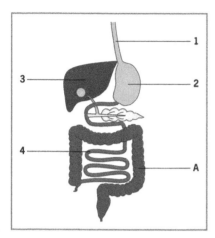

Figure 1 *The human digestive system*

    i)   Name the structure labelled A, and state its function.   **(2 marks)**

    ii)   Nikoli is 7 years old and his mother is beginning to worry that his legs are showing signs of bowing outwards, so she takes him to the doctor and the doctor suggests he might be lacking vitamin D. Identify ONE way Nikoli could increase his intake of vitamin D.   **(1 mark)**

    iii)   Which numbered structure in Figure 1 would vitamin D have an effect on?   **(1 mark)**

    iv)   Explain how increasing his intake of vitamin D would affect the structure identified in a) iii) above and help treat Nikoli's condition.   **(1 mark)**

b) Table 1 gives the body mass index (BMI) of five people. A person with a healthy weight would have a body mass index between 18.5 and 24.9 kg per m².

Table 1 *Body mass index of five people*

Name	Body mass index in kg per m²
Akeem	37.9
Zane	5.4
Alex	28.6
Romain	43.0
Mitchell	22.5

    i)   Which person has the healthiest body mass index?   **(1 mark)**

    ii)   Draw a bar graph to represent the data in Table 1.   **(3 marks)**

iii) Which two people in Table 1 are most likely to be suffering from malnutrition? **(2 marks)**

iv) Name a disease that EACH person identified in b) iii) might be suffering from and identify the main factors that could have led to the development of EACH disease named. **(4 marks)**

Total 15 marks

2 **a)** Distinguish between respiration and breathing. **(2 marks)**

b) Figure 2 shows part of the human respiratory system.

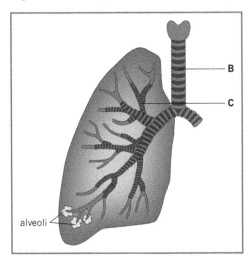

Figure 2 *Part of the human respiratory system*

i) Name the structures labelled B and C. **(2 marks)**

ii) Outline how the intercostal muscles, ribcage and diaphragm function during inhalation. **(3 marks)**

iii) Identify TWO features of the alveoli that make them efficient in carrying out gaseous exchange. **(2 marks)**

c) A study was carried out into the link between smoking levels and lung cancer. The researchers recorded the number of deaths from lung cancer per 100 000 individuals in the population, and the smoking levels of each person dying. The results for men aged 60 to 69 years are given in Table 2 below.

Table 2 *Death rates from lung cancer among men aged 60 to 69 years related to smoking levels*

Level of smoking		Death rate per 100 000 population
Never smoked		12
Smoked 20 cigarettes per day for:	30 years	234
	40 years	487
Smoked 40 cigarettes per day for:	30 years	576
	40 years	608

i) Which individuals are most at risk of dying from lung cancer? **(1 mark)**

ii) Give TWO conclusions that the researchers could have drawn from the results. **(2 marks)**

d) Tamara used to be a very good sprinter; however, she started to smoke heavily and now finds that whenever she tries to run she quickly becomes breathless and at times she even collapses.

    i) Write a chemical equation to summarise what causes Tamara to collapse. **(1 mark)**

    ii) Other than lung cancer, suggest TWO ways that Tamara's heavy smoking contributes to her breathlessness. **(2 marks)**

                                          Total 15 marks

3   **a)** Figure 3 shows the internal structure of the heart.

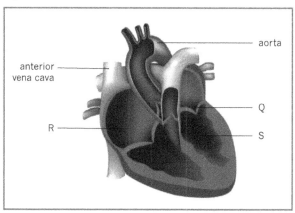

Figure 3 *The internal structure of the heart*

    i) Identify the parts labelled R and S. **(2 marks)**

    ii) What is the function of the structure labelled Q? **(1 mark)**

    iii) Complete Table 3 to compare the aorta with the anterior vena cava.

Table 3 *Differences between the aorta and the anterior vena cava*

	Aorta	Anterior vena cava
Pressure of blood carried		
Thickness of the walls		

                                          (2 marks)

    iv) Humans have a double circulation. Explain what this means. **(2 marks)**

  b) Jerome visits his doctor and is told that his blood pressure is 170/105 mm Hg.

    i) What diagnosis will Jerome's doctor give? **(1 mark)**

    ii) Identify THREE factors that could have led to Jerome's condition. **(3 marks)**

  c) Sabrina spends all day sitting working at her computer and by the end of the day she notices that her feet and ankles appear swollen.

    i) By reference to her lymphatic system, explain why Sabrina's feet and ankles are swollen. **(3 marks)**

    ii) What suggestion would you give to Sabrina to avoid the same thing happening again? **(1 mark)**

                                          Total 15 marks

4 **a)** State TWO functions of the skeleton, other than movement. **(2 marks)**

    b) Figure 4 is a diagram of a knee joint.

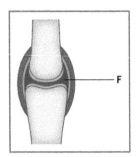

Figure 4 *A knee joint*

      i) Name the type of joint shown in Figure 4. **(1 mark)**

      ii) Identify F and state its main function. **(2 marks)**

      iii) How does movement of the knee joint differ from movement at the hip joint? **(2 marks)**

      iv) Jordan is told by his doctor that he needs to have one of his knees replaced. Suggest TWO reasons why this might be necessary. **(2 marks)**

    c) Shakira works as a shop assistant and goes to the gym each day after work.

      i) Explain how Shakira's elbow joint works as she bends and straightens it repeatedly during her daily workout using dumbbells. **(4 marks)**

      ii) Shakira wears high-heeled shoes to work each day. Suggest TWO adverse effects this might have on her body. **(2 marks)**

                                                   Total 15 marks

5 **a)** **i)** What is meant by the term 'excretion'? **(2 marks)**

      ii) Name ONE excretory organ, other than the kidney, found in the human body and identify ONE substance that it excretes. **(2 marks)**

    b) Figure 5 is a diagram of a nephron found in a human kidney.

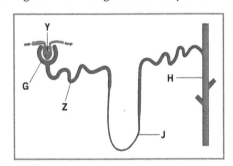

Figure 5 *Diagram of a nephron*

      i) Identify the structures labelled G, H and J in Figure 5. **(3 marks)**

      ii) Briefly describe the process that takes place in EACH of the structures labelled Y and Z. **(4 marks)**

c) Table 4 shows the composition of Andrew's urine 1 hour after he drank 2 large glasses of water and again 1 hour after he played a 90-minute game of football in the heat of the day, without drinking.

Table 4 *Composition of Andrew's urine*

Component	% in Andrew's urine after drinking	% in Andrew's urine after playing football
Urea	2.0	6.0
Salt	0.3	1.0
Water	95	90

i)   Which activity caused Andrew's urine to have the HIGHEST concentration?   **(1 mark)**

ii)   Name the hormone secreted by Andrew's pituitary gland when there is not enough water in his body fluids.   **(1 mark)**

iii) Explain how the hormone named in c) ii) above functioned to prevent Andrew losing too much water in his urine when his body fluids became too concentrated.   **(2 marks)**

Total 15 marks

6 a) Identify the TWO main divisions of the nervous system.   **(2 marks)**

b) Figure 6 is a diagram of a neurone.

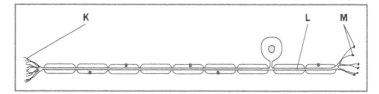

Figure 6 *A neurone*

i)   Name the parts labelled K and L.   **(2 marks)**

ii)   State the function of L.   **(1 mark)**

iii) How do impulses travel from the structures labelled M to adjacent neurones in the brain?   **(1 mark)**

c) Complete Table 5 below, which gives information about three different regions of the brain.

Table 5 *Functions of three regions of the brain*

Region of the brain	One function
Medulla oblongata	•
	• Controls conscious thought
Cerebellum	•

(3 marks)

d) i) Dana's dress has a hole in it that needs mending, so she cuts a piece of cotton thread and threads her needle. Are her actions voluntary or involuntary? Give ONE reason to support your answer. **(2 marks)**

ii) Dana starts to mend the hole, but accidently pricks her finger causing her to immediately pull her hand away from the needle. Complete Figure 7 below by drawing and labelling THREE neurones involved in bringing about Dana's action. **(3 marks)**

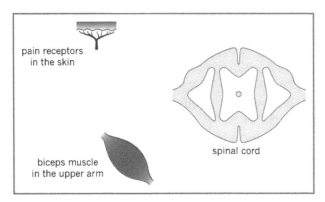

Figure 7 *Parts of the nervous system*

iii) What term is used to describe Dana's action in d) ii) above? **(1 mark)**

Total 15 marks

7 **a)** Figure 8 shows the male and female reproductive systems.

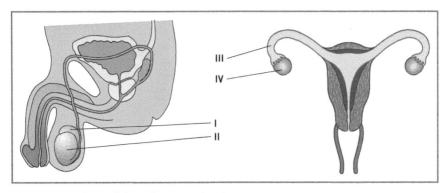

Figure 8 *Male and female reproductive systems*

i) Complete Table 6 below by writing the name and ONE function of EACH of the structures labelled I and III

Table 6 *Name and function of parts of the human reproductive systems*

	Name of structure	One function
I		
III		

(4 marks)

ii) Suggest TWO reasons why structures labelled II and IV in Figure 8 may be described as having similar functions. **(2 marks)**

iii) Place arrows on the male reproductive system to show the pathway taken by sperm as it travels out of the male body. **(2 marks)**

b) Figure 9 shows the number of births to teenage mothers aged 16 and 17 years over five-year periods from 1980 to 2009 in a certain Caribbean territory.

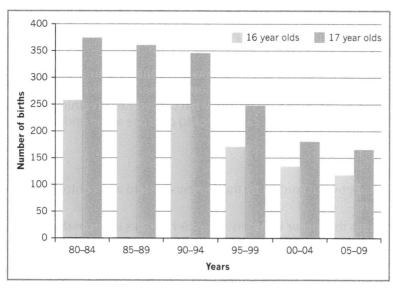

Figure 9 *Number of births to mothers aged 16 and 17 years between 1980 and 2009*

i) In which five-year period was the total number of births the HIGHEST? **(1 mark)**

ii) Between which two five-year periods was the GREATEST decrease in the number of births recorded? **(1 mark)**

iii) Describe TWO trends shown in Figure 9. **(2 marks)**

iv) It is thought that increased use of contraception among teenagers, particularly condoms, could possibly account for the overall trend in teenage pregnancy numbers in the country. Explain how condoms act as a method of birth control and give ONE advantage and ONE disadvantage of their use. **(3 marks)**

Total 15 marks

Structured essay questions

8 **a)** Alexa is advised by her doctor that after her baby is born she should feed him on breast milk for the first 6 months of his life because breast milk is a complete food for babies.

i) Why is breast milk considered to be a complete food for babies? **(2 marks)**

ii) Alexa takes her doctor's advice and breastfeeds her baby, Jay, from birth. Describe how the milk is digested as it passes through Jay's digestive system. **(6 marks)**

iii) There is a tendency for babies fed on powdered milk to gain weight more rapidly than breastfed babies. Suggest TWO reasons for this. **(2 marks)**

b) Alexa is also told that Jay must develop teeth before he can digest solid foods properly.

i) Explain why Jay needs to develop teeth before he can properly digest any solid food in his diet. **(3 marks)**

ii) Why is it important that the enamel of Jay's teeth is the hardest substance found in his body? **(2 marks)**

Total 15 marks

9 **a)** Define the term 'homeostasis' and outline how negative feedback mechanisms play an important role in homeostasis. **(4 marks)**

b) Jason goes on a hiking expedition into the mountains and loses his way as it begins to get dark. He is forced to spend the night high up in the mountains and begins to get very cold. Explain how his body responds to conserve as much heat as possible. **(6 marks)**

c) On Sports Day, Britnee ran the 1500 m race as fast as she could. During the race she was aware that her breathing rate was significantly higher than normal and as she crossed the finish line she collapsed. Explain what caused her breathing rate to increase as she was running and what caused her to collapse at the end of the race. **(5 marks)**

Total 15 marks

10 **a)** Give THREE differences between control by the nervous system and control by the endocrine system. **(3 marks)**

b) **i)** Describe the changes that occur in Aiden's eyes as he looks up from the smart phone in his hand to watch a bird in the top of a tree. **(4 marks)**

ii) As Aiden gets older, he finds it harder and harder to focus on his smart phone. Suggest the possible cause of Aiden's difficulty and explain what he must do to correct it. **(4 marks)**

c) Aiden is also found to have developed an underactive pituitary gland. By referring to TWO different hormones produced by Aiden's pituitary gland, explain how this reduced activity could affect his body. **(4 marks)**

Total 15 marks

11 **a)** **i)** Describe the events taking place in Rasheeda's ovaries and uterus during one complete menstrual cycle. **(5 marks)**

ii) Name TWO hormones, other than those secreted by Rasheeda's pituitary gland, that control her menstrual cycle and outline the role played by EACH. **(4 marks)**

b) Rasheeda misses her period and decides to go to the doctor because she thinks she might be pregnant. Her doctor confirms her suspicions. Outline the role that the placenta, umbilical cord and amniotic fluid play in the development of Rasheeda's baby during her pregnancy. **(6 marks)**

Total 15 marks

Section C – Heredity and variation

10 Cell division and inheritance

Cells contain all the information they need to control their activities coded as genetic information in their **genes**. These genes are passed on to new cells, including gametes, during **cell division**. **Genetics** is a branch of science that seeks to understand how characteristics are passed from one generation to the next; in other words, how they are **inherited.**

An introduction to chromosomes, DNA, genes and alleles

Chromosomes and DNA

Chromosomes are thread-like structures that are found in the nuclei of cells and are composed of DNA and protein molecules.

Deoxyribonucleic acid or DNA is a large molecule that contains the genetic instructions for the development and functioning of living organisms.

Chromosomes are present in the nuclei of all living cells. Each chromosome is composed of a single **deoxyribonucleic acid (DNA) molecule** wrapped around **proteins** called **histones**. DNA molecules contain **genetic information** in the form of **genes**. In any cell that is not dividing, chromosomes are present as long, thin strands known as **chromatin threads**, which are spread throughout the nucleus. Chromosomes become visible when a cell begins to divide due to the threads coiling, which causes them to become shorter and thicker.

Chromosomes are passed on from one generation to the next in **gametes** and each species has a distinctive **number** of chromosomes per body cell, e.g. every human cell has 46 chromosomes. The number of chromosomes in each cell is known as the **diploid number**

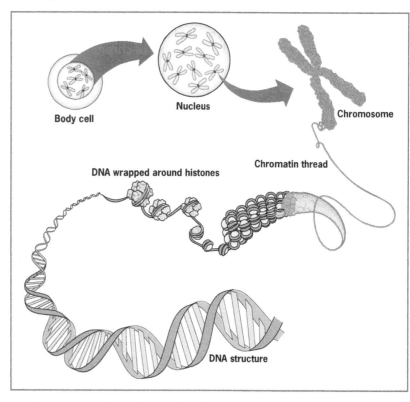

★ **Figure 10.1** *The relationship between a chromosome, chromatin threads and DNA*

or **2*n* number.** Chromosomes exist in pairs known as **homologous pairs.** Every human cell has 23 pairs, one member of each pair being of **maternal origin** and the other of **paternal origin**. With the exception of the pair of sex chromosomes, members of each homologous pair are similar in shape, size and genetic composition.

Genes and alleles

*A **gene** is the basic unit of heredity and is composed of DNA. It occupies a fixed position on a chromosome and determines a specific characteristic.*

*An **allele** is either of a pair (or series) of alternative versions of a gene that occupy the same position on a particular chromosome and that control the same characteristic.*

Genes are specific sections of chromosomal DNA molecules and are the basic units of **heredity**. Each human body cell has over 30 000 genes and each gene controls a particular characteristic. Genes work by controlling the production of **proteins** in cells, mainly the production of **enzymes**. Each gene controls the production of a specific protein.

All the cells of one individual contain an **identical combination** of genes. It is this combination which makes each individual **unique** since no two individuals, except identical twins or organisms produced asexually, have the same combination of genes. Within any cell some genes are **active** while others are inactive, e.g. in a nerve cell, genes controlling the activity of the nerve cell are active and genes that would control the activity of a muscle cell are inactive.

A gene controlling a particular characteristic can have different forms, or versions, depending on the information they contain. These different versions are known as **alleles** and each gene usually has **two** different alleles.

Diploid and haploid cells

A **diploid cell** is a cell that contains **two** complete sets of chromosomes. Diploid cells contain the **diploid** or **2n number** of chromosomes. A **haploid cell** is a cell that contains **one** complete set of chromosomes. Haploid cells contain the **haploid** or *n* **number** of chromosomes, which is **half** the diploid number.

Cell division

When a cell divides, **chromosomes** with their **genes** are passed on to the new cells produced, known as **daughter cells**. There are two types of cell division: **mitosis** and **meiosis**.

Mitosis

Mitosis is the type of cell division that results in the formation of two daughter cells, each with the same number and kind of chromosomes as the parent cell.

Mitosis occurs in **all body (somatic) cells** except in the formation of gametes. During mitosis, **two genetically identical** cells are formed. Each cell contains the **diploid number** of chromosomes. All cells produced by mitosis from a single parent cell are collectively called a **clone**.

Mitosis is divided into **four** stages: **prophase**, **metaphase**, **anaphase** and **telophase**. When a cell is not dividing it is in **interphase** and the final division of the cytoplasm is known as **cytokinesis**.

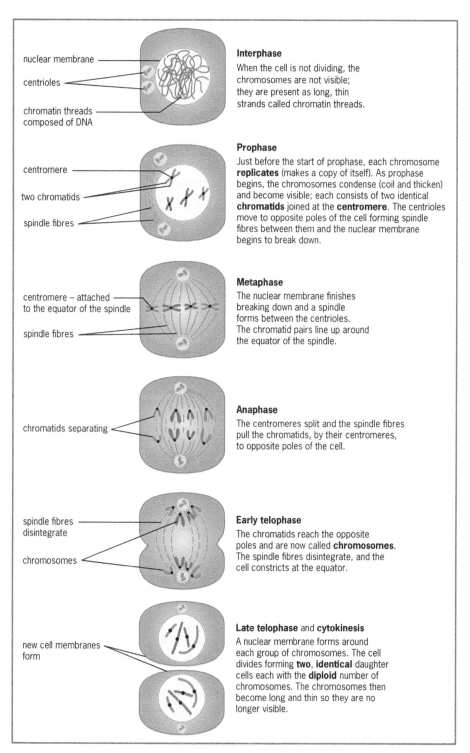

Interphase
When the cell is not dividing, the chromosomes are not visible; they are present as long, thin strands called chromatin threads.

nuclear membrane

centrioles

chromatin threads composed of DNA

Prophase
Just before the start of prophase, each chromosome **replicates** (makes a copy of itself). As prophase begins, the chromosomes condense (coil and thicken) and become visible; each consists of two identical **chromatids** joined at the **centromere**. The centrioles move to opposite poles of the cell forming spindle fibres between them and the nuclear membrane begins to break down.

centromere

two chromatids

spindle fibres

Metaphase
The nuclear membrane finishes breaking down and a spindle forms between the centrioles. The chromatid pairs line up around the equator of the spindle.

centromere – attached to the equator of the spindle

spindle fibres

Anaphase
The centromeres split and the spindle fibres pull the chromatids, by their centromeres, to opposite poles of the cell.

chromatids separating

Early telophase
The chromatids reach the opposite poles and are now called **chromosomes**. The spindle fibres disintegrate, and the cell constricts at the equator.

spindle fibres disintegrate

chromosomes

Late telophase and **cytokinesis**
A nuclear membrane forms around each group of chromosomes. The cell divides forming **two**, **identical** daughter cells each with the **diploid** number of chromosomes. The chromosomes then become long and thin so they are no longer visible.

new cell membranes form

★ **Figure 10.2** *The process of mitosis in an animal cell with four chromosomes; two of paternal origin (blue) and two of maternal origin (red)*

Mitosis is **important** for the following reasons.

- It ensures that each daughter cell has the **same number** and **type** of **chromosomes** as the parent cell.
- It ensures that each daughter cell has an **identical** combination of **genes**.
- It is the method by which all cells of a multicellular organism are formed, hence it is essential for **growth** and to **repair** or **replace** damaged tissues.
- It is the method by which organisms reproduce **asexually**, forming offspring that are **identical** to each other and to the parent.

Meiosis (reduction division)

Meiosis is the type of cell division that results in the formation of four daughter cells, each with half the number of chromosomes as the parent cell.

Meiosis occurs only in the **reproductive organs** during the production of **gametes**. During meiosis, **four genetically non-identical** cells are formed. Each cell contains the **haploid number** of chromosomes, hence it is also called **reduction division**. During meiosis, the cell divides **twice**, known as **meiosis I** and **meiosis II**, and each division takes place in the same four stages as mitosis.

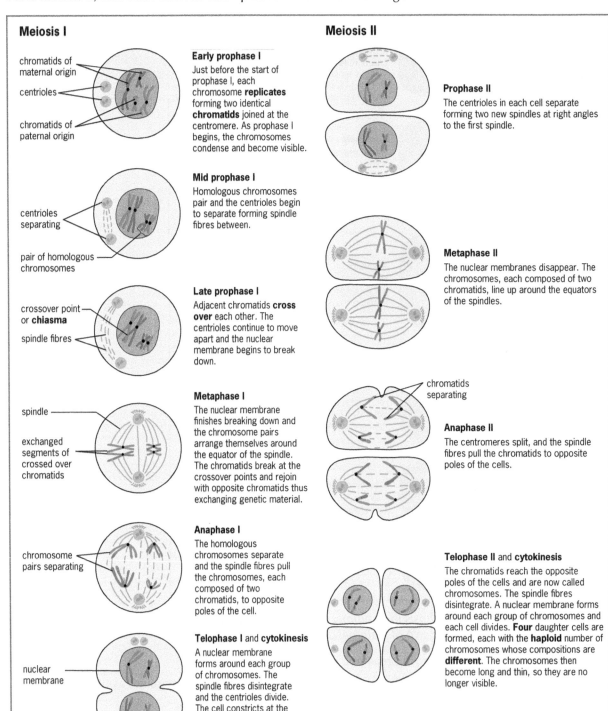

Meiosis I

chromatids of maternal origin

centrioles

chromatids of paternal origin

Early prophase I
Just before the start of prophase I, each chromosome **replicates** forming two identical **chromatids** joined at the centromere. As prophase I begins, the chromosomes condense and become visible.

centrioles separating

pair of homologous chromosomes

Mid prophase I
Homologous chromosomes pair and the centrioles begin to separate forming spindle fibres between.

crossover point or chiasma

spindle fibres

Late prophase I
Adjacent chromatids **cross over** each other. The centrioles continue to move apart and the nuclear membrane begins to break down.

spindle

exchanged segments of crossed over chromatids

Metaphase I
The nuclear membrane finishes breaking down and the chromosome pairs arrange themselves around the equator of the spindle. The chromatids break at the crossover points and rejoin with opposite chromatids thus exchanging genetic material.

chromosome pairs separating

Anaphase I
The homologous chromosomes separate and the spindle fibres pull the chromosomes, each composed of two chromatids, to opposite poles of the cell.

nuclear membrane

Telophase I and cytokinesis
A nuclear membrane forms around each group of chromosomes. The spindle fibres disintegrate and the centrioles divide. The cell constricts at the equator forming two cells.

Meiosis II

Prophase II
The centrioles in each cell separate forming two new spindles at right angles to the first spindle.

Metaphase II
The nuclear membranes disappear. The chromosomes, each composed of two chromatids, line up around the equators of the spindles.

chromatids separating

Anaphase II
The centromeres split, and the spindle fibres pull the chromatids to opposite poles of the cells.

Telophase II and cytokinesis
The chromatids reach the opposite poles of the cells and are now called chromosomes. The spindle fibres disintegrate. A nuclear membrane forms around each group of chromosomes and each cell divides. **Four** daughter cells are formed, each with the **haploid** number of chromosomes whose compositions are **different**. The chromosomes then become long and thin, so they are no longer visible.

★ **Figure 10.3** *The process of meiosis in an animal cell with four chromosomes*

Meiosis is **important** for the following reasons.

- It ensures that each daughter cell or **gamete** has the **haploid** number of chromosomes. The **diploid** number can then be restored at **fertilisation** (see Figure 10.4).

- It ensures that each daughter cell or **gamete** has a **different** combination of genes. This leads to **variation** among offspring (see page 124).

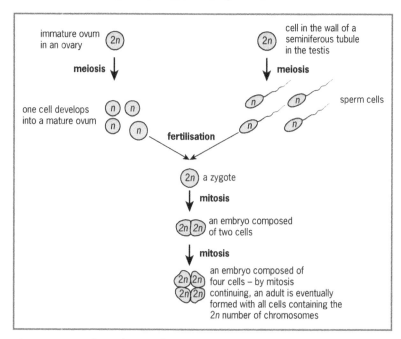

Figure 10.4 *The relationship between mitosis and meiosis*

Inheritance

Inheritance is the passing on of genetic information from parents to their offspring.

Most human characteristics are controlled by **many genes** and this makes it very difficult to predict how they are inherited. However, a few are controlled by a **single gene** which usually has **two alleles**, and it is much easier to predict how these characteristics are inherited.

Definitions of some important terms used in genetics

In addition to the definitions of **chromosome**, **DNA**, **gene** and **allele** given on pages 113 and 114, the following definitions of **genetic terms** are important when discussing how characteristics are **inherited**.

- *Genotype: the combination of alleles present in an organism.*
- *Phenotype: the observable characteristics of an organism.*
- *Homozygous: having two identical alleles in corresponding positions on a pair of homologous chromosomes.*
- *Heterozygous: having two different alleles in corresponding positions on a pair of homologous chromosomes.*
- *Dominant allele: the allele which, if present, produces the same phenotype whether its paired allele is identical or different.*
- *Recessive allele: the allele which only shows its effect on the phenotype if its paired allele is identical.*

- *Dominant trait:* an inherited characteristic that results from the presence of a single dominant allele. It is seen in an individual with one or two dominant alleles.
- *Recessive trait:* an inherited characteristic that results from the presence of two recessive alleles. It is only seen in an individual with no dominant allele.

Monohybrid inheritance

Monohybrid inheritance is the inheritance of a **single characteristic** controlled by a **single gene**, e.g. **albinism** and **blood groups**. Like chromosomes, genes exist in **pairs**; one gene of each pair is of **maternal origin** and one is of **paternal origin**. The pairs occupy equivalent positions, known as **loci**, on homologous chromosomes, and each gene controlling a particular characteristic usually has **two** different forms or **alleles**.

The **composition of genes** within the cells of an organism makes up the organism's **genotype**. The **observable characteristics** of an organism make up its **phenotype**.

The principles of monohybrid inheritance can be explained using **albinism** as an example.

Albinism

People with **albinism** produce very little or no melanin in their skin, eyes and hair. The gene controlling the production of the pigment melanin has **two** different **alleles** which can be represented using letters:

- **N** represents the allele that stimulates melanin production
- **n** represents the allele that fails to stimulate melanin production

The allele stimulating melanin production, **N**, is **dominant**, i.e. if it is present it shows its effect on the phenotype. The allele for albinism, **n**, is **recessive**, i.e. it only has an effect on the phenotype if there is no dominant allele present. **Three** combinations of these alleles are possible; **NN**, **Nn** and **nn**. If the two alleles are the same, the organism is said to be **homozygous**. If the two alleles are different, the organism is said to be **heterozygous**. Heterozygous individuals are **carriers** because they can pass on a recessive allele.

Table 10.1 *Possible combinations of the alleles controlling melanin production*

Genotype (combination of alleles)	How the alleles appear on homologous chromosomes	Phenotype (appearance)
NN **Homozygous dominant** (pure breeding)	N / N	Normal pigmentation of the skin, eyes and hair
Nn **Heterozygous** (carrier)	N / n	Normal pigmentation of the skin, eyes and hair
nn **Homozygous recessive** (pure breeding)	n / n	Albino – very pale skin that does not tan, white or light blond hair and very pale blue eyes

Gametes produced in meiosis contain only **one chromosome** from each homologous pair. As a result, they contain only **one allele** from each pair. When fertilisation occurs, chromosomes and the alleles they carry **recombine** to form pairs in the zygote. **Genetic-cross diagrams** can be drawn to show how characteristics controlled by one gene with two alternative alleles are passed on from one generation to the next.

Examples of possible crosses to show the inheritance of albinism

1 If one parent is **homozygous dominant** and one is **homozygous recessive**:

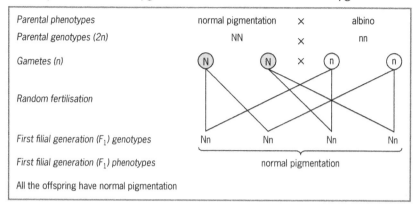

Parental phenotypes	normal pigmentation	×	albino	
Parental genotypes (2n)	NN	×	nn	
Gametes (n)	(N) (N)	×	(n) (n)	
Random fertilisation				
First filial generation (F_1) genotypes	Nn Nn		Nn Nn	
First filial generation (F_1) phenotypes		normal pigmentation		

All the offspring have normal pigmentation

2 If one parent is **heterozygous** and one is **homozygous recessive**, showing the use of a **Punnett square** to predict the outcome of the cross:

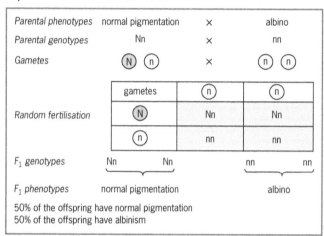

Parental phenotypes	normal pigmentation	×	albino
Parental genotypes	Nn	×	nn
Gametes	(N) (n)	×	(n) (n)

gametes	(n)	(n)
(N)	Nn	Nn
(n)	nn	nn

F_1 genotypes: Nn   Nn   nn   nn

F_1 phenotypes: normal pigmentation   albino

50% of the offspring have normal pigmentation
50% of the offspring have albinism

3 If both parents are **heterozygous**, i.e. carriers:

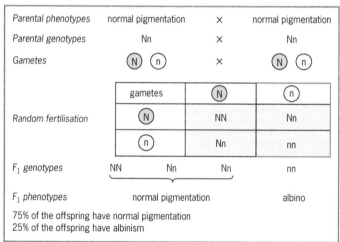

Parental phenotypes	normal pigmentation	×	normal pigmentation
Parental genotypes	Nn	×	Nn
Gametes	(N) (n)	×	(N) (n)

gametes	(N)	(n)
(N)	NN	Nn
(n)	Nn	nn

F_1 genotypes: NN   Nn   Nn   nn

F_1 phenotypes: normal pigmentation   albino

75% of the offspring have normal pigmentation
25% of the offspring have albinism

Tongue rolling

Some people **can** roll their tongues into a tube and some people **cannot**, and at one time it was accepted that tongue rolling was controlled by a single gene with two alleles, the allele for rolling (**R**) being dominant to the allele for non-rolling (**r**). However, based on current evidence, it is now accepted that the inheritance of tongue rolling is **more complex** than originally thought, though it is still often used to illustrate monohybrid inheritance.

ABO blood groups

ABO blood groups are controlled by **three** alleles, I^A, I^B and I^O.

- I^A and I^B are both dominant to I^O.
- I^A and I^B are **co-dominant**, meaning that if an individual has both alleles, both will have an influence on the phenotype.

Only **two** alleles are present in any cell.

Table 10.2 *Possible combinations of alleles controlling ABO blood groups*

Genotype	Phenotype
$I^A I^A$	Blood group A
$I^A I^O$	Blood group A
$I^B I^B$	Blood group B
$I^B I^O$	Blood group B
$I^A I^B$	Blood group AB
$I^O I^O$	Blood group O

Example of a possible cross showing the inheritance of ABO blood groups

If one parent is **heterozygous** with **blood group A** and the other is **heterozygous** with **blood group B**.

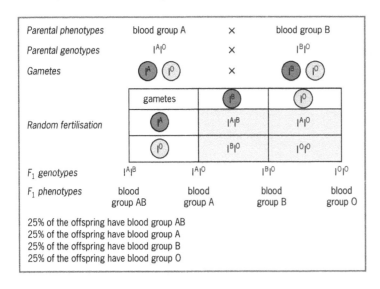

The inheritance of sex in humans

In each cell, one pair of chromosomes is composed of the **sex chromosomes**. There are two types, **X** and **Y**, and they determine the individual's sex. Genotype **XX** is **female**; genotype **XY** is **male**. Only the **male** can pass on the **Y** chromosome, consequently the **father** is the parent who determines the sex of his offspring.

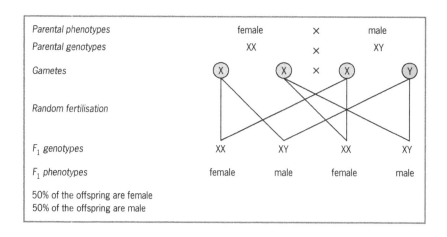

Parental phenotypes		female	×	male		
Parental genotypes		XX	×	XY		
Gametes	X	X	×	X	Y	
Random fertilisation						
F_1 genotypes		XX	XY	XX	XY	
F_1 phenotypes		female	male	female	male	

50% of the offspring are female
50% of the offspring are male

Sex-linked inheritance

The sex chromosomes carry genes, called **sex-linked genes**, which have nothing to do with determining an individual's sex. The characteristics controlled by these genes are called **sex-linked characteristics** or **traits**. Some of these genes also cause **disease**.

Since chromosome X is **longer** than chromosome Y, it carries more genes. Males only have one X chromosome and any allele that is carried on the X chromosome, whether dominant or recessive, which has no counterpart on the Y will be expressed in the male's phenotype. However, for any recessive allele to be expressed in a female's phenotype, two recessive alleles must be present. As a result, sex-linked traits are more likely to be seen in males than in females. Examples include **haemophilia** and **colour blindness**, and the sex-linked disease **Duchenne muscular dystrophy**.

Haemophilia

Haemophilia is a sex-linked condition where the blood fails to clot at a cut. The **dominant** allele, **H**, causes blood to clot normally; the **recessive** allele, **h**, causes haemophilia. These alleles are carried on the **X** chromosome only, therefore males are much more likely to be haemophiliacs than females. If the single X chromosome in a male carries the recessive allele he will have haemophilia, whereas both X chromosomes must carry the recessive allele in a female for her to have the condition.

Table 10.3 *Possible combinations of alleles controlling blood clotting*

Genotype	Phenotype
$X^H X^H$	Female, normal blood clotting
$X^H X^h$	Female, normal blood clotting (carrier)
$X^h X^h$	Female, haemophiliac
$X^H Y$	Male, normal blood clotting
$X^h Y$	Male, haemophiliac

Example of a possible cross showing the inheritance of haemophilia

A cross between a **female** with **normal blood clotting** who is a **carrier**, and a **male** with **normal blood clotting**.

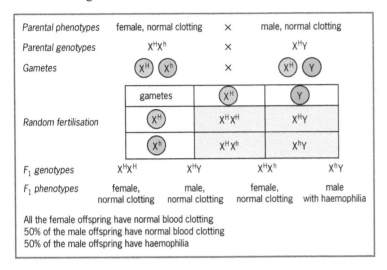

Parental phenotypes	female, normal clotting ×	male, normal clotting
Parental genotypes	$X^H X^h$ ×	$X^H Y$
Gametes	X^H X^h ×	X^H Y

gametes	X^H	Y
X^H	$X^H X^H$	$X^H Y$
X^h	$X^H X^h$	$X^h Y$

Random fertilisation

F_1 *genotypes*	$X^H X^H$	$X^H Y$	$X^H X^h$	$X^h Y$
F_1 *phenotypes*	female, normal clotting	male, normal clotting	female, normal clotting	male with haemophilia

All the female offspring have normal blood clotting
50% of the male offspring have normal blood clotting
50% of the male offspring have haemophilia

Colour blindness

Colour blindness (also known as red–green colour blindness) is a sex-linked condition where the sufferer is unable to distinguish differences between certain colours, mainly red and green. The **dominant** allele, **R**, allows normal vision and the **recessive** allele, **r**, causes colour blindness. These alleles are carried on the **X** chromosome only, so colour blindness is inherited in the same way as haemophilia.

Duchenne muscular dystrophy

Duchenne muscular dystrophy is a sex-linked disease where the sufferer is unable to produce a **protein** called dystrophin in their muscles. It is caused by a **recessive** allele which is carried on the **X** chromosome only, so it is inherited in the same way as haemophilia. It causes progressive muscle weakness and loss of muscle function, and goes on to affect the **heart** and **respiratory muscles**. Only a few individuals with the disease live beyond their 30s.

Revision questions

1 Distinguish between the following:

   a chromosome and DNA   **b** gene and allele   **c** diploid and haploid

2 Define the following terms:

   a mitosis   **b** meiosis

3 Outline the process of mitosis.

4 Give THREE reasons why mitosis is important to living organisms.

5 In what ways does meiosis differ from mitosis?

6 Give TWO reasons why meiosis is important to living organisms.

7 Distinguish between the following pairs of terms:

    a genotype and phenotype   **b** dominant trait and recessive trait

    c homozygous and heterozygous

8 Assuming that tongue rolling is controlled by a single gene with two alternative alleles, and that the allele for rolling the tongue is dominant to the allele for non-rolling, predict the chances of a heterozygous woman and a homozygous recessive man having a child who is homozygous recessive. Use appropriate symbols and a genetic-cross diagram to support your answer.

9 PTC is a chemical that tastes bitter to some people and is tasteless to others. The allele for tasting PTC, **T**, is dominant. Use a genetic-cross diagram to show how a couple who can both taste PTC can produce a child who is unable to taste PTC.

10 Is it possible for a female of blood group A and a male of blood group AB to have a child of blood group B? Use appropriate symbols and a genetic-cross diagram to support your answer.

11 Is it the mother or the father that determines the sex of their children? Explain your answer by means of a genetic-cross diagram.

12   **a** What are sex-linked characteristics?

    b Colour blindness is caused by an X-linked, recessive allele. Is it possible for a mother with normal vision and a father with colour blindness to have a child with colour blindness? Use a genetic-cross diagram to help explain your answer (X^R = normal vision; X^r = colour blindness).

11 Variation and genetic engineering

All living organisms show **variation** and much of this variation is passed on from one generation to the next via genes. This variation is extremely important because it provides the raw material for **natural selection**. Since the structure of DNA was discovered in 1953, gene technology, including **genetic engineering**, has accelerated to improve food production and the production of medicinal drugs.

Variation

No two living organisms are exactly alike, not even identical twins. **Variation** refers to the **differences** that exist between individuals and it arises from a combination of **genetic causes** and **environmental causes**. In other words, an individual's **phenotype** (observable characteristics) is determined by their **genotype** (composition of genes) and the influences of their **environment**:

$$\text{phenotype} = \text{genotype} + \text{environmental influences}$$

Genetic variation

Genetic variation is controlled by **genes** and **can** be passed on from one generation to the next, i.e. it can be **inherited**. It arises in several ways:

- **Meiosis.** Every gamete produced by meiosis has a different combination of genes as a result of:
  - **Chromatids** of homologous chromosomes crossing over and **exchanging genes**, which occurs randomly.
  - **Chromosomes** arranging themselves around the equators of the spindles in totally **random** ways during both meiosis I and meiosis II.
- **Sexual reproduction.** During **fertilisation**, male and female gametes fuse in completely **random** ways to create a different combination of genes in each zygote.
- **Mutations.** A mutation is a **change** in the structure of a single **gene**, the structure of part of a **chromosome** containing several genes, or in the **number of chromosomes** in a cell. Mutations cause new characteristics to develop in organisms. Mutations occurring in body cells cannot be inherited, whereas mutations occurring in a gamete or zygote can be inherited. Many mutations are harmful; however, a few produce **beneficial characteristics** which help the organism survive. The following are examples of mutations in humans.

  - **Albinism** is caused by a mutation in a gene controlling the production of melanin. People with **albinism** produce very little or no melanin in their skin, eyes and hair (see page 118).

  - **Down syndrome** occurs when an individual has an **extra chromosome 21** in each of their cells because pair 21 fails to separate properly during meiosis and both chromosomes pass into one gamete. Individuals with Down syndrome usually have flattened facial features, a short wide neck, small ears, a bulging tongue, slanted eyes, short, stocky arms and legs, poor muscle tone and slow learning capabilities.

  - **Klinefelter's syndrome** occurs in **males** when the male has an **extra X chromosome**, therefore having the genotype **XXY**. Males with the syndrome have small testes that produce reduced amounts of testosterone. Without treatment it can lead to delayed or incomplete puberty, decreased muscle mass, a reduced amount of facial and body hair, and infertility.

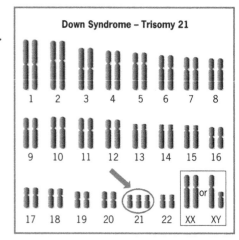

Figure 11.1 *Composition of chromosomes in the cell of a person with Down syndrome*

- **Turner's syndrome** occurs in **females** when one of the **X chromosomes** is **missing** or **partially missing**. Their genotype can be written as **XO**. Females with the syndrome have a short stature and underdeveloped ovaries, resulting in a lack of menstruation and infertility.

The importance of genetic variation

Genetic variation is **important** in living organisms for the following reasons.

- It helps organisms **adapt** to their environment, and to any changes in their environment, which improves their chances of **survival**.
- It provides the raw material on which **natural selection** can work (see page 126).
- It makes it **less likely** that adverse changes in environmental conditions will wipe out an entire species.

Environmental variation

Environmental variation is caused by different factors in an organism's environment. It is not caused by genes and **cannot** be passed on from one generation to the next. Environmental factors that affect human characteristics include:

- The type and quantity of **food** they eat.
- The **diseases** they suffer from.
- The **drugs** they take.
- The **climate** they are exposed to, especially the amount of sunlight.
- Their **upbringing** and **living conditions**.
- The **education** they receive.
- The amount of **exercise** they get and their daily activities.

Continuous and discontinuous variation

Within a **species**, characteristics show **two** basic types of variation: **continuous variation** and **discontinuous variation**.

Continuous variation

Continuous variation is where characteristics show **continuous gradation** between individuals from one extreme to the other without a break. Most individuals usually display characteristics that fall in the middle of the range, with fewer at the two extremes, i.e. the characteristics show a **normal distribution** pattern. Examples include height, weight, foot size, hand span, hair colour, skin colour and intelligence.

Characteristics showing continuous variation are usually controlled by **many genes** and can be affected by **environmental factors**.

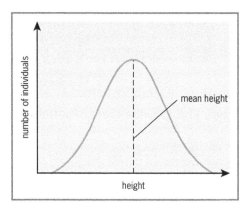

Figure 11.2 *A normal distribution curve showing height*

Discontinuous variation

Discontinuous variation is where characteristics show **clear-cut differences** between individuals. Individuals can be placed into distinct categories based on the characteristic in question and there are no intermediates. Examples include sex, ABO blood groups, Rhesus blood groups and tongue-rolling ability. Characteristics showing discontinuous variation are usually controlled by a **single gene** and environmental factors have little, if any, influence on them.

Natural selection

Natural selection is the process by which organisms that are best adapted to their environment tend to survive, reproduce and pass on genes for their beneficial characteristics to their offspring, so entire populations become better adapted to their environments over time.

Organisms generally produce **more offspring** than the environment can support, therefore there is a constant **struggle for survival**. Within any species, individuals that possess variations that make them **best suited** to their environment have the best chance of survival in the struggle, i.e. there is **survival of the fittest**. The organisms that survive are likely to **reproduce** and they can then pass the genetic information for their beneficial characteristics on to their offspring. Over time, this process of **natural selection** enables species to remain well adapted to their environment or to **change** and **improve** by becoming better adapted; in other words, it allows species to **evolve.**

Natural selection can be seen in the development of **antibiotic resistance** in bacteria and the prevalence of **sickle cell anaemia** in people of African descent.

Antibiotic resistance in bacteria

In natural populations of **bacteria**, a few individuals may possess genes which make them **resistant** to antibiotics. These genes arise from **random mutations**. When exposed to antibiotics, these resistant organisms have a **selective advantage** as shown in Figure 11.3. This has caused some species of **bacteria** to become **resistant** to almost all commonly used antibiotics, enabling them to survive antibiotic treatment. **Overuse** of antibiotics has speeded up the development of this resistance.

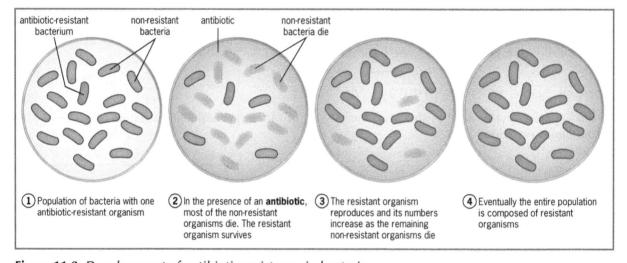

① Population of bacteria with one antibiotic-resistant organism

② In the presence of an **antibiotic**, most of the non-resistant organisms die. The resistant organism survives

③ The resistant organism reproduces and its numbers increase as the remaining non-resistant organisms die

④ Eventually the entire population is composed of resistant organisms

Figure 11.3 *Development of antibiotic resistance in bacteria*

Sickle cell anaemia

Sickle cell anaemia is a hereditary blood disease caused by an **abnormal, recessive allele**. A person with **two** abnormal alleles produces abnormal **haemoglobin S** instead of normal haemoglobin A. As a result, the person's red blood cells become **sickle-shaped** when oxygen supplies are low and this often leads to death at a young age. People with only **one** abnormal allele produce about 35–45% haemoglobin S, and develop **sickle cell trait.**

People with the disease are at a **selective disadvantage**. However, the abnormal allele has remained within populations, especially in regions of **Africa** where **malaria** is common, because people with **sickle cell trait** show **resistance** to malaria and this gives them a **selective advantage**. They have a better chance of surviving malaria, reproducing and passing on their sickle cell allele to their children.

Genetic engineering

Genetic engineering or genetic modification is the process by which the DNA of an organism is altered in order to alter the characteristics of the organism in a particular way.

The **uses** of genetic engineering include the following.

- To improve the **quality** of a food product, e.g. by increasing nutritional value.
- To improve **yields** of livestock and crops, e.g. by increasing size or growth rate, or by making organisms hardier.
- To **protect** agricultural crops against environmental threats, e.g. pathogens, pests, herbicides and low temperatures.
- To make organisms produce **materials** that they do not usually produce, e.g. vaccines and medicinal drugs.

Two main techniques, **recombinant DNA technology** and **gene editing**, are employed in genetic engineering.

- **Recombinant DNA technology** involves changing the traits of one organism by inserting the genetic material of a different organism into its DNA. The organism receiving the genetic material is called a **transgenic organism** or **genetically modified organism (GMO)**.

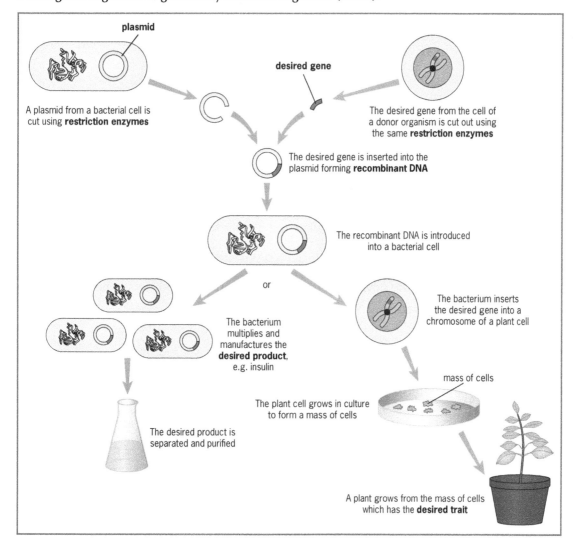

Figure 11.4 *Steps involved in recombinant DNA technology*

- **Gene editing** involves making highly specific changes in the DNA of living organisms to customise the organism's genetic makeup. It is usually carried out using a system known as **CRISPR-Cas9** in which **Cas9** acts like a pair of **molecular scissors** to cut a DNA molecule and **CRISPR guides** Cas9 to the specific part of the DNA molecule to be cut. Once cut, the DNA molecule can then be manipulated and edited. DNA editing has, so far, been used to correct genetic errors associated with disease in **animals** and to modify the genetic makeup of **crop plants**. Scientists are working to determine if it is safe and effective to use to treat single gene disorders such as sickle cell anaemia and cystic fibrosis, and more complex diseases such as cancer and heart disease.

Uses of genetic engineering in medical treatment

Genetic engineering is used to produce many **drugs** used in medical treatment. Examples include the following.

Insulin

The gene that controls **insulin** production in humans is transferred from cells in the pancreas that produce insulin into bacteria. The gene stimulates the bacteria to produce human insulin which is used to treat **diabetes**.

Human growth hormone (HGH)

The gene controlling the production of **HGH** is transferred into bacteria and it stimulates the bacteria to produce the hormone which is used to treat **growth disorders** in children.

Hepatitis B vaccine

The gene controlling the production of **hepatitis B antigens** by the hepatitis B virus is transferred from the virus into yeast cells. The gene stimulates the cells to produce the **antigens**, which are used as a **vaccine** against hepatitis B.

Other medicinal drugs and vaccines produced by genetic engineering

- **Blood clotting drugs** for haemophiliacs.
- **Follicle stimulating hormone (FSH)** used to stimulate the ovaries to release ova in women that are infertile.
- **Interferons** used to treat viral infections and certain cancers.
- **Anticoagulants** used to prevent the development of life-threatening blood clots in heart patients.
- **Human papilloma virus (HPV) vaccine.**

Uses of genetic engineering in food production

Genetic engineering is used to **improve** food production. Examples include the following.

Golden rice

Two genes, one from maize and one from a soil bacterium, are transferred into rice plants. These genes stimulate the rice grains to produce **beta-carotene** which the body converts to **vitamin A**. Golden rice should help fight vitamin A deficiency, which is a leading cause of blindness, and often death, of children in many underdeveloped countries.

Figure 11.5 *Golden rice*

Bovine somatotrophin (BST) hormone

The gene that controls the production of **BST hormone** is transferred from cattle into bacteria. The gene stimulates the bacteria to produce the hormone, which is then injected into cattle to increase **milk** and **meat** production.

Chymosin (rennin)

The gene that controls the production of **chymosin** is transferred from calf stomach cells into bacteria or fungi. The gene stimulates the microorganisms to produce chymosin, which is used in **cheese** production. This has considerably increased the production of cheese worldwide.

Possible advantages of genetic engineering

- **Yields** can be **increased** by genetic engineering, which should increase the world food supply and reduce food shortages.
- The **nutritional value** of foods can be increased by genetic engineering, which should reduce deficiency diseases worldwide.
- The need for **chemical pesticides** that harm the environment can be reduced by genetically engineering crops to be resistant to pests.
- When used in agriculture, it is a much **faster** and more **efficient** way to get the same results than traditional methods such as selective breeding.
- **Vaccines** produced by genetic engineering are generally **safer** than vaccines containing live and weakened, or dead pathogens.
- **Larger quantities** of drugs in a **safer** and **purer** form can be produced than were previously produced from animal sources, resulting in more people worldwide having ready access to safe, life-saving drugs.
- It overcomes **ethical concerns** of obtaining certain drugs from animals, e.g. insulin used to be obtained from pigs and cows.
- It has the potential to **treat** and **cure** diseases, especially hereditary diseases, for which there are currently no cures.

Possible disadvantages of genetic engineering

- Plants genetically engineered to be toxic to a pest may also be toxic to **useful organisms**, especially insects which bring about pollination. This could reduce reproduction in crops, reducing food production.
- Plants genetically engineered to be resistant to pests and herbicides could create **unpredictable environmental issues**, e.g. they could lead to the development of insecticide-resistant insects and herbicide-resistant 'superweeds'.
- Once a genetically modified organism is released into the environment it cannot be **contained** or **recalled**. Any negative effects are irreversible.
- The number of **allergens** in foods could be increased by transferring genes causing allergic reactions between species.
- **Unfavourable** or possibly **dangerous traits** could be introduced into microorganisms, e.g. resistance to antibiotics, production of toxins or the tendency to cause disease. This could then increase the spread and severity of disease worldwide, or lead to new diseases developing for which there are no treatments or cures.
- As yet **unknown health risks** may occur as a result of eating genetically modified plants and animals.
- Large companies with funds and technology to develop genetically modified organisms could make **large profits** at the expense of smaller companies and poorer nations.

- Future steps in genetic engineering might allow the genetic makeup of higher organisms, including humans, to be altered, e.g. to produce 'designer babies'. Difficult **moral** and **ethical issues** then arise, e.g. do humans have the right to manipulate the course of nature or how far should we go in changing our own genes and those of other animals?

Revision questions

1 Distinguish between genetic and environmental variation.

2 **a** What is a mutation?

  b By reference to albinism and Down syndrome, explain how mutations cause variation.

3 Give THREE reasons why variation is important to living organisms.

4 Identify FOUR environmental factors that can cause variation in humans.

5 Outline the differences between continuous and discontinuous variation. Support your answer with TWO examples of EACH type of variation.

6 **a** What is natural selection and why is it important to living organisms?

  b Use the development of antibiotic-resistant bacteria to help explain the principles of natural selection.

7 **a** What is meant by the term 'genetic engineering'?

  b Identify the TWO main techniques used in genetic engineering.

8 Outline how genetic engineering can be used to produce insulin to treat diabetes.

9 Outline TWO ways genetic engineering is being used to improve food production.

10 Discuss THREE possible advantages and THREE possible disadvantages of using genetic engineering.

Exam-style questions – Chapters 10 to 11

Structured questions

1 **a)** Distinguish between a chromosome and a gene. **(2 marks)**

b) Figure 1 shows a dividing cell.

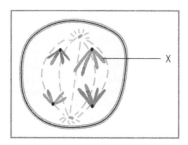

Figure 1 *A dividing cell*

  i) Name the structure labelled X. **(1 mark)**

  ii) Identify the type of cell division that the cell in Figure 1 is undergoing. **(1 mark)**

  iii) Give TWO reasons for your answer to **b) ii)** above. **(2 marks)**

  iv) Name ONE place in the human body where the type of cell division shown in Figure 1 would occur. **(1 mark)**

  v) How many chromosomes would each daughter cell possess when the cell shown in Figure 1 has finished dividing? **(1 mark)**

  vi) Give TWO reasons why this type of cell division is important. **(2 marks)**

c) **i)** All living organisms show variation. What is meant by the term 'variation'? **(1 mark)**

  ii) Distinguish between continuous variation and discontinuous variation. **(2 marks)**

  iii) Explain what happens to cause a person to be born with Down syndrome. **(2 marks)**

Total 15 marks

2 Some people produce wet earwax, while other people produce dry earwax. The allele for producing wet wax is dominant, and the type of wax produced is NOT sex-linked. Selena produces wet wax whereas her husband, Ario, produces dry wax. Figure 2 below shows the phenotypes of Selena, Ario and their five children.

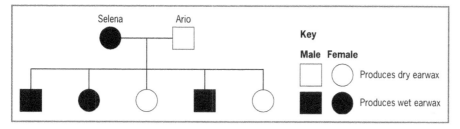

Figure 2 *The inheritance of earwax type in Selena and Ario's family*

a) i) What is meant by the term 'dominant allele'? (2 marks)

ii) Complete the following Punnett square to show the possible genotypes of Selena and Ario's children.

Use **E** to represent the dominant allele for producing wet wax and **e** to represent the recessive allele for producing dry wax.

gametes		

(4 marks)

iii) What is the chance that Selena and Ario's next child will produce dry wax? (1 mark)

iv) What term is used to describe Selena's genotype? (1 mark)

b) i) Identify the type of variation shown in Figure 2. (1 mark)

ii) Identify ONE other human characteristic that shows the same type of variation. (1 mark)

iii) Tara and Ashlee are identical twins. Explain, using suitable examples, how it is possible for them to have differences in their phenotypes even though they have the same genotypes. (3 marks)

iv) Why is it important that living organisms show variation? (2 marks)

Total 15 marks

Structured essay question

3 **a) i)** Haemophilia is caused by an X-linked recessive allele. Use a genetic-cross diagram to determine the genotype of the offspring of a cross between a female carrier of haemophilia and a normal male.

Use X^HX^h to denote the genotype of the female carrier and X^HY to denote the genotype of the normal male. (4 marks)

ii) State the phenotype of EACH offspring in a) i) above. (4 marks)

b) i) Kemar suffers from type I diabetes. Explain how genetic engineering is used to help treat Kemar's condition. Your answer must include the name of the product produced by genetic engineering and an explanation of how the product is made. (5 marks)

ii) Give TWO concerns that people might have about the use of genetic engineering to change the traits of organisms. (2 marks)

Total 15 marks

Section D – Diseases and their impact on humans

12 Health and disease

The World Health Organization (WHO) is a specialised agency of the United Nations (UN) responsible for **international public health**. The constitution of the WHO states that its main objective is 'the attainment by all people of the highest possible level of health'. According to the WHO, **healthy people** are able to function well physically, mentally and socially, and a **disease** is any condition that leads to the loss of good health.

Health is a state of complete physical, mental and social well-being and not merely an absence of disease and infirmity.

A disease is a condition that impairs the normal functioning of part or all of an organism, and leads to a loss of good health.

An introduction to disease

Types of disease

Diseases can be classified into the following **two** types.

- **Communicable diseases**, which are also known as **pathogenic** or **infectious diseases**.
- **Non-communicable diseases** or **NCDs**.

Communicable diseases

Communicable diseases are diseases that can be passed from one person to another and are caused by **pathogens**. Pathogens are **microscopic parasites** that cause disease in their hosts and include **viruses**, **bacteria**, **fungi** and **protozoans**. Some infectious diseases are **contagious** because they are spread by **direct** or **indirect contact** with an infected person. Not all infectious diseases are contagious, e.g. dengue is spread by mosquitoes, not by contact with an infected person.

Communicable diseases include **viral infections**, e.g. COVID-19 and influenza, **bacterial infections**, e.g. cholera and tuberculosis, **fungal infections**, e.g. athlete's foot and thrush, **sexually transmitted infections** (**STIs**), e.g. HIV/AIDS and gonorrhoea, and **vector-borne diseases**, e.g. malaria and dengue fever.

Non-communicable diseases or NCDs

Non-communicable diseases are diseases that cannot be passed from person to person and are not caused by pathogens. Many of these are described as being **chronic diseases**, meaning that they are long-term medical conditions that can worsen over time. There are several different **types** of NCDs.

- **Nutritional deficiency diseases** are caused by the shortage or lack of a particular **nutrient** in the diet, e.g. rickets, iron deficiency anaemia and protein-energy malnutrition or PEM (see pages 24–25 and 28).
- **Degenerative diseases** are caused by a gradual **deterioration** of body tissues or organs over time which prevents them from functioning normally, e.g. Alzheimer's disease, Parkinson's disease and osteoporosis.
- **Inherited disorders** are passed on from one generation to the next via genes and are caused by an **abnormal gene**, e.g. sickle cell anaemia, cystic fibrosis and Huntington's disease.

- **Lifestyle diseases** are linked to the way people **live** their lives, e.g. obesity, diabetes and hypertension (see pages 142–144).
- **Mental health problems** are disorders that affect how a person feels, thinks, behaves and interacts with other people, e.g. depression, anxiety disorders, neurosis, stress, schizophrenia and eating disorders.

Signs and symptoms of disease

Signs and **symptoms** are **abnormalities** that indicate a person is suffering from a disease.

Signs of a disease can be detected by someone other than the person affected by the disease.

Symptoms of a disease are experienced or felt by the person affected by the disease.

Signs are **objective.** They can be **observed** by another person and they are often **measurable**, e.g. an elevated temperature, high blood pressure, increased pulse or breathing rate, sugar in the urine, an increase in the number of white blood cells in the blood, a rash and swelling.

Symptoms are **subjective.** They cannot be observed by anyone else and they cannot be measured, e.g. headache, nausea, fatigue, pain, itching, dizziness, ringing in the ears and anxiety.

Treatment and control of disease

When **treating** a disease, the aim is to **relieve the symptoms** and to **cure** the disease if possible. When **controlling** a disease, the aim is to **prevent further development** and **spread** of the disease so that the incidence of it within the population is gradually reduced. Treating a disease is always one method to control it. The ultimate goal of treating and controlling any disease is to totally **eradicate** it from the human population.

Respiratory diseases

Respiratory diseases are diseases that affect any of the structures and organs of the **respiratory system.** They include asthma, influenza, bronchitis, emphysema, lung cancer, pneumonia and cystic fibrosis.

Asthma

The effects of asthma on the respiratory tract

Asthma is a **chronic inflammation** of the walls of the bronchi and bronchioles which causes these airways to be sensitive and makes them **narrower**, leading to breathing difficulties. During an **asthma attack**, the muscles around the walls contract, their lining becomes inflamed and mucus secretion increases. This causes the airways to become even narrower and breathing to become extremely difficult. Severe asthma attacks can be life-threatening.

Causes of asthma

The following factors play an important role in **increasing** a person's chances of developing asthma.

- Having a **history** of asthma in the **family.**
- Being exposed to **tobacco smoke** and other **irritants** or **allergens**, or having certain **respiratory infections** as an infant or in early childhood.
- Being prone to develop **allergies.**
- Being born to a mother who **smoked** during **pregnancy.**

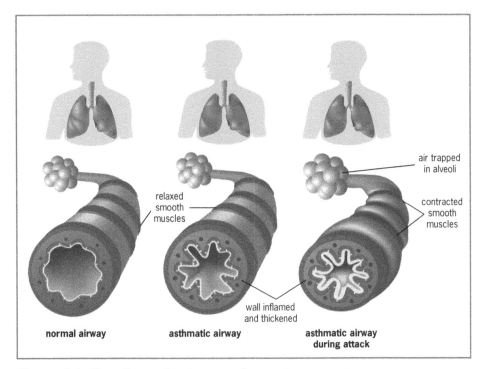

Figure 12.1 *The effects of asthma on the respiratory system*

Asthma attacks are usually brought on by exposure to some kind of **trigger**, including:

- **Allergens**, e.g. pollen, dust mites, animal fur and fungal spores.
- **Airborne irritants**, e.g. smoke, fumes, dust and other air pollutants.
- **Respiratory infections** such as colds and flu.
- **Anxiety** or **stress**.
- Inhaling **cold**, **dry** air.
- **Physical activity**.

Signs/symptoms of asthma

There are **four** main signs/symptoms of asthma and these **worsen** during an asthma attack:

- **Shortness** of **breath**.
- **Wheezing**.
- A **tight feeling** in the chest and **chest pain**.
- **Coughing**.

Treatment modality for asthma

There is currently **no cure** for asthma; however, it can be **treated** by using medications that are usually inhaled via an **inhaler**. Two types of inhaler can be used.

- **Preventer inhalers** contain **steroids** and are used once a day to reduce inflammation and sensitivity of the airways, which stops symptoms from developing. They provide **long-term** relief.
- **Reliever inhalers** are used to **quickly** relieve asthma symptoms during an **asthma attack**. They usually work by **relaxing** the muscles around the airways.

Prevention and control of asthma

- Do not smoke during pregnancy and reduce exposure of infants and young children to cigarette smoke and other irritants, allergens and respiratory infections.
- Draw up a **personal action plan** with a healthcare professional and stick to the plan.
- Reduce exposure to specific asthma triggers.
- Avoid contact with persons with colds and flu.

Influenza (flu) and bronchitis

Cause of influenza and its effects on the respiratory system

Influenza is caused by a **virus** which is spread by airborne droplets. It causes **inflammation** of the **lining** of the nose, throat and airways, and increases **mucus** production. The mucus build-up leads to a **stuffy nose** and **cough**, and it increases a person's chance of developing pneumonia. Other signs and symptoms of influenza, given in Table 12.1, are caused by the **immune system's response** to the virus.

Causes of bronchitis and its effects on the respiratory system

Bronchitis occurs when the **walls** of the bronchi and bronchioles become **inflamed** and **swollen**, and **mucus** production increases, both of which make breathing difficult. Bronchitis may be **acute** or **chronic**, and the signs/symptoms of both types are very similar.

- **Acute bronchitis** is usually caused by a **virus**; often the same ones that cause colds and flu can lead to a person developing acute bronchitis. It can last for a few days up to three weeks.
- **Chronic bronchitis** is usually caused by **smoking**, or long-term exposure to air pollution, chemical fumes or dust. It either does not go away or keeps coming back for extended periods.

Table 12.1 *Signs/symptoms, treatment, prevention and control of influenza and bronchitis*

	Influenza	Bronchitis
Signs/symptoms	• Stuffy or runny nose. • Cough. • Sore throat. • Fever (elevated temperature) and chills. • Muscle or body aches. • Headache. • Fatigue (tiredness). • Swollen lymph glands.	• A cough that usually brings up mucus. • Chest congestion or chest discomfort. • Shortness of breath. • Wheezing sounds when breathing. • A slight fever and chills. • Mild headache and body aches.
Treatment modality	• Antiviral drugs. • Drugs to relieve the symptoms, e.g. fever reducers, painkillers and cough medicines. • Bed rest.	• Drugs to relieve the symptoms, e.g. cough medicines, bronchodilators and painkillers. • Lots of fluids to drink. • Bed rest.

	Influenza	Bronchitis
Prevention and control	• Annual **influenza vaccination**. • Avoid crowded areas and contact with persons with influenza. • Wash hands often with soap and water or use alcohol-based hand sanitisers, and avoid touching the face. • Cough or sneeze into a tissue or elbow and wash hands afterwards.	• Use the same control measures as used for influenza, including having an annual **influenza vaccination**. • Avoid contact with persons with colds and influenza. • Stop smoking and avoid secondhand smoke. • Wear a face mask when in the presence of lung irritants or avoid them completely.

Gastrointestinal diseases

Gastrointestinal diseases affect the structures and organs of the **digestive system**. They include cholera, gastroenteritis, oesophageal reflux, pancreatitis, irritable bowel syndrome and coeliac disease.

Cholera and gastroenteritis

Cause of cholera

Cholera is an infectious disease caused by a **bacterium** known as *Vibrio cholerae*. When food or water contaminated by faeces from an infected person is consumed, the bacteria quickly release a **toxin** into the intestines which can cause **severe diarrhoea** that can be life-threatening.

Cause of gastroenteritis

Gastroenteritis is an inflammation of the lining of the intestines. The most common cause is one of two **viruses: norovirus** in adults and **rotavirus** in children. It can also be caused by **bacteria** such as *Salmonella* or *E. coli*, and occasionally by a **parasite** such as *Giardia*. A person can become infected by close contact with an infected person, touching a contaminated surface or object, or ingesting contaminated food or water.

Table 12.2 *Signs/symptoms, treatment, prevention and control of cholera and gastroenteritis*

	Cholera	Gastroenteritis
Signs/ symptoms	• Severe watery diarrhoea. • Vomiting. • Dehydration; signs and symptoms include irritability, fatigue, sunken eyes, dry mouth, extreme thirst, dry and shrivelled skin, very little urination, dark-coloured urine, low blood pressure, rapid heartbeat and muscle cramps.	• Watery diarrhoea. • Abdominal cramps and pain. • Nausea. • Vomiting. • A mild fever. • Loss of appetite.
Treatment modality	• **Antibiotics** to kill the bacterium. • Replace lost fluids by drinking rehydration solutions or receiving rehydration fluids intravenously.	• Plenty of fluids to drink, including rehydration fluids if necessary. • Small amounts of plain food to eat, e.g. clear soups, rice and pasta. • Paracetamol to relieve pain and reduce fever. • Plenty of rest.

	Cholera	Gastroenteritis
Prevention and control	• **Cholera vaccination.** • Use only bottled, boiled or chemically treated water for drinking, food preparation, brushing teeth and washing. • Dispose of faeces in the correct way to prevent contamination of food and water supplies. • Chlorinate drinking water supplies.	• **Rotavirus vaccine** for children younger than one year old. • Wash hands regularly. • Practise good food hygiene (see page 26). • Drink bottled, boiled or chemically treated water. • Disinfect surfaces and objects that could have been contaminated.

Sexually transmitted infections or STIs

Sexually transmitted infections or **STIs** are passed on from one person to another during **unprotected sexual intercourse** with an infected person. They include gonorrhoea, syphilis, genital herpes, chlamydia, human papilloma virus or HPV infection and HIV/AIDS.

Gonorrhoea, syphilis, genital herpes and chlamydia

Table 12.3 *Causes, signs/symptoms and treatment of gonorrhoea, syphilis, genital herpes and chlamydia*

Infection	Cause	Signs/symptoms	Treatment modalities
Gonorrhoea	**Bacterium** known as *Neisseria gonorrhoeae*	• **In females:** abnormal vaginal discharge, pain or burning sensation when urinating, pain or tenderness in the lower abdomen and bleeding between periods. • **In males:** abnormal discharge from the tip of the penis, pain or burning sensation when urinating and pain or swelling in the testes. If left untreated, it can lead to infertility in both males and females.	• **Antibiotics** to kill the bacterium.
Syphilis	**Bacterium** known as *Treponema pallidum*	Syphilis develops in stages: • **Primary syphilis:** painless, round sores called **chancres** develop on the genitals at the point of infection and last for 3 to 6 weeks. • **Secondary syphilis:** a red, non-itchy rash then spreads over the body and may be accompanied by patchy hair loss, fever, sore throat and swollen lymph glands. These symptoms eventually go away. • **Latent syphilis:** no symptoms occur for years. • **Tertiary syphilis:** if left untreated, damage can occur to the brain, nerves, heart, blood vessels and other organs many years after the original infection.	• **Antibiotics** to kill the bacterium.

Infection	Cause	Signs/symptoms	Treatment modalities
Genital herpes	**Virus** known as the herpes simplex virus or HSV	• Recurrent painful blisters on the genitals and surrounding areas. • Flu-like symptoms may accompany the initial outbreak (appearance of the blisters) and become reduced in severity during subsequent outbreaks.	• **Antiviral drugs** to reduce symptoms. • No cure exists.
Chlamydia	**Bacterium** known as *Chlamydia trachomatis*	• **In females**: abnormal vaginal discharge, burning sensation when urinating, pain during sexual intercourse, itching or soreness in or around the vagina and bleeding between periods. • **In males**: abnormal discharge from the tip of the penis, burning sensation when urinating, itching or burning around the opening of the penis and pain or swelling in the testes. If left untreated it can damage the reproductive organs and cause infertility, especially in females.	• **Antibiotics** to kill the bacterium.

Human papillomavirus or HPV infection

Cause and signs/symptoms of HPV infection

Human papillomavirus infection is caused by a **virus**. There are over 100 varieties of the virus, and more than 40 of these are **sexually transmitted**. Many types affect the mouth, throat or genital area.

Often, HPV infection does not cause any **noticeable** signs/symptoms. However, some varieties can cause **genital warts** to develop inside the vagina or on the cervix in females, and on the penis or scrotum in males. Other varieties can cause **cervical**, **vaginal** or **vulval cancer** in females, **penile cancer** in males, and **anal** or **throat cancer** in both females and males.

Treatment and prevention of HPV infection

There is currently **no** treatment available for the virus itself. **Genital warts** can be treated with medications applied to the warts; however, getting rid of the warts does not get rid of the virus, so the warts may return. **Cervical cancer** can be detected by having a regular **cervical** or **Pap smear** test, and if cancer is detected, it can be treated by methods such as chemotherapy, radiotherapy or surgery. A **vaccine** is available to prevent the development of **genital warts** and **cancers** caused by **nine** types of the virus.

Prevention and control of STIs

The following methods can be employed to **prevent** or **control** the spread of **all STIs**.

• **Abstain** from sexual intercourse or keep to **one**, uninfected sexual partner.

• Use **condoms** during sexual intercourse.

• Visit a doctor or healthcare facility to be **tested** if an infection is suspected.

• **Trace** and **treat** all sexual contacts of infected persons.

• Set up **education programmes** to educate populations about sexually transmitted infections and how to prevent their spread.

Currently **no vaccine** exists for gonorrhoea, syphilis, genital herpes or chlamydia.

HIV/AIDS

HIV stands for **human immunodeficiency virus**. Over time, if HIV is not treated, it can lead to the development of **AIDS**, which stands for **acquired immune deficiency syndrome**.

Methods of transmission of HIV

HIV is **transmitted** from person to person in body fluids. Methods of transmission include the following.

- Having **unprotected sexual intercourse** with a person infected with HIV.
- Using **needles** or **cutting instruments** that are contaminated with HIV.
- From an **infected mother** to her baby during pregnancy, birth or breastfeeding.
- Receiving **transfusions** of blood or blood products that are contaminated with HIV.
- Contact between **broken skin**, **wounds** or **mucous membranes** and HIV-infected blood or body fluids.

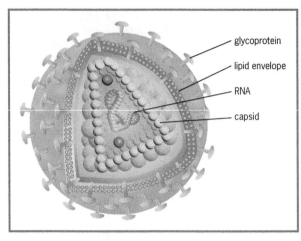

Figure 12.2 *Structure of the human immunodeficiency virus*

Mode of action of HIV

When the **virus** enters the blood, the virus particles bind to certain white blood cells known as **helper T lymphocytes**, **CD4⁺ T cells** or simply **T cells**. The virus particles enter these T cells and begin to replicate (make copies of themselves). The new HIV particles burst out of the cells and this destroys the T cells. The new particles go on to attack more T cells and this starts to **weaken** the immune system.

Signs/symptoms of HIV/AIDS

HIV/AIDS develops in **three stages** and the signs/symptoms depend on the stage of infection.

- **Primary infection** is the **first stage**. **Flu-like** symptoms, which last for 1 to 2 weeks and then go away, may develop 2 to 6 weeks after infection, and not everyone develops these symptoms.
- **Asymptomatic stage** is the **second stage**. Most people remain without symptoms for 10 years or more. However, the virus is damaging the person's immune system by destroying T cells, and the infected person can transmit the virus to other people without realising.
- **Symptomatic stage** is the **third stage**, when symptoms of **AIDS** begin to develop because the immune system has been severely damaged. These symptoms include weight loss, prolonged fever, severe tiredness, night sweats, chronic diarrhoea, swollen lymph glands and skin rashes. The damage to the immune system also leaves the person vulnerable to **opportunistic infections**, e.g. pneumonia and tuberculosis, and to some types of **cancer**, e.g. lymphoma and Kaposi's sarcoma.

Treatment modality for HIV/AIDS

There is currently **no cure** for HIV/AIDS; however, it can be **treated** by using **antiretroviral therapy** or **ART** where the patient takes a combination of three or more **antiretroviral drugs** daily for the rest of their life. ART helps prevent patients from developing AIDS and reduces their risk of transmitting HIV.

ART can cause **side effects** in some people. These include nausea, vomiting, diarrhoea, dry mouth, headaches, rashes, dizziness, emotional problems, difficulty sleeping, heart disease, liver, kidney and pancreas damage, loss of bone density, and elevated blood sugar and cholesterol levels.

Prevention and control of HIV/AIDS

The measures outlined on page 139 can be used to prevent and control the spread of HIV. Additionally, the following **specific measures** can be taken.

- Do not use intravenous drugs or share cutting instruments.
- Use sterile needles for all injections.
- Test all human products to be given intravenously for HIV.
- Prevent mother to baby transmission by ensuring pregnant women with HIV receive ART and their babies receive HIV medication after birth.
- Persons who are at a high risk of HIV infection, such as those with an HIV positive partner, should take **pre-exposure prophylaxis** or **PrEP**, a daily HIV drug which reduces their risk of being infected.

No vaccine currently exists against HIV.

Ethical considerations of HIV/AIDS

The HIV/AIDS epidemic has presented a host of **ethical** and **moral** issues related to human life and dignity. The disease has particularly affected vulnerable groups such as male homosexuals, sex workers and intravenous drug users, and often leads to **stigma** and **discrimination**.

The **stigma** experienced by those living with HIV/AIDS, in which they are labelled as being part of a **socially unacceptable** group, leads to acts of **discrimination**, in which these people are **treated differently** from others. This stigma and discrimination can affect a person's emotional well-being and mental health, break down self-confidence and lead to feelings of shame, isolation and despair. **Fear** of stigma and discrimination can also keep people from being tested, seeking medical care, disclosing their HIV status and taking antiretroviral drugs. This then contributes to the continued spread of HIV and can be experienced by people in all sections of society.

Effects of STIs on a pregnant mother and her foetus/baby

Untreated STIs pose a significant risk for a pregnant mother and her baby. If a **pregnant woman** is infected with an STI it increases her chances of having a miscarriage, or of her baby being born prematurely (early) and with low birth weight, or being stillborn (born dead).

HIV and **syphilis** can pass across the **placenta**. Babies infected with **HIV** are at risk of developing **AIDS** and those infected with **syphilis** are at risk of developing serious problems with major organs, which can be fatal. **Gonorrhoea**, **chlamydia** and **genital herpes** can pass from mother to baby during **birth**. **Gonorrhoea** can cause the baby to develop eye infections, blindness and infections of the blood and joints, while **chlamydia** can lead to the baby developing eye infections, blindness and pneumonia. Active **herpes** blisters on the genitals of a mother at the time of delivery can lead to **neonatal herpes**, a potentially deadly infection.

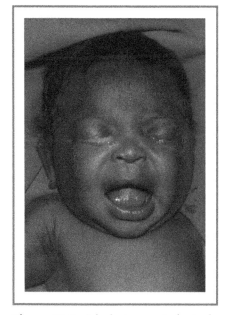

Figure 12.3 *A baby's eyes infected with gonorrhoea during birth*

Lifestyle-related diseases

Lifestyle-related diseases are **non-communicable diseases**. They are associated with the way people **live** their lives and include obesity, diabetes mellitus and cardiovascular disease or CVD.

Obesity

Obesity is characterised by an excessive accumulation and storage of **fat** in the body.

Causes and signs/symptoms of obesity

Obesity occurs when a person consumes more food than they use on a daily basis. The excess food is converted to **fat** and **stored** under the skin and around organs. It is generally **caused** by a combination of **two** factors.

- The excessive consumption of energy-rich foods high in **carbohydrates**, particularly **sugar**, and/or **fat**, especially animal fat that is rich in saturated fatty acids.
- A lack of **physical activity**.

Certain **risk factors** can contribute to a person developing obesity, including a history of obesity in the family, family influences, unhealthy lifestyle choices, certain medical conditions and medications, social and economic factors, increasing age, pregnancy and stopping smoking.

A person with obesity has a body mass index (**BMI**) greater than 30.0 kg per m². Apart from being very overweight, other **signs/symptoms** include breathlessness, increased sweating, inability to cope with physical activity, feeling very tired every day, back and joint pains, and elevated blood pressure and cholesterol levels. Obesity increases a person's risk of developing **hypertension**, **coronary heart disease**, **type 2 diabetes**, **osteoarthritis** and some **cancers**, and a person's risk of suffering from a **heart attack** or **stroke**.

Treatment and prevention of obesity

Persons with obesity must take steps to **lose weight**. The following are the **two** most important steps.

- Changing to a **healthy diet** that is **low** in **carbohydrates** and **saturated fats**. The diet should contain plenty of high-fibre foods such as fruits, vegetables and whole grains.
- **Increasing physical activity** to a minimum of 150 minutes of moderately intense activity per week such as fast walking and swimming.

Diabetes mellitus

Diabetes mellitus is a condition in which the **blood sugar level** is consistently **high** over a prolonged period. There are **two** types of diabetes mellitus.

- **Type 1** or **insulin-dependent diabetes** is the most common type in children and young adults. About 10% of people with diabetes worldwide have type 1.
- **Type 2** or **non-insulin dependent diabetes** occurs most often in older adults. About 90% of people with diabetes worldwide have type 2. Being overweight or obese, or having a family history of type 2 diabetes increases a person's chances of developing the condition.

There is **no cure** for diabetes, and if it is not managed it can lead to complications such as cardiovascular disease, damage to the nerves, kidneys, eyes and feet, and various skin problems.

Table 12.4 *Causes, signs/symptoms, treatment, prevention and control of diabetes mellitus*

	Type 1 diabetes	Type 2 diabetes
Causes	The pancreas does not produce insulin because the insulin-producing cells have been damaged, usually by the body's own immune system.	The pancreas does not produce enough insulin and/or the body cells develop insulin resistance and do not respond to the insulin.
Signs/symptoms	The main signs/symptoms of **both types** are very similar. • A blood glucose level that is consistently higher than the normal 80 mg per 100 cm³ of blood. • Glucose present in the urine. • Frequent urination. • Excessive thirst. • Excessive hunger. • Unexplained weight loss. • Fatigue. • Blurred vision. • Numbness or tingling in the hands and feet. • Slow healing of cuts and sores.	
Treatment, prevention and control	• **Insulin therapy**, which involves taking insulin by means of regular insulin injections or using an insulin pump. • Regular monitoring of blood glucose levels and daily monitoring of carbohydrate consumption.	• **Oral medications** that help lower blood glucose levels. Some people also take insulin. • Maintain a healthy weight.
	The following apply to **both types** of diabetes. • Consume a healthy diet that is low in sugar and saturated fats, and high in fibre. • Take regular, moderate exercise. • Attend regular checkups with a doctor or healthcare provider.	

Cardiovascular disease or CVD

Cardiovascular disease refers to a group of conditions that affects the **heart** and **blood vessels**, including **hypertension**, **coronary heart disease** and other **heart diseases** covered on pages 60 and 61.

• **Hypertension** or **high blood pressure** occurs when the blood pressure in the arteries is consistently high, in other words, **140/90 mm Hg** or **higher** (see page 60).

Coronary heart disease or **CHD** is a condition caused by a build-up of fatty **atheromas** or **plaques** in the walls of the **coronary arteries** that supply the muscle cells of the heart with oxygen. These atheromas are formed by a process known as **atherosclerosis** (see page 60).

Table 12.5 *Causes, signs/symptoms, treatment, prevention and control of hypertension and coronary heart disease*

	Hypertension	Coronary heart disease
Causes	The following can lead to the development of both **hypertension** and **coronary heart disease.** • Being overweight or obese. • Being physically inactive. • Consuming too much saturated fat and salt in the diet. • Smoking. • Drinking too much alcohol. • Being under stress. The following can also lead to the development of **coronary heart disease.** • Having high blood pressure. • Having diabetes.	
Signs/symptoms	• Blood pressure of 140/90 mm Hg or above. • In many cases there are no symptoms. It is known as the 'silent killer'. • Can cause headaches, nose bleeds, heart failure, heart attack, stroke, kidney failure and impaired vision.	• Chest pain, known as **angina**. • Shortness of breath. • Can lead to heart failure or a heart attack.
Treatment, prevention and control	• Prescription drugs to lower blood pressure.	• Coronary artery bypass surgery. • A daily low-dose aspirin tablet to help prevent clot formation.
	The following apply to both **hypertension** and **coronary heart disease.** • Consume a healthy diet that is low in saturated fats and salt, and high in fibre. • Take regular, moderate exercise. • Maintain a healthy weight. • Manage stress. • Reduce alcohol consumption. • Stop smoking. • Attend regular checkups with a doctor or healthcare provider.	

Obesity and secondary hypertension

Secondary hypertension is caused by another condition or disease such as obesity, and if the disease is treated, then the person's blood pressure is usually lowered significantly. People with **obesity** are 2 to 6 times more likely to develop **hypertension** than those whose weight is within a healthy range, therefore it is recommended that all obese people **lose weight**.

The importance of diet and exercise to lifestyle-related diseases

Diet and **exercise** are important in the treatment, prevention and control of lifestyle-related diseases. Eating a **healthy**, **balanced diet** ensures that excess carbohydrates and fats are not consumed. This then limits weight gain and helps reduce obesity, diabetes, hypertension and heart disease. In particular, the diet should be **low** in saturated fats and salt, and **high** in dietary fibre supplied by fresh fruits, vegetables and whole grains. It should also contain low-fat dairy products and lean protein such as fish, skinless poultry and lean meat, and healthy fats such as olive oil.

Regular, **aerobic exercise**, e.g. swimming, walking and aerobics, also limits weight gain and increases metabolism, improves circulation, lowers heart rate and blood pressure, and maintains fitness. Exercise has the added benefit of improving mental health as it reduces stress, anxiety and depression, and boosts self-esteem.

Cancer

Cancer refers to a group of related diseases that result from changes to the DNA of cells somewhere in the body. This produces **abnormal cells** which start to divide in an uncontrolled way, producing more abnormal cells that replace normal cells and usually produce a **tumour** or **cancerous lump**. Some of the abnormal cells may also spread or **metastasise** to other parts of the body. Tumours do not form in some types of cancer, e.g. leukaemia and other cancers of the blood.

According to the WHO, the most common cancers are **lung cancer**, **breast cancer**, **colorectal cancer** (cancer of the **colon** and **rectum**), **prostate cancer**, **skin cancer** and **stomach cancer**.

Causes of cancer

The main **risk factors** that can increase a person's chances of developing cancer include the following.

- **Lifestyle factors**, e.g. smoking, excessive exposure to the sun's ultraviolet radiation, drinking too much alcohol, being overweight or obese, consuming an unhealthy diet, a lack of physical activity and having unprotected sex.
- Having a **family history** of cancer.
- Exposure to certain **bacteria** and **viruses**, e.g. HIV, HPV, and hepatitis B and C.
- Exposure to certain **environmental factors**, e.g. radiation, and certain harmful chemicals, e.g. asbestos, some pesticides and secondhand smoke.

The term **carcinogen** is used to describe any substance or agent that causes cancer.

Signs/symptoms of cancer

The specific **signs/symptoms** of the different types of cancer vary, and include the following.

- Unexplained **pain** that does not improve with treatment.
- Unexplained **weight loss**.
- Extreme **tiredness** that does not improved with rest.
- Having a **fever** that lasts for several days or weeks.
- The appearance of an unusual **lump** or **tissue mass**, such as occurs with breast cancer.
- Changes in the **skin** such as new moles or marks appearing, or sores that do not heal, could be a sign of skin cancer.
- A **cough** or **hoarseness** that does not go away could be a sign of lung cancer or cancer of the larynx.
- Unusual **bleeding**, e.g. blood in the faeces could be a sign of colorectal cancer.
- **Anaemia** could be a sign of leukaemia.

The signs/symptoms of cancers of the **reproductive system** are summarised in Table 9.2 on page 95.

Treatment modalities and ways to reduce the risk of developing cancer

Cancer treatment aims to cure the cancer, shrink a tumour or slow the growth and spread of the cancer. A single method or combination of methods may be used.

- **Surgery** is used to **remove** the cancerous tumour, or as much of it as possible, from the body.

- **Radiation therapy** or **radiotherapy** uses high doses of **radiation** to kill the cancer cells.
- **Chemotherapy** uses **drugs** to kill the cancer cells.
- **Immunotherapy** helps the body's **immune system** to fight the cancer.
- Other treatment methods include **bone marrow transplant**, also known as **stem cell transplant**, **hormone therapy** and **targeted drug therapy**.

To **reduce the risk** of developing cancer, a person should:

- Stop smoking, protect against exposure to too much sunlight, reduce alcohol consumption, reduce obesity and maintain a healthy weight, eat a healthy diet, get plenty of exercise, practise safe sex and limit exposure to carcinogens in the environment.
- Get immunised against HPV and hepatitis.
- Know the medical history of one's family and get regular screenings for cancer.

The impact of diseases on human populations

Throughout history, **epidemics**, and more recently **pandemics**, have had major impacts on human populations.

*An **epidemic** is the widespread occurrence of an infectious disease within a population, community or region in a particular period of time.*

*A **pandemic** is the widespread occurrence of an infectious disease that spreads across multiple countries and/or continents.*

Both **infectious** or **communicable diseases** and **non-communicable diseases** or **NCDs** can have negative **socio-economic impacts** on human populations, including:

- Increased demands on **health services** and increased **healthcare costs** as more people have to seek treatment.
- **Job losses** and **loss of earnings** as those infected are unable to work.
- Reduced **productivity** of businesses due to a reduction in their workforce.
- **Impoverishment** of families and reduced **living standards**.
- Shortened **lifespans** and loss of **human resources**.
- Reduced **foreign exchange earnings** for countries.

Revision questions

1   Define the following terms:
    a health   **b** disease

2   Using examples, distinguish between the following terms as they relate to disease:
    a communicable and non-communicable   **b** signs and symptoms

3   **a** Explain how asthma affects the respiratory system.
    b Identify THREE factors that can increase a person's chances of developing asthma and explain how asthma is treated.

4   Distinguish between influenza and bronchitis in terms of:
    a their causes   **b** their symptoms

5. Explain how EACH of the following gastrointestinal diseases is caused and measures that can be put in place to control the spread of EACH:

   a cholera   **b** gastroenteritis

6. **a** What is an STI?

   b Describe the causative agent, signs/symptoms and treatment measures for gonorrhoea.

   c Excluding treatment measures, outline FOUR measures that can be taken to control the spread of STIs.

7. **a** What is the relationship between HIV and AIDS?

   b Outline FOUR ways HIV can be transmitted and describe the effects it has on the body.

8. By referring to specific examples, explain why it is important that a pregnant woman is tested and, if necessary, treated for any STIs that she might have.

9. Identify the TWO main causes of obesity and explain why it is important for persons who are obese to reduce their weight.

10. **a** Distinguish between type 1 and type 2 diabetes in terms of their causes.

    b Identify TWO signs that a doctor might use to diagnose diabetes in a patient and THREE symptoms that a person with diabetes might experience.

11. Identify the TWO main types of cardiovascular disease and outline the measures used to treat and control the two types.

12. **a** Explain how cancer develops.

    b Outline how cancer can be treated and identify FOUR ways a person can reduce their risk of developing cancer.

13. **a** Distinguish between an epidemic and a pandemic.

    b Discuss the impact of diseases on the human population.

Vectors and disease

*A **vector** is an organism that carries pathogens in or on its body and transmits the pathogens from one host to another.*

A vector is not usually harmed by the pathogen. **Rats**, **houseflies** and **mosquitoes** are examples of vectors.

- **Rats** can transmit diseases such as **leptospirosis** and **salmonella** when a person comes into direct or indirect contact with rat faeces, urine or saliva, or gets bitten by a rat. They can also spread diseases such as the **plague** via ticks and fleas that have fed on the blood of a rat carrying the pathogens.
- **Houseflies** can transmit diseases such as **gastroenteritis** and **cholera** (see pages 137–138).
- **Mosquitoes** can transmit diseases such as **malaria**, **dengue fever**, **chickungunya** and **Zika virus disease** (see pages 149–150).

Life cycle of a mosquito

There are **four distinct stages** in the life cycle of a mosquito.

- **Egg** – The adult female lays eggs in standing water and the eggs float on the surface of the water.

- **Larva** – The larva hatches from the egg. This is the **feeding** and **growing stage**. The larvae hang from the water's surface and breathe air through breathing tubes. They **moult** (shed their skin) several times, which enables them to grow as they feed on microorganisms and organic matter in the water.

- **Pupa** – The pupa develops from the larva. This is the non-feeding, resting stage in which **larval tissue re-organises** into adult tissue. The pupae hang from the surface of the water and breathe air through two breathing tubes.

- **Adult** or **imago** – The adult emerges from the pupa onto the surface of the water. The adult is the **flying** and **reproductive stage**. The adults live in and around human residences where they rest in cool, dark places during the day, and fly and feed on nectar and sugars from plants in the evenings. After mating, the female requires a **blood meal** to mature her eggs before she lays them. She usually obtains this blood from a human.

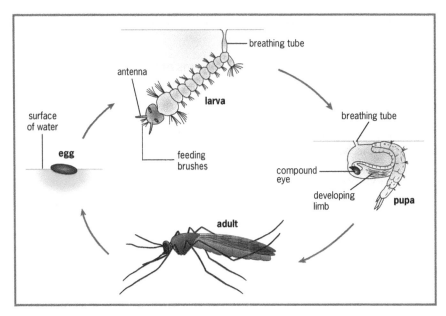

★ **Figure 12.4** *The life cycle of a mosquito*

Transmission of pathogens by mosquitoes

A female mosquito can transmit **pathogens** from one person to another when she bites an **infected person** to obtain a **blood meal**.

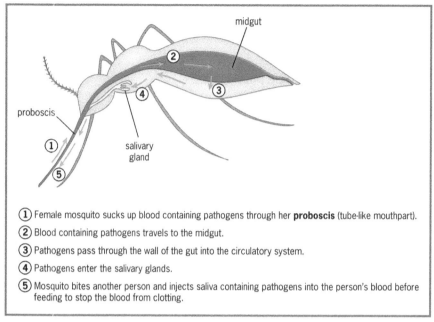

① Female mosquito sucks up blood containing pathogens through her **proboscis** (tube-like mouthpart).

② Blood containing pathogens travels to the midgut.

③ Pathogens pass through the wall of the gut into the circulatory system.

④ Pathogens enter the salivary glands.

⑤ Mosquito bites another person and injects saliva containing pathogens into the person's blood before feeding to stop the blood from clotting.

Figure 12.5 *Transmission of pathogens by a mosquito*

Mosquito-borne diseases

The *Anopheles* mosquito transmits **malaria** while the *Aedes aegypti* mosquito transmits **dengue fever**, **chikungunya** and **Zika virus disease** or **Zika fever**.

Table 12.6 *Causative agents, signs/symptoms and treatment of mosquito-borne diseases*

Disease	Causative agent	Signs/symptoms	Treatment
Malaria	**Protozoan** known as *Plasmodium*	• Feeling cold and shivering followed by a high fever and severe sweating lasting several hours. • Headache, muscle aches, nausea, vomiting and weakness. • Can be fatal, or attacks of high fever and weakness can return periodically for years.	• Antimalarial drugs to kill the protozoan, e.g. quinine, chloroquine and hydroxychloroquine. • Fever reducers and painkillers.
Dengue fever	**Dengue virus** or **DENV** which has four types: DENV-1, DENV-2, DENV-3, DENV-4	• High fever, lasting several days. • Severe headaches. • Pain behind the eyes. • Severe joint and muscle pain. • Skin rash. • **Severe dengue** or **haemorrhagic dengue** can cause bleeding from the nose, gums, beneath the skin and internally, and can be fatal.	• Fever reducers and painkillers, except aspirin and anti-inflammatories such as ibuprofen. • Drink plenty of fluids. • Get plenty of rest.

Disease	Causative agent	Signs/symptoms	Treatment
Chikungunya	Chikungunya virus	• Fever. • Joint pain that can last for months, particularly affecting the wrists, hands, ankles and feet, and can be debilitating. • Joint swelling. • Headaches and muscle pain. • Skin rash.	• Fever reducers and painkillers. • Drink plenty of fluids. • Get plenty of rest.
Zika virus disease or Zika fever	Zika virus	• Mild fever. • Skin rash. • Conjunctivitis. • Headaches, and joint and muscle pain. • Zika infection during pregnancy can cause birth defects, particularly **microcephaly** (abnormally small head).	• Fever reducers and painkillers. • Drink plenty of fluids. • Get plenty of rest.

Note: After recovery from **dengue fever**, a person has **long-term immunity** to the **type** of virus that infected him or her, but has no immunity to the other types.

Prevention and control of mosquito-borne diseases

A variety of measures can be put in place to **prevent** and **control** mosquito-borne diseases.

- Control **mosquitoes** (see Table 12.7, page 152).
- Protect against being **bitten** by mosquitoes by wearing long-sleeved shirts and long trousers, using insect repellant, placing screens on windows and doors, and sleeping under mosquito nets.
- Implement **education programmes** to educate the public about the diseases and how to prevent them.
- Take **antimalarial drugs** to protect against developing **malaria**.

The life cycle of a housefly

The life cycle of a housefly has the same **four distinct stages** as that of a mosquito.

- **Egg** – The adult female lays eggs in decaying organic matter such as compost, faeces, manure and the bodies of dead animals.
- **Larva** or **maggot** – The larva hatches from the egg. This is the **feeding** and **growing stage**. The larvae **moult** several times, which enables them to grow rapidly as they feed on the organic matter. The larvae burrow deep into the organic matter after the last moult.
- **Pupa** – Once deep in the organic matter, the skin of the larva hardens and darkens and it changes into the pupa. This is the non-feeding, resting stage in which **larval tissue re-organises** into adult tissue.
- **Adult** or **imago** – The adult emerges from the pupa. The adult is the **flying** and **reproductive stage**. Adults fly and feed on decaying organic matter and human food. After mating, the female lays her eggs in decaying organic matter.

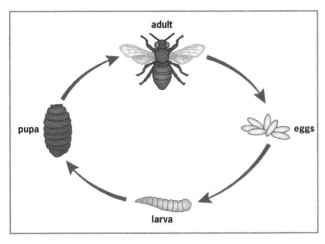

★ **Figure 12.6** *The life cycle of a housefly*

Transmission of pathogens by houseflies

Houseflies pick up **pathogens** on their legs, body and mouthparts when they feed on **organic waste**, including **faeces**, or they suck them up into their guts as they feed. They then transfer these pathogens to **human food** when they walk on the food to feed, or they regurgitate them onto the food in their saliva and digestive juices as they feed, or they pass them onto the food in their faeces and vomit spots.

Control of vectors of disease

The importance of controlling vectors

Controlling vectors is crucial to reduce the incidence of infection from vector-borne diseases, some of which can be fatal. This is **important** because some vector-borne diseases currently have **no effective cure** or **medical measures** available to **prevent** them, such as vaccines and drugs. Even for those with effective treatments or preventative measures available, issues such as cost, delivery of the measures, correct diagnosis and drug resistance make controlling the diseases through medical measures an unrealistic alternative to prevention by vector control.

Methods of controlling vectors

Vectors can be controlled by **four** main methods.

- **Chemical control** involves using chemicals to kill the vectors, e.g. insecticides and poisoned baits.
- **Biological control** involves using natural enemies of the vectors to kill them, e.g. predators.
- **Mechanical control** involves using physical means to control the vectors, e.g. barriers and traps.
- **Sanitary control** involves removing conditions which attract the vectors, e.g. removing all garbage.

Table 12.7 *Methods used to control vectors*

Pest	Methods of control
Mosquitoes	To control mosquito **larvae** and **pupae**: • Add **insecticides** to breeding areas to kill larvae and pupae. • Introduce **fish**, e.g. tilapia, into breeding areas to feed on larvae and pupae. • **Drain** all areas of standing water and remove all containers that collect water. • Spray **oil**, **kerosene** or non-toxic **lecithins** onto still-water breeding areas to prevent larvae and pupae from breathing. To control **adult** mosquitoes: • Spray with **insecticides** to kill the adults. • Remove **dense vegetation** to reduce protection for adults during daylight hours. • Place **mosquito screens** over windows and doors to prevent adults entering buildings, and place **mosquito nets** over beds at night.
Houseflies	• Spray adults with **insecticides** to kill them. • Use **fly traps** to kill adults. • **Dispose** of all human and animal waste properly. • **Treat** all sewage. • **Cover** food so that adults cannot land on it.
Rats	• Use **rat bait** to kill them. • Introduce **cats** or other animals that prey on them. • Use **rat traps** to trap and kill them. • **Rodent-proof** buildings.

Revision questions

14 **a** What is a vector?

b Identify THREE different vectors and name TWO diseases transmitted by EACH.

15 Explain how a mosquito transmits Zika fever.

16 Give FOUR signs/symptoms of chikungunya, and state how the disease can be treated.

17 With the aid of a labelled diagram, describe the life cycle of a housefly.

18 **a** Why is it important to control vectors of disease?

b Describe the different control measures for mosquito larvae and for adult mosquitoes.

13 Hygiene, defence against disease and drugs

The human body is surrounded by microorganisms, some of which are **pathogenic**. However, there are measures that can be taken to reduce the likelihood that these pathogens will enter the body and cause disease, and if they do enter, the body has **natural defences** against them, such as the **immune system**. Many medical conditions, including those caused by pathogens, can be treated using **drugs**. Some drugs are, however, illegal and all drugs can have harmful effects on the body if they are used incorrectly.

Personal hygiene

Personal hygiene refers to the practices carried out by individuals in order to maintain **cleanliness** of their bodies and clothing to preserve overall **good health** and **well-being**.

Maintaining good personal hygiene is **important** because it helps to:

- Ensure good overall health.
- Prevent the spread of infections.
- Eliminate bad breath and body odour.
- Prevent dental caries.
- Promote greater confidence and self-esteem.
- Promote social and professional acceptance.

Body and hair hygiene

Active people or people in high environmental temperatures **sweat** to cool their bodies. When water evaporates from the sweat it leaves salts, urea and dead skin cells on the surface of the skin. **Bacteria** then break down these substances and produce unpleasant smelling chemicals that cause **body odour** or **BO**. They can also cause **infections**. To **reduce** body odour and the likelihood of infections:

- **Wash** the **body** daily using soap and water, especially the armpits, genitals and between the toes.
- **Wash** the **hair** with shampoo at least once a week.
- **Dry** the skin and hair thoroughly after washing.
- Apply **deodorant** to the clean, dry skin of the armpits.
- Change and wash **clothing** frequently.

Genital hygiene

Keeping the **genitals** and surrounding area clean is particularly important as they can become infected very easily. To maintain **genital hygiene**:

- Thoroughly **wash** the genitals daily using mild soap and water, especially during **menstruation** in females.
- **Wipe** the female genitalia from front to back to prevent any faeces reaching the vaginal area.
- Change female **sanitary products** regularly.
- Pull the male **foreskin** back and clean beneath it daily or carry out **male circumcision** (removal of the foreskin).

Hand hygiene

Maintaining clean **hands** is one of the best ways to stop the spread of pathogens:

- **Wash** hands regularly using soap and water for at least 20 seconds, especially **before** preparing and eating food, and **after** using the toilet, coughing, sneezing, blowing one's nose, touching dirty objects or handling pets.
- Keep fingernails **short** and **clean**.

Oral hygiene

Guidelines for the care of **teeth** and **gums** to prevent **tooth decay** and **gum disease** are given on page 32.

Controlling the growth of microorganisms

Controlling the growth of microorganisms is essential to reduce the risk of **infection** and to help stop the spread of **disease**. Two techniques that can be used are **sterilisation** and **disinfection**.

Sterilisation

Sterilisation is the complete destruction of all microorganisms, including their spores, which are present in a specified region.

Sterilisation often uses **high temperatures** to **denature** the enzymes of the microorganisms, thereby killing them.

- **Autoclaving** or **steam sterilisation** is used to sterilise **liquids, equipment** and **instruments** such as hospital equipment and surgical instruments. It uses **pressurised steam** in an **autoclave**, which is similar to a pressure cooker. Inside the autoclave, the high pressure ensures that high temperatures of above **121 °C** are maintained in order to destroy all microorganisms and their spores.
- **Boiling** involves heating items to be sterilised, such as **surgical instruments**, in a water bath at **100 °C** for 15 to 20 minutes. **Drinking water** can also be purified by boiling. Boiling kills all microorganisms and some spores.
- **Ultra-high temperature treatment** or **UHT** is used to sterilise liquid **food** items such as milk, soups, sauces and baby foods. The food is heated to temperatures higher than **135 °C** for a few seconds, cooled rapidly and packaged in pre-sterilised containers. The flavour of the food can be affected, but it destroys almost all microorganisms and their spores.
- **Pasteurisation** is used to sterilise **food** or **drink** items. The items are heated to **72 °C** for 15 to 25 seconds and cooled rapidly. **Milk** is commonly treated in this way. The quality of the product is maintained, and the method destroys most of the microorganisms, but not their spores.
- **Canning** is used to sterilise a wide variety of **foods**. Containers such as metal cans and glass bottles are filled with the food, covered with lids and heated in a steam bath or boiling water bath at **100 °C**, or in a pressure canner at **121 °C**. After heating, the lids are immediately sealed onto the containers to make them airtight and prevent microorganisms from re-entering. This method destroys microorganisms and their spores.

Disinfection

*Disinfection involves using **chemicals** to reduce the numbers of microorganisms present in a specified region to a level where they cannot cause infection.*

Disinfection does not necessarily kill all microorganisms, and it does not destroy resistant spores. Disinfection can be carried out using **disinfectants** and **antiseptics**.

Disinfectants are chemicals used to destroy, or to inhibit the growth of, microorganisms in or on non-living objects.

Disinfectants can be used to destroy microorganisms in water, and on surfaces such as counter tops and floors. Examples include **pure alcohols**, **chlorine-releasing compounds**, e.g. sodium hypochlorite found in household bleaches, and **quaternary ammonium salts** found in disinfectants. Disinfectants can be harmful to living tissue.

*Antiseptics are chemicals used to destroy, or to inhibit the growth of, microorganisms on **living tissue**.*

Antiseptics can be used to destroy microorganisms in a cut or wound, on unbroken skin before an injection or surgery, in the mouth, and on hands if soap and water are not available. Examples include **hydrogen peroxide**, **rubbing alcohol** and **iodine solution**.

Antibiotics and antifungal agents

Antibiotics and **antifungal agents** are chemicals used to destroy or inhibit the growth of **specific types** of microorganisms living within or on the body.

*Antibiotics are chemical substances that are used to destroy, or to inhibit the growth of, **bacteria** within or on the body.*

Antibiotics are only used to treat infections caused by **bacteria**. They are not effective against viruses, and their overuse is leading to **antibiotic resistance** (see page 126). Some are **highly specialised** and are only effective against certain specific bacteria. Others attack a wide range of bacteria, including ones that are beneficial to the body.

*Antifungal agents or **fungicides** are chemicals that are used to destroy, or to inhibit the growth of, **fungi** within or on the body.*

Antifungal agents are used to treat infections caused by **fungi**, e.g. athlete's foot, thrush and ringworm.

The body's defences against pathogenic diseases

The **immune system** protects the body against infections in different ways. White blood cells known as **phagocytes** are able to engulf and digest pathogens by **phagocytosis**, outlined in Figure 5.2 on page 53. Other white blood cells known as **lymphocytes** produce **antibodies** against the specific **antigens** of the pathogens to destroy the pathogens or neutralise their toxins.

*An **antigen** is a substance that is recognised as being foreign to the body and it stimulates the lymphocytes to produce antibodies.*

*An **antibody** is a specific protein that is produced by lymphocytes in response to the presence of a specific antigen.*

*An **antitoxin** is an antibody that is produced in response to a specific toxin, and it is able to neutralise this toxin.*

Antigens are usually **proteins** on the surface of **bacteria**, **viruses** and **fungi**, or **toxins** produced by these cells. When **antigens** are detected in the body, **lymphocytes** produce specific **antibodies**, including **antitoxins**, against them. The **antibodies** bind to the **antigens** and cause the pathogens to clump together so that the phagocytes can engulf them, or they cause the pathogens to disintegrate. The **antitoxins** neutralise any toxins produced. Antibody production is an essential part of the body's **immune response**.

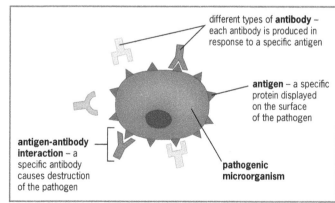

Figure 13.1 *The antigen-antibody interaction*

Immunity

Immunity is the body's temporary or permanent resistance to a disease.

Immunity can be **innate** or **acquired**.

- **Innate immunity** refers to the inborn ability of the body to resist disease. It is provided by physical barriers such as the skin and phagocytes in the blood, and is present from **birth**.

- **Acquired immunity** or **adaptive immunity** refers to the immunity that the body gains over time. There are **four** different types and, apart from one type, they are **not** present at birth.

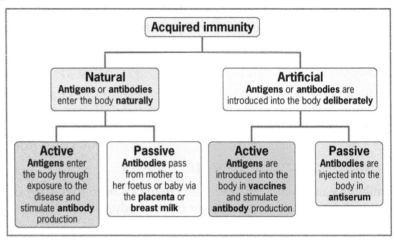

Figure 13.2 *Types of acquired immunity summarised*

Acquired immunity

Natural active immunity

Natural active immunity is acquired by a person being exposed to a pathogenic disease. When a pathogen enters the body, lymphocytes make specific antibodies in response to the specific antigens of the pathogen. These **antibodies** destroy the pathogens or neutralise their toxins. This takes time and while it is happening, the person experiences **signs** and **symptoms** of the disease. When enough antibodies have been produced to destroy the pathogens or neutralise their toxins, the person recovers. The antibodies then gradually disappear from the blood and some lymphocytes develop into **lymphocyte memory cells** which remember the specific antigens.

When the same pathogen re-enters the body, the memory lymphocytes recognise the antigens, multiply and produce **large quantities** of the specific antibodies **rapidly**. The antibodies destroy the pathogens, or neutralise their toxins, so quickly that the person does not develop signs and symptoms of the disease. The person has become **immune** to the disease.

This type of immunity is known as **active immunity** because the antibodies are produced by the body of the person exposed to the pathogen. It may provide **short-term** protection, e.g. against the common cold, or **long-term** protection, e.g. chickenpox is rarely caught twice.

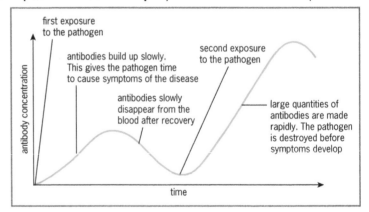

Figure 13.3 *Antibody production during the acquisition of active immunity*

Natural passive immunity

Natural passive immunity is acquired by the transfer of antibodies from a mother to her foetus or baby. The antibodies can be passed from the mother to her foetus across the **placenta** and from the mother to her baby in **breast milk**, especially in **colostrum**, the first breast milk formed after birth. This is known as **passive immunity** because the antibodies are produced by the body of another organism. The immunity provided is only **short-term** because no lymphocyte memory cells are produced in the baby's body, and the antibodies gradually disappear from the blood.

Artificial active immunity

Artificial active immunity is acquired by the deliberate introduction of the specific **antigens** into a person's body. This process is known as **vaccination** and the preparation containing the antigens is called a **vaccine**.

*A **vaccine** is a biological preparation that stimulates a person's immune system to develop immunity to a specific infectious disease.*

***Vaccination** is the administration of a vaccine which is capable of stimulating a person's immune system to develop immunity to a specific infectious disease.*

***Immunisation** is the process by which a person is made immune to an infectious disease, typically by receiving a vaccine.*

A **vaccine** may contain weakened or dead pathogens, fragments of pathogens, specific antigens from the coats of pathogens or toxins that have been made harmless. A vaccine does not cause disease, but it stimulates lymphocytes to make the specific **antibodies** or **antitoxins** needed. **Lymphocyte memory cells** also develop so that an **immune response** is set up whenever the specific pathogen enters the body. Vaccines may provide **short-term** protection, e.g. against cholera, or **long-term** protection, e.g. against tuberculosis and polio.

Artificial passive immunity

Artificial passive immunity is acquired when **antiserum** containing **specific antibodies** or **antitoxins** is injected into a person's body for **immediate relief** of symptoms of a specific disease. The antiserum is produced in the body of another organism, e.g. a horse. The immunity provided is only **short-term** because no memory cells are produced, and the antibodies will gradually disappear from the blood. For example, antiserum containing antibodies against tetanus can be given if tetanus is suspected.

Revision questions

1 Why is it important to maintain good personal hygiene?

2 Outline THREE measures used to maintain EACH of the following:

a body and hair hygiene   **b** genital hygiene   **c** hand hygiene

3 Distinguish between the following terms:

a sterilisation and disinfection

b disinfectant and antiseptic

c antibiotic and antifungal agent

4 Describe THREE methods of sterilisation

5 Define the terms 'antigen', 'antibody' and 'antitoxin'.

6 Name the cells that produce antibodies and explain how antibodies work to protect the body against pathogens.

7 Identify and explain the type of immunity that is gained in the situations described:

a Kryssie contracted chickenpox when she was a child and she does not get sick several years later when there is another outbreak of chickenpox in her community.

b Enrique was injected with antiserum after a rusty nail punctured the sole of his foot.

c Shiann was vaccinated against influenza before travelling overseas in winter.

Drug use and misuse

A **drug** is any chemical substance that alters the functioning of the body physically and/or psychologically.

Drug misuse is using a drug for purposes other than those for which it was intended or in larger quantities than prescribed.

Classification of drugs

Drugs can have **physiological effects** on the body because they affect the way organs and systems function, which affects the person's **physical health.** They can also have **psychological effects** because they affect the way a person's brain functions, which affects the person's **mental health.**

Drugs can be **classified** into **four** categories. Some can fall into more than one category.

- **Stimulants** are drugs that **speed up** the body's functions and the functioning of the central nervous system. They make a person feel more awake, alert and anxious, e.g. nicotine, caffeine, amphetamines, cocaine and ecstasy.
- **Depressants** are drugs that **slow down** the body's functions and the functioning of the central nervous system. They make a person feel calm and relaxed, e.g. alcohol, sedatives and heroin.
- **Hallucinogens** are drugs that alter a person's **perception of reality.** They can lead to irrational or bizarre behaviour, aggression and/or paranoia, e.g. ecstasy, LSD (acid) and magic mushrooms.
- **Narcotics**, also known as **opioids**, are drugs that give **relief** from moderate to severe **pain.** They can also cause impaired judgement and a feeling of euphoria, e.g. codeine, morphine and heroin.

Drug dependence

Drug dependence develops when a person takes a drug repeatedly over a period of time and needs the drug to function normally. Drug dependence can lead to **drug tolerance** and/or **drug addiction. Drug tolerance** occurs when a person needs to use increasing quantities of a drug to produce the same initial effect. **Drug addiction** occurs when a person cannot stop using a drug, despite the harmful consequences. Drug dependence can be **physical** or **psychological.**

- **Physical dependence** occurs when the body adapts to the drug and the body's cells cannot function without it. The person will experience **withdrawal symptoms** if drug use stops suddenly; these are often painful and include tremors, nausea, vomiting, diarrhoea, insomnia and body aches.
- **Psychological dependence** occurs when a person becomes emotionally and mentally attached to a drug. The drug becomes central to a person's life and the person feels that he or she cannot function without it.

Prescription drugs

A **prescription drug** is a legal drug that requires a **prescription** from a medical practitioner to be dispensed. Prescription drugs can be **misused** by taking the drugs in a manner or dose other than prescribed, taking someone else's prescription drugs or taking the drugs to feel euphoria (get a high). Misuse of prescription drugs can lead to **drug dependence.**

Table 13.1 *The use and misuse of some prescription drugs*

Prescription drug	Examples (brand name*)	Uses	Effects on the body
Prescription opioids	Codeine, methadone, morphine	Relief of moderate to severe pain.	Bind to opioid receptors of neurones in the brain and this blocks the feeling of pain. Other effects include drowsiness, confusion, nausea, slowed breathing and euphoria. **Misuse** can lead to death.
Sedatives/ tranquillisers	Lorazepam (Ativan*), diazepam (Valium*)	To treat anxiety, sleep disorders and panic disorders.	Slow down the central nervous system activity, causing a feeling of relaxation and sleepiness. Other effects include dizziness, slowed heartbeat and breathing rate, slurred speech, blurred vision, difficulty focusing and thinking, and poor muscular coordination. **Misuse** can lead to memory loss, anxiety, depression and liver failure.
Painkillers or pain relievers	Paracetamol or acetaminophen (Panadol*, Tylenol*), aspirin, ibuprofen (Advil*)	Relief of mild to moderate pain.	Work in different ways to reduce pain. **Misuse** can lead to stomach ulcers, stomach and intestinal bleeding, liver and kidney damage and cardiovascular problems.

Medical marijuana

Medical marijuana is made from the dried parts of the cannabis plant containing chemicals called **cannabinoids**. In counrties where it has been legalised, it is used to treat a variety of conditions, e.g. chronic pain, glaucoma, multiple sclerosis and Parkinson's disease. **Misuse** of medical marijuana can have similar effects to **recreational marijuana** (see page 160). However, it contains less of the psychoactive cannabinoid known as THC, and more of the non-psychoactive cannabinoid known as CBD, so the user does not experience the euphoria associated with recreational marijuana.

Antibiotics

Antibiotics are prescribed to treat infections caused by **bacteria**. **Misuse** of antibiotics can lead to the development of **antibiotic-resistant** strains of bacteria which are making infections caused by bacteria harder to treat. Some people are also **allergic** to antibiotics and in these cases, their use can be fatal.

Non-prescription drugs

Some **non-prescription drugs** are **legal** and include **over-the-counter drugs** such as cough medicines, painkillers and laxatives, **alcohol** and **tobacco**; the latter two can only be used legally by persons over a certain age which varies from country to country. Other non-prescription drugs are **illegal**, e.g. **cocaine**, **methamphetamine**, **ecstasy** and **marijuana** (in most countries). **All** non-prescription drugs can be **misused**.

Cocaine and methamphetamine

Cocaine is a white powder that is usually inhaled or 'snorted' through a tube. **Crack** is a chemically altered form of cocaine that is smoked. **Methamphetamine** is a synthetic drug, also known as 'speed', 'meth' and 'ice'. It can be used in tablet form, snorted in powdered form, injected or smoked. Both are highly addictive **stimulants** that have similar effects on the body.

Both drugs increase heart rate, breathing rate, blood pressure and body temperature, which can lead to a heart attack, stroke or respiratory failure. They cause euphoria, anxiety, paranoia, confusion, violent or erratic behaviour and hallucinations, decrease appetite and increase wakefulness which leads to insomnia. **Cocaine** can also give feelings of well-being, increased energy, alertness and power, and lead to damage to the nasal passages, weight loss, seizures, schizophrenia and other mental disorders. **Methamphetamine** can increase physical activity, and cause convulsions and extreme weight loss.

Figure 13.4 *Cocaine powder on dried coca leaves*

Ecstasy

Ecstasy, also known as MDMA or 'Molly', is a synthetic **hallucinogen** and **stimulant** that is taken in tablet form. It increases heart rate and blood pressure, and can cause a sharp rise in body temperature and dehydration that can result in heat stroke, kidney damage and even death. It causes hallucinations, lowers the user's inhibitions, enhances sensory perception, increases anxiety and leads to psychosis, confusion, depression, and problems with attention, memory and sleep.

Heroin

Heroin is an **opioid** drug. It is a highly addictive **narcotic** and **depressant** obtained from the seed pod of the opium poppy plant. It can be injected, sniffed, snorted or smoked, and it produces an immediate 'rush' of euphoria and the user feels extremely relaxed. It slows heart rate and breathing rate and can stop a person from breathing. It dulls pain and reduces coordination, stress and anxiety, and can lead to destructive health issues, e.g. mental health problems and depression. **Dependence** is established very quickly and **withdrawal symptoms** are severe.

Marijuana (cannabis)

Marijuana, also known as cannabis, 'ganja', 'herb', 'weed' or 'pot', is usually smoked. It can be classified as a **stimulant**, **depressant** or **hallucinogen**. It initially produces a feeling of well-being, enhanced sensory perception and euphoria known as a 'high'. It can then leave the user anxious, afraid or paranoid, and its use can also cause sleepiness, bloodshot eyes, increased heart rate, poor judgement and coordination, problems with concentration, learning and memory, and hallucinations. Heavy use can lead to respiratory system damage, reduced fertility and mental health problems.

Figure 13.5 *Marijuana flowers are dried, rolled into joints and smoked*

Alcohol

Alcohol is a **depressant** and persons who are dependent on alcohol are called **alcoholics. Alcoholism** is classed as a **disease** and severe alcoholism can lead to death. Babies born to mothers who consume large quantities of alcohol during pregnancy may develop **foetal alcohol syndrome** or **FAS**, which is characterised by **mental impairment.**

Short-term effects of alcohol use include impaired muscular skills, reduced muscular coordination, slowed reflexes, impaired mental functioning, concentration and judgement, blurred vision and slurred speech, memory lapses, drowsiness, increased urine production leading to dehydration, and loss of consciousness.

Long-term effects of alcohol use include fatty liver disease, alcoholic hepatitis and cirrhosis (scarring) of the liver, increased blood pressure causing heart disease, heart attack and stroke, stomach ulcers and other intestinal disorders, cancer of the mouth, throat and oesophagus, malnutrition, nervous system disorders, brain damage, long-term memory loss and delirium tremens (DTs).

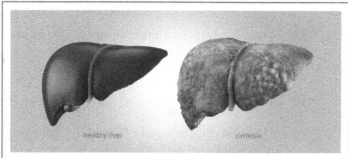

Figure 13.6 *A healthy liver on the left and a liver with cirrhosis on the right*

Social and economic effects of drug misuse

Drug misuse can have a devastating impact on **individuals**, **families** and **communities**. It harms the **user** physically and psychologically, and can lead to loss of self-worth and emotional stability, personal neglect, health issues, loss of earnings or job loss, and financial problems. Financial problems can cause the user to turn to crime or prostitution. Crime can lead to arrest and imprisonment, and prostitution exposes the user to STIs. Use of intravenous drugs exposes the user to HIV/AIDS and hepatitis C, and babies born to addicts may have developmental problems or be addicts themselves. Higher suicide rates and anti-social behaviour are also associated with drug use.

Drug misuse upsets relationships with **family** and **friends**, and can lead to neglect or abuse of family members, especially children and the elderly, resulting in unstable and disturbing family environments. It may also cause children to lose one or both parents, and ultimately leads to dysfunctional families.

The cost to **society** of drug misuse is high. It can lead to reduced productivity and weakened economies. Automobile accidents resulting from drug use can cause serious injury and loss of life, and violent crimes associated with drug use cause injury, loss of life and communities to live in fear. More and more resources have to be used to treat and rehabilitate drug users and addicts, to fight drug-related crimes, and to apprehend, convict and imprison traffickers and pushers of illegal drugs. Ultimately, economies suffer, standards of living are reduced and human resources are lost by drug misuse.

Revision questions

8 What is a drug?

9 Construct a table that classifies drugs into FOUR categories, outlines the effects that drugs in EACH category have on the body and gives ONE example of an illegal drug belonging to EACH category.

10 Provide a suitable definition for 'drug dependence' and distinguish between physical dependence and psychological dependence.

11 Explain how prescription drugs can be misused and state the function of EACH of the following prescription drugs:

   a antibiotics   **b** sedatives   **c** opioids

12 What is medical marijuana and how does it differ from recreational marijuana?

13 Describe the effects of EACH of the following on the human body:

   a cocaine   **b** heroin

14 Why is alcohol considered a drug?

15 List FIVE short-term effects and FIVE long-term effects of alcohol misuse.

16 Describe the effects of drug misuse on:

   a the user   **b** society as a whole

Exam-style questions – Chapters 12 to 13

Structured questions

1 **a)** **i)** Define the term 'non-communicable disease'. **(1 mark)**

   ii) Name TWO non-communicable lifestyle-related diseases that are prevalent in the Caribbean. **(2 marks)**

   iii) Explain why diet and exercise are important measures in the prevention and treatment of the diseases named in **a) ii)** above. **(3 marks)**

b) Dengue fever is a vector-borne disease that has affected many countries in the Caribbean.

   i) Name the vector that is responsible for the spread of dengue fever. **(1 mark)**

   ii) State TWO signs/symptoms of dengue fever, other than fever. **(2 marks)**

   iii) Describe THREE measures that can be taken by community members to control the spread of dengue fever. **(3 marks)**

c) Scientists recently announced the development of a dengue vaccine. Explain how this vaccine will work to provide immunity to dengue fever. **(3 marks)**

Total 15 marks

2 **a)** **i)** What is meant by the term 'drug misuse'? **(1 mark)**

   ii) Name TWO drugs, other than heroin, which are commonly misused in the Caribbean. **(2 marks)**

b) A study was carried out in a particular country to assess heroin use within various age groups. Table 1 below shows the results of the study.

Table 1 *Heroin addicts in various age groups*

Age group	Number of addicts
15–24	475
25–34	1035
35–44	354
45–54	198
55 or older	81

   i) Construct a bar graph using the data in Table 1. **(3 marks)**

   ii) Discuss the trends shown by the number of heroin addicts in the various age groups. **(3 marks)**

   iii) Explain THREE socio-economic implications of the findings of the study for the country. **(3 marks)**

c) Some medical practitioners have been known to regularly prescribe antibiotics to treat influenza. Explain the dangers associated with this practice. **(3 marks)**

Total 15 marks

Structured essay questions

3   **a)**   Sterilisation and disinfection are both methods that are used to prevent harmful microorganisms from affecting us.

       i)   Describe TWO differences between sterilisation and disinfection.   **(4 marks)**

       ii)   Suggest how sterilisation and disinfection could be used when caring for a patient in a hospital. Provide ONE situation for EACH method.   **(2 marks)**

       iii)   Your classmate, Jordan, suggests that antiseptics are the same as disinfectants. Explain to Jordan that they are different, stating ONE difference between them.   **(2 marks)**

   b)   Your new friend, Jess, has poor hygiene and it is affecting her self-esteem. Advise Jess on measures she should take to maintain good personal hygiene. Include in your answer:

     •   THREE reasons for maintaining good personal hygiene

     •   TWO methods of maintaining good skin hygiene

     •   TWO methods of maintaining good genital hygiene   **(7 marks)**

                                                          Total 15 marks

4   **a)**   Lisa suddenly suspects that her friend, Asher, is having an asthma attack. Suggest TWO reasons for Lisa's suspicions, identify TWO factors that might have triggered Asher's attack and explain what is happening in his respiratory system during the attack.   **(6 marks)**

   b)   **i)**   HIV/AIDS and syphilis are both sexually transmitted infections (STIs); however, it is much harder to control the spread of HIV/AIDS than the spread of syphilis. Identify THREE factors that make the spread of HIV/AIDS difficult to control and explain how HIV affects the body.   **(6 marks)**

       ii)   Cervical cancer is believed to be caused by another STI. Identify this infection and explain TWO measures that Zwena can take to protect herself from cervical cancer.   **(3 marks)**

                                                           Total 15 marks

Section E – The impact of health practices on the environment

14 Pollution, water and water treatment

Humans are constantly harming their environment by releasing unpleasant or harmful substances, or forms of energy, known as **pollutants**, into the natural environment. These pollutants contaminate land, air and water. All living organisms need **water** to survive, and pollution of water resources makes them unsafe for human use. As a consequence, various forms of **treatment** are required to ensure water is safe for use in agriculture, industry and people's homes.

Pollution and its effects

Pollution is the contamination of the natural environment by the release of unpleasant or harmful substances, or forms of energy, into the environment.

A pollutant is any unpleasant or harmful substance, or form of energy, that causes contamination of the natural environment when released.

Based on their **origin**, most pollutants can be classified as **domestic, industrial** or **agricultural pollutants**.

- **Domestic pollutants** are released from **homes.** They include sewage from the bathroom and kitchen, detergents from the bathroom, kitchen and laundry room, pesticides and food waste, including cooking oils.
- **Industrial pollutants** are released from **industries**. They include carbon monoxide, carbon dioxide, sulfur dioxide, oxides of nitrogen, smoke, dust and other particulate matter, heavy metals, oils, hot water and noise.
- **Agricultural pollutants** are associated with **agricultural practices**. They include fertilisers, pesticides such as herbicides, insecticides and fungicides, manure and methane.

Air pollution

Air pollution is caused by the release of pollutants into the **atmosphere**. Most air pollution in urban areas is associated with **industrial activities**, particularly the **combustion** or **burning** of fossil fuels, whereas much of the air pollution in rural areas is associated with **agricultural practices**.

Table 14.1 *Examples of air pollutants and their effects*

Pollutant	Origin	Harmful effects
Carbon dioxide **(CO$_2$)**	• Combustion of fossil fuels in industry, motor vehicles, power plants and aeroplanes.	• Builds up in the upper atmosphere where it is enhancing the **greenhouse effect**, which is contributing to **global warming** (see page 14). • Some is absorbed by oceans, causing **ocean acidification.** This is a lowering of the pH of ocean water, which harms aquatic organisms, particularly corals and shellfish.

Pollutant	Origin	Harmful effects
Carbon monoxide (CO)	• Combustion of fossil fuels in industry and motor vehicles. • Bush fires and cigarette smoke.	• Combines with haemoglobin in the blood more readily than oxygen. This reduces the amount of **oxygen** being carried to body cells and causes dizziness, headaches and visual impairment, and can lead to unconsciousness and death.
Sulfur dioxide (SO$_2$)	• Combustion of fossil fuels in industry and power plants. *Pollution from industry*	• Causes **respiratory disorders**, e.g. bronchitis and asthma, increases the risk of **cardiovascular disease**, reduces the growth of plants and corrodes buildings. • Combines with water vapour, smoke and other air pollutants forming **smog**, which causes respiratory disorders and irritates the skin and eyes. • Dissolves in rainwater turning it acidic, i.e. it forms **acid rain**. Acid rain lowers the pH of the soil, damages plants, harms animals, corrodes buildings and causes bodies of water such as lakes, streams and rivers to become acidic, which harms aquatic organisms.
Oxides of nitrogen (NO and NO$_2$)	• Combustion at high temperatures in industry, motor vehicles and power plants.	• Contribute to the formation of **smog** (see above). • Cause **lung damage** and even low concentrations irritate the skin, eyes and respiratory system. • Reduce the growth of plants, cause leaves to die and dissolve in rainwater forming **acid rain** (see above).
Methane (CH$_4$)	• Extraction, processing and transportation of fossil fuels. • Livestock farming, rice agriculture and landfills.	• Builds up in the upper atmosphere, enhancing the **greenhouse effect** and **global warming**.
Carbon particles in smoke, and other particulate matter	• Combustion of fossil fuels in industry. • Wild fires and cigarette smoke. • Mining and quarrying.	• Cause **respiratory disorders**, including bronchitis, asthma, lung disease, emphysema and lung cancer, and increase the risk of **cardiovascular disease**. • Contribute to the formation of **smog**. • Coat leaves, reducing photosynthesis, and blacken buildings.
Noise	• Traffic, aircraft, industry, construction and social events.	• Impairs hearing and leads to poor concentration, low productivity, sleep disturbances, stress and hypertension.

Water pollution

Water pollution can be caused by pollutants being **released directly** into **bodies of water**, e.g. lakes, streams, rivers, estuaries and oceans, from industrial, agricultural and domestic sources, or by being **washed off** the land into the water. Discharge of **improperly treated sewage** is one of the **main** causes of water pollution.

Table 14.2 *Examples of water pollutants and their effects*

Pollutant	Origin	Harmful effects
Suspended solid particles	• Soil erosion, which leads to silt and soil being washed into bodies of water. • Improperly treated sewage and industrial waste.	• Reduce **light penetration**, which reduces photosynthesis in aquatic plants. • **Clog** fish gills and **smother** bottom-dwelling organisms. • Sediment build-up **blocks** waterways.
Organic matter	• Improperly treated sewage and industrial waste. • Manure and other farmyard waste.	• Aerobic bacteria decompose the organic matter, which reduces the amount of **dissolved oxygen** in the water and leads to the death of fish and other aquatic organisms.
Pathogens	• Improperly treated sewage and animal manure.	• Can cause a variety of **infectious diseases**, e.g. typhoid, cholera, gastroenteritis and dysentery.
Pesticides, including herbicides	• Used mainly in agriculture to control pests, pathogens and weeds.	• Become **higher in concentration** up food chains and can harm top consumers, e.g. large fish and fish-eating birds.
Plant nutrients, e.g. nitrates and phosphates	• Chemical and organic fertilisers used in agriculture. • Improperly treated sewage and synthetic detergents.	• Cause **eutrophication** (see page 168). • High levels of nitrates in drinking water can harm human health (see page 172).
Heavy metal ions, e.g. mercury and lead	• Industrial waste.	• May be directly **toxic** to aquatic organisms, or become **higher in concentration** up food chains, harming the top consumers. • Harmful to human health (see page 173).
Oil	• Industrial waste. • Runoff from roads and car parks. • Oil tankers and offshore oil rigs.	• Chemical constituents can be **toxic** to aquatic organisms. • Forms slicks on the surface of water which prevent **oxygen** from dissolving and block out light for photosynthesis. • **Coats** sea birds and mammals causing birds to be unable to fly and both to be unable to keep warm. • **Smothers** and **kills** plants and animals living on the shore.
Hot water (thermal pollution)	• Water used in power plants and industry to cool equipment.	• May **kill** aquatic organisms directly or lower their resistance to **pathogens** by causing sudden changes to water temperature. • Reduces the amount of **oxygen** dissolved in the water, leading to the death of aquatic organisms.

Eutrophication is the nutrient enrichment of the aquatic environment, mainly by nitrates and phosphates. This causes the rapid growth of green plants and algae which turn the water in lakes, ponds and rivers green. When the plants and algae die, they are decomposed by **aerobic bacteria** which multiply and use up the **dissolved oxygen** in the water. This then causes other aquatic organisms, e.g. fish, to die.

Figure 14.1 *Eutrophication*

Plastics

Plastics enter bodies of water mainly as a result of improper garbage and sewage disposal. Most plastics are **non-biodegradable** (see page 176) so they will remain and accumulate for hundreds of years. Plastics are **directly harmful** to aquatic organisms, e.g. turtles, whales, fish and aquatic birds, due to entanglement, suffocation and ingestion. In addition, many plastics gradually break down into **microplastic** particles and the tiniest of these can enter the bodies of aquatic organisms where they can be harmful to tissues and organs. Organisms that ingest pieces of plastic often die of starvation because their stomachs become filled with the pieces and they stop eating.

Social and economic effects of pollution

Pollution, especially **air pollution**, is a leading cause of **disease** globally and this places huge socio-economic burdens on societies (see page 146). Additionally, pollution has a negative impact on **tourism**, which can weaken tourism-based economies. **Water pollution** can harm any sector of the economy that relies on clean water, including tourism, commercial fishing and recreational businesses. It also increases the costs associated with water treatment, and can cause disease. **Air pollutants** reduce the growth of plants, which reduces crop yields and can lead to food shortages. Large sums of **money** have to be spent to **clean up** pollution, which further damages economies and hampers economic growth.

Methods of controlling pollution

A variety of measures can be put in place to **control pollution** of air, water and land.

- Use **renewable energy** sources, e.g. solar and wind, which do not cause pollution, instead of burning fossil fuels.
- Clean gaseous emissions from factories before releasing them into the environment.

- Install pollution control devices in the exhausts of motor vehicles and make vehicles more energy efficient, or switch to using ones that do not use fossil fuels, e.g. electric vehicles.
- Purify all effluent from factories.
- Treat all sewage in sewage treatment plants, and use the sludge as fertiliser and the water to irrigate crops after treatment is complete.
- Collect and recycle or reuse all recyclable waste such as glass, plastic, metals and paper.
- Compost all waste of plant origin, e.g. vegetable peelings and crop residues.
- Use farmyard waste and waste from food industries to produce biogas, a renewable energy source.
- Use natural, biodegradable pesticides or biological control instead of synthetic pesticides.
- Use organic fertilisers, which cause less pollution, instead of inorganic chemical fertilisers.
- Develop public education programmes for people of all ages about the consequences of pollution and ways to reduce it.
- Pass and enforce legislation, with strict penalties, that limits the release of air, water and land pollutants by industry.
- Set national noise standards, and implement and enforce legislation, to control noise pollution at all levels within communities to meet these standards.
- Sign international agreements with fixed goals aimed at controlling pollution.

Revision questions

1 Define the following terms:

   a pollution   **b** pollutant

2 Construct a table that identifies the THREE groups of pollutants based on their origin and names THREE pollutants in EACH group.

3 Identify the main sources and outline the harmful effects of the following air pollutants:

   a carbon dioxide   **b** noise   **c** carbon monoxide

4 Distinguish between acid rain and smog in terms of:

   a how they are formed   **b** their harmful effects

5 Dawn wants to know why her teacher said that agriculture contributes to water pollution. Explain to her how the overuse of chemical fertilisers and the overuse of pesticides can EACH affect aquatic environments.

6 For EACH of the following water pollutants, identify the major source(s) and outline the harmful effects of the pollutants:

   a suspended solids   **b** organic matter   **c** oil

7 Discuss the socio-economic effects of pollution.

8 Identify FOUR methods of controlling air pollution and FOUR methods of controlling water pollution.

The cycling and treatment of water

The water cycle

The cycling of water in nature is known as the **water cycle** or **hydrological cycle** and it is important because it ensures that all living organisms have a continuous supply of water to keep their cells **hydrated** and to act as a **solvent** for chemical reactions. It also ensures that plants have a steady supply of water for **photosynthesis** and aquatic organisms have a **constant environment** in which to live.

The **water cycle** involves the following **processes**.

- **Evaporation** – Water **evaporates** from bodies of water, e.g. streams, rivers, ponds, lakes, seas and oceans, and also from the soil, and it forms water vapour which enters the atmosphere.

- **Transpiration** and **exhalation** – Plants lose water vapour to the atmosphere from their leaves when they **transpire**, and animals lose water vapour when they **exhale**.

- **Condensation** – Water vapour in the atmosphere cools and **condenses** to become water droplets that form **clouds**.

- **Precipitation** – Water from clouds **falls back** into bodies of water or onto land as rain, hail, sleet and snow.

- **Surface runoff** – Some water falling onto land **runs off** the surface of the land into bodies of water.

- **Infiltration** – Some water falling onto land moves **downwards** through the soil.

- **Percolation** – The water then moves through cracks and pores in rocks such as limestone, and into groundwater, and it may eventually return to bodies of water.

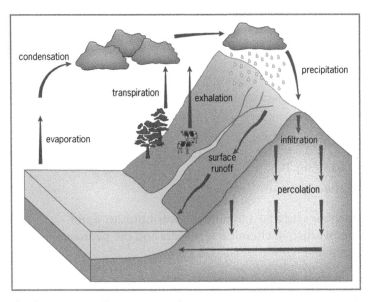

★ **Figure 14.2** *The water cycle*

Water purification

Water piped to homes usually comes from surface water sources, e.g. **rivers**, **lakes** and **reservoirs**, or from groundwater sources, e.g. **aquifers**. To make the water **potable**, i.e. safe to drink and use in food preparation, it must be **treated** to remove harmful contaminants, including bacteria, viruses, dissolved chemicals and suspended solid particles. As well as being **safe** for human consumption after treatment, the water should also be **clear** and not discoloured, and it should have an **acceptable taste** and **odour**.

Large-scale purification of water

Large-scale treatment provides potable water for use in towns and cities. This involves **four** steps.

- **Screening** – Water from water sources passes through grid screens which remove floating and suspended materials.
- **Flocculation** and **sedimentation** – Certain chemicals, e.g. **alum**, are mixed with the water to cause fine suspended solid particles to clump together into larger particles called **floc**. The water is then pumped into a settlement tank where the floc is allowed to settle.
- **Filtration** – The clear water above the floc is passed through **filter beds**, usually composed of sand, gravel and charcoal. This removes any remaining particles and some microorganisms. Harmless microorganisms in the filter beds also remove any organic matter by feeding on it.
- **Chlorination** – **Chlorine gas** or **monochloroamine** is added to the filtered water to kill any remaining microorganisms. **Fluoride** is sometimes added to help reduce tooth decay. The water is then pumped to storage tanks for distribution to consumers.

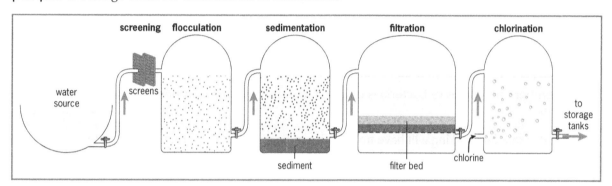

★ **Figure 14.3** *Large-scale water purification*

Small-scale water purification in the home

Several methods can be used to treat water in the **home**, especially if clean water is not available.

Boiling

Bringing water to a **rolling boil** for at least 1 to 3 minutes kills harmful microorganisms, including bacteria, viruses and parasitic protozoans. After boiling, the water should be covered and allowed to cool.

Water purification tablets

Water purification tablets contain chemicals that release **chlorine**, **chlorine dioxide** or **iodine** when dissolved, and are effective in killing bacteria, viruses and protozoans. They are useful following a natural disaster, e.g. a hurricane, or in remote areas where safe drinking water is not available.

Chlorine bleach

If water purification tablets are not available, **chlorine bleach** can be used to kill microorganisms. It is recommended that two drops of bleach are added to each litre of water.

Filtration

Filtration involves passing water through a **filter** to remove unwanted particles. **Domestic filters** usually contain a **filter cartridge** of variable pore size, the smallest being capable of filtering out bacteria and protozoans. Others contain **activated charcoal** which can absorb certain chemical contaminants, dissolved organic compounds, odours and unpleasant tastes.

Testing water for bacteria

Coliform bacteria are commonly found in human and animal intestines. Their presence in water may suggest **faecal contamination**, which could then indicate the presence of disease-causing pathogens, e.g. bacteria, viruses and parasites. To detect the presence of coliform bacteria, an **agar plate** can be used. Hot agar containing nutrients is poured into a sterile Petri dish and allowed to cool, forming a gel. If a sample of water is poured into the plate, the nutrients will allow any bacteria present to grow and each **one** will form a **colony** on the plate.

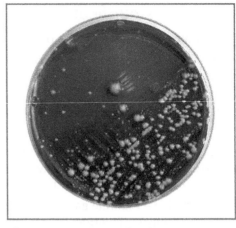

Figure 14.4 *Bacterial colonies on an agar plate*

The following **steps** are used to test a sample of water for coliform bacteria.

- A sample of water to be tested is collected in a sterile container.
- A small, measured quantity of the water, usually 1 cm³, is poured onto a sterile agar plate. The plate is covered with a lid and the lid is sealed in place with tape.
- The plate is then incubated at 35 °C for 24 hours.
- The number of colonies of bacteria is counted to determine the number of bacteria per cm³ of water.

Water that is **safe for drinking** will have **no colonies** of bacteria growing on the agar plate.

The impact of human activities on water supplies

Water supplies worldwide face a host of serious **threats** caused primarily by **human activity**.

- Humans remove **excessive quantities** of water from water supplies for agricultural, industrial and domestic use, a lot of which is wasted.
- Human activities release **waste** and **harmful substances** into water supplies, which make the water unsuitable for use without treatment.
- **Deforestation** carried out by humans reduces transpiration and precipitation, which are needed to replenish water supplies.
- **Deforestation**, **agriculture** and **mining** lead to an increase in soil erosion, which increases the amount of particulate matter entering water sources.
- **Climate change**, brought about by a variety of human activities, is increasing water scarcity in many countries.
- Building of **dams** and **reservoirs** greatly reduces water availability for populations living in river basins downstream from the dam or reservoir.

These activities **reduce** the **quantities** of water available for consumption and for agricultural, industrial and domestic use, and **increase** the **costs** associated with the treatment of contaminated water.

Harmful effects of contaminated water on human health

Consuming **contaminated water** is detrimental to humans because one or more contaminants it contains can be harmful to **human health**.

- **Pathogens** cause infectious diseases, e.g. typhoid, cholera, gastroenteritis and dysentery.
- **Pesticides** can cause cancer, and can harm the nervous and endocrine systems.
- High levels of **nitrates** reduce the amount of oxygen carried by red blood cells. This is particularly harmful to bottle-fed babies because it can lead to **blue baby syndrome**, which can be fatal.

- **Heavy metals ions**, e.g. mercury, lead, arsenic and cadmium ions, damage many body tissues and organs, especially those of the nervous system, resulting in mental illness and brain damage.
- **Radioactive waste** from nuclear power plants, hospitals and laboratories can damage DNA, causing mutations which can lead to cancer, birth defects and even death.

Revision questions

9   Explain how EACH of the following processes is involved in the cycling of water: evaporation, transpiration, condensation, precipitation and infiltration.

10   **a** What is meant by the term 'potable'?

    b Outline the processes involved in large-scale water purification.

11   Describe TWO ways of purifying water in the home.

12   Your teacher asks you to outline the steps used to test water for the presence of bacteria. List the steps you would include in your answer.

13   Discuss THREE impacts of human activities on water supplies.

14   Explain, giving THREE reasons, why contaminated water is detrimental to humans.

15 Treatment and disposal of human waste

Human activities produce waste and harmful materials which must be properly treated and disposed of in order to keep the environment clean and healthy, and to reduce the spread of disease. Some of this waste is in liquid form with suspended solids in it and is known as **sewage**. Some is in solid form and is known as **solid waste.**

Sewage and sewage treatment

Sewage disposal practices

Sewage is **wastewater** from homes, schools, hospitals, businesses and industry, and rainwater that runs into drains from the streets. It is usually heavily contaminated with **microorganisms**, including pathogens, dissolved and suspended **organic matter** and suspended, **solid particulate matter.**

Sewage must be **properly disposed of** to prevent contamination of the environment and health issues that arise from its **improper disposal.**

Proper sewage disposal practices

Proper sewage disposal involves disposing of sewage in a way that humans and animals, especially vectors of disease, cannot come into contact with it, and in a way that it does not contaminate water supplies and the environment. It can be disposed of either in an **on-site sewage system**, e.g. a **septic tank** or **suckwell**, or in a **sewage disposal system** which consists of a network of underground pipes, known as **sewers**, that transport the sewage to a **sewage treatment plant** (see page 175).

Improper sewage disposal practices

Improper sewage disposal involves disposing of **partially treated sewage** or **untreated sewage**, also known as **raw sewage**, directly into the environment. It can be deliberately released, usually into bodies of water, or it can enter from poorly maintained sewage and drainage systems, e.g. sewers that are cracked and leaking, or drains that are blocked.

The impact of improper sewage disposal practices

Improper disposal of sewage has a **negative effect** on human health and the environment.

- Untreated sewage released into bodies of **water** has a variety of effects.
  - **Pathogens** can cause **disease**, e.g. cholera, typhoid, gastroenteritis and dysentery.
  - The breakdown of **organic matter** reduces the amount of **dissolved oxygen** in the water, which can lead to the death of aquatic organisms.
  - **Particulate matter** can reduce light penetration and photosynthesis in plants, which affects aquatic **food chains.** It also clogs the gills of fish and smothers bottom-dwelling organisms.
  - **Plant nutrients**, especially nitrates and phosphates, contribute to **eutrophication** (see page 168).
  - **Toxic chemicals** can be directly **harmful** to aquatic organisms.
- Untreated sewage released onto **land** promotes the breeding of **vectors**, e.g. flies and rats, which transmit **diseases** (see page 147).
- Untreated sewage gives off a foul **odour**, which contaminates the environment.

Sewage treatment

Sewage treatment is the process that removes contaminants from sewage to produce **effluent** (treated wastewater) and semi-solid **sludge**. The process involves several steps.

Pre-treatment

The sewage is passed through **screens** to remove large objects, e.g. plastic bottles, cans, rags, paper and twigs, a process known as **screening**. The sewage then passes slowly through a **grit chamber** or **grit pit** where smaller solid materials, e.g. grit and sand, settle out. These processes are **important** so that the solid objects do not damage or clog the pumps and sewage lines of the treatment plant.

Primary treatment

The sewage water flows into **sedimentation tanks** where any remaining solid particles settle and form **sludge**. The sludge is removed, treated and used to make **fertiliser** or to make **methane** in a sludge digester. It can also be disposed of in a landfill or incinerated.

Secondary treatment

The sewage water from the sedimentation tank, known as **effluent**, still contains suspended and dissolved **organic matter** which is removed by harmless **microorganisms** in one of two ways.

- The **biological filter method** involves passing the effluent through a bed of stones in a **trickling filter**. The stones are covered with a film of **aerobic bacteria** and **protozoans**.
- The **activated sludge method** involves passing the effluent into an **aeration tank** where it is mixed with **activated sludge** consisting of large numbers of **aerobic bacteria** and **protozoans**. **Compressed air** is bubbled through the mixture and paddles help the mixing process.

In both methods, the **microorganisms** break down the organic matter into harmless substances. When breakdown is complete, the effluent passes into a final **settlement tank** where any remaining solids and microorganisms settle, forming **sludge**. The effluent is now safe to release into bodies of water, or it can be further treated.

Tertiary treatment

The **quality** of the effluent from the secondary treatment can be **raised** for domestic, agricultural or industrial use, or safe discharge into fragile environments. It can be **filtered** to remove any remaining particulate matter or toxins, **harmless bacteria** can be added to remove nitrates and phosphates, and it can be **disinfected** to remove any remaining pathogens.

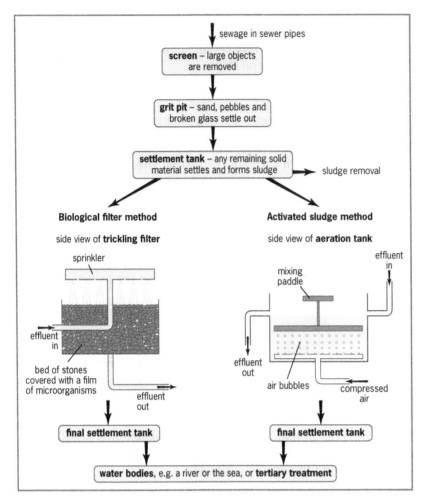

Figure 15.1 *Sewage treatment process*

Solid waste and its disposal

Biodegradable and non-biodegradable solid waste

Solid waste is discarded **solid material**. It can come from domestic, commercial, institutional and industrial sources and can be divided into **biodegradable waste** and **non-biodegradable waste.**

- **Biodegradable waste** can be broken down by living organisms, mainly bacteria and fungi, into harmless materials that can be recycled into the environment. It includes food waste, most paper, garden and farmyard waste, and some plastics.

- **Non-biodegradable waste** cannot be broken down by living organisms. It remains in the environment and acts as a source of pollution. It includes metal, glass, rubber, construction materials and most plastics.

Disposal of domestic refuse

Domestic refuse is **solid waste** originating from households, including paper and packaging, cans, glass and plastic items, textiles, food waste and garden waste. It must be **disposed of** properly. **Landfills** usually provide the most economical option for disposal; however, other methods can be used, including **incineration**, **composting** and **recycling**. Some communities also dump their refuse in **open dumps**.

Collection of refuse

Before collection, households should **store** their refuse in durable **bins** with **tight-fitting lids**, and it should be **collected** at least once per week. Refuse not stored correctly and not collected on a regular basis attracts vectors, e.g. rodents, flies and mosquitoes, which can breed and spread disease. It also creates an **eyesore**, gives off unpleasant **odours** and can **pollute** water running through it during rain.

Separation of refuse

Refuse should be **separated** into different types either before collection or before disposal. **Organic waste**, e.g. food and garden waste, should be separated and **composted**, and **recyclable materials**, e.g. paper, glass, metal and plastic, should be separated and **recycled**. This **reduces** the **volume** of solid waste entering landfills and has many other **advantages** (see page 181).

Figure 15.2 *Incorrectly stored and uncollected refuse endangers human health and the environment*

Figure 15.3 *Colour-coded bins for separating recyclable waste*

Incineration, composting and landfills

Table 15.1 evaluates the use of **incineration**, **composting** and a **landfill** as methods that can be used to dispose of domestic refuse.

Table 15.1 *Evaluation of some methods of domestic refuse disposal*

Method	Outline of method	Advantages	Disadvantages
Incineration	Solid **combustible waste** is burned in **incinerators** at very high temperatures, leaving an inert residue which is disposed of in a landfill.	• Can reduce the volume of uncompacted waste entering landfills by more than 90%. • High temperatures kill harmful pathogens in the waste. • Heat produced can be used to generate electricity or to heat water. • Incinerators occupy relatively small areas of land.	• Incinerators are relatively expensive to build and operate. • Energy requirements to operate incinerators are high. • Waste gases are produced which can contribute to air pollution and cause respiratory problems.

Method	Outline of method	Advantages	Disadvantages
Composting	**Biodegradable waste** is broken down by **aerobic bacteria** in compost heaps or composters at home, or in a commercial composting facility.	• Produces organic fertiliser which is rich in minerals that can be used as a soil conditioner or mulch. • Reduces the need for synthetic chemical fertilisers that can be harmful to the soil and pollute water. • Reduces the volume of waste entering landfills.	• Can be time-consuming as the compost needs 'turning' daily. • Compost heaps can give off unpleasant odours and attract pests and vectors of disease. • Composting requires relatively large areas of land.
Landfill	See below.	• Once constructed, it is relatively economical and easy to use to dispose of refuse. • Many different types of waste can be disposed of. • Produces methane that can be used as a fuel. • The site can be re-landscaped and put to good use once the landfill is full.	• The initial costs of construction are high. • Requires continuous maintenance to prevent leachate and toxic gases entering the environment. • If allowed to escape, waste gases can produce unpleasant odours and contribute to air pollution, and leachate can contaminate soil and water sources. • Uses up valuable land and is unsightly when in operation.

The difference between a landfill and an open dump

A **landfill** is a carefully maintained structure where waste is disposed of in a controlled and regulated way. The landfill is constantly monitored and is separated from the surrounding environment.

An **open dump** is a place where refuse is simply dumped and left to break down. It is not controlled, monitored or regulated, and is not separated from the surrounding environment.

Open dumps are **illegal** in most developed countries. They attract vectors of disease, give off unpleasant odours and toxic gases which contribute to air pollution, contaminate water supplies, are unsightly and contribute to land pollution, and they pose fire hazards. However, they provide a source of **income** in some countries for those who pick through the waste for items they can use or sell.

Operations at a landfill

Landfills consist of large, deep pits in which compacted solid waste is buried in layers. The pit is lined with impermeable material which forms the **bottom liner** to prevent liquids, known as **leachate**, seeping into the ground and contaminating soil and water sources. Two sets of **pipes** are installed, one to drain off the **leachate** and carry it to a treatment plant, and the other to remove **waste gases**, e.g. methane.

On arrival at the landfill, the refuse is **sorted** to remove materials that can be **recycled**. The remaining refuse is placed in a **refuse cell** of the landfill, **compacted** by heavy equipment such as bulldozers, covered with **soil** at the end of each day and compacted further. This reduces its volume, keeps vectors out and contains odours. Cells are arranged in rows and layers.

Any biodegradable **organic material** is broken down anaerobically by bacteria and fungi, and this produces **gases** such as **methane**, which are removed via pipes. The methane is then extracted and used as a **fuel**, e.g. to generate electricity. Any non-biodegradable materials remain and their volume reduces over time. When the landfill is **full**, it is capped, the topsoil is replaced and vegetation is planted. The land can then be reused, e.g. for recreational purposes or agriculture.

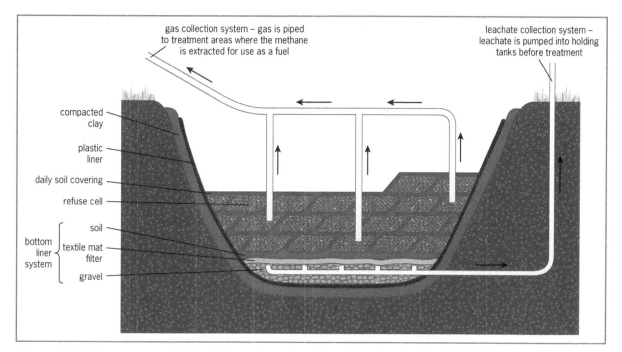

Figure 15.4 *The concept of a landfill*

The importance of landfills in the Caribbean

Disposing of solid waste in properly maintained and operated **landfills** is the most **cost-effective** way Caribbean countries can correctly manage their solid waste. It ensures that the waste is **isolated** from the surrounding environment to prevent the spread of **disease**, to keep valuable **water supplies** clean and uncontaminated, and to prevent **pollution** of land and air. Ultimately, this ensures that countries of the Caribbean can enjoy clean, unpolluted environments that can improve health, tourism, international investment and economic growth.

The impact of solid waste on the environment

If solid waste is **not disposed of properly**, it becomes a serious threat to the environment.

- **Toxic chemicals** can leach out and contaminate the soil, aquatic environments and water sources.
- **Pathogens** and intestinal **parasites** or their eggs, which may be present, can enter water supplies and contaminate potable (drinking) water.
- **Greenhouse gases**, e.g. methane and carbon dioxide, can be released into the atmosphere and contribute to the **greenhouse effect** (see page 14).
- **Hydrogen sulfide gas** can be released into the air. This is extremely **toxic**; even low concentrations irritate the eyes and respiratory system.
- **Plastics** can wash into waterways and oceans where they are harmful to aquatic organisms.
- Solid waste provides a breeding ground for **pests** and **vectors** which can spread disease.
- Solid waste creates an **eyesore** and **unpleasant odours** which impact negatively on tourism.

Reduce, reuse and recycle

The **volume** of **solid waste** that has to be disposed of can be decreased considerably by practising the **3Rs** of waste management, **reduce**, **reuse** and **recycle**.

Reduce

Reduce means to cut down on what is produced, what is purchased and what is used.

If this is achieved, then there should be less waste to be discarded, reused or recycled. For example, the **manufacture** and **use** of disposable items and excessive packaging materials should be reduced to a minimum. **Electronic mail** or **e-mail** should be used whenever possible and businesses should aim to become as '**paperless**' as possible by working electronically whenever they can.

Reuse

Reuse means to use the same item again, preferably many times, for the same purpose or for a different purpose.

Items such as **glass bottles** and **cloth shopping bags** can be reused many times for the same purpose. Old **tyres** can be reused to make tyre gardens or chipped, mixed with construction rubble and used to build roads. **Newspapers** can be reused as packaging material or shredded to make animal bedding. **Old clothing** can be used as rags for cleaning.

Recycle

Recycle means to separate, recover and reprocess materials into new raw materials that can then be used to make new products.

Many materials can be **recycled**.

- **Paper** and **cardboard** can be pulped and the pulp used to make new paper, cardboard or plasterboard.

- **Glass** can be crushed, melted and formed into new glass items.

- **Metals** can be shredded, melted, purified and solidified, and then used to make new metal items.

- **Plastics** can be shredded, melted and turned into new plastic items or fibres for clothing.

- **Food** and **garden waste** can be composted to make soil conditioner and mulch, and **agricultural waste** can be used to make **biogas** (see page 49).

- Used **cooking oil**, **animal fats** and **restaurant grease** can be reacted with an alcohol to make **biodiesel** for use in vehicles and machinery that normally use diesel obtained from petroleum. Biodiesel reduces an engine's overall emissions by up to 75% and reduces the use of fossil fuel.

Figure 15.5 *The 3Rs of waste management*

Operations at a recycling centre

Recycling centres are responsible for sorting and separating **mixed** recycling. This can be done automatically by machines and/or by hand.

At a typical centre, the **unsorted recycling** is loaded onto conveyers and any non-recyclables are removed and disposed of, including plastic bags. The **paper** and **cardboard** are then removed and compressed to make bales. **Ferrous metal** (iron-containing) items are then removed using large magnets, followed by **plastic** items. **Aluminium** cans are then removed, and finally **glass** is removed at the end of the conveyer. The metal and plastic items are compressed and made into bales, and the glass is usually crushed. The materials are then **transported** to manufacturers.

Advantages of practising the 3Rs

Practising the **3Rs** of waste management has many **advantages.**

- It **reduces** the **volume** of solid waste that must be disposed of in landfills and incinerators.
- It **reduces** the **loss** of potentially useful materials.
- It **conserves natural resources**, many of which are running out.
- It **reduces energy consumption**, mainly because processes used to obtain raw materials such as mining and refining are not involved.
- It **reduces pollution** of air, land and water that results from waste disposal measures.

The impact of environmental issues on humans

Environmental issues are affecting humans in a variety of ways.

Food security

Global warming is affecting **food security** by causing changes in temperature and rainfall patterns, increasing the frequency and severity of extreme weather events, e.g. floods and droughts, increasing the prevalence of pests and disease of livestock and crops, and changing ocean temperatures, which affects the distribution and productivity of fished species. All these changes affect **world food production** and this will lead to food shortages, higher food prices, hunger and starvation.

Water security

Erratic rainfall, severe droughts and flooding caused by **climate change**, together with **water pollution** and **deforestation**, are all having a negative impact on the quantity and quality of **water supplies** worldwide. As water supplies decrease, so does **food production**, and as pollution increases, so does the spread of **water-borne diseases**.

Land security

Global warming is causing once-fertile lands to turn into deserts (desertification) or to become permanently flooded, and coastal lands to erode or flood due to sea level rises. Similarly, **deforestation, poor agricultural practices** and **land pollution**, especially by indiscriminate and illegal dumping of waste, are all contributing to **land degradation**. As land becomes degraded, food production is reduced, water resources become stressed and people lose their livelihoods. This can lead to people being displaced from affected areas and becoming **environmental refugees.**

Human health

Environmental risk factors such as air, land and water **pollution**, exposure to hazardous **chemicals** and **ultraviolet radiation**, and **climate change** causing heat waves, floods and changes in the distribution of infectious diseases and allergens, all contribute to the development of over 100 different communicable and non-communicable diseases worldwide. These risk factors disproportionately affect **socially disadvantaged** and **vulnerable** population groups.

1. What is sewage and what are its THREE main contaminants?

2. Distinguish between proper and improper sewage disposal practices.

3. Discuss THREE impacts of improper sewage disposal practices.

4. Outline how sewage from households is treated to produce TWO products that are safe to use in agriculture.

5. Distinguish between biodegradable waste and non-biodegradable waste, and give TWO examples of EACH type.

6. Identify THREE methods of disposal of domestic refuse other than recycling, and give TWO advantages and TWO disadvantages of EACH method.

7. Suggest THREE reasons why dumping of refuse in open dumps has been made illegal in many countries.

8. a Describe a landfill and the operations that take place at a landfill.
   b Why are landfills important to the countries of the Caribbean?

9. Discuss THREE impacts of solid waste on the environment.

10. a Outline the principles of practising the 3Rs of waste management.
    b Suggest FOUR advantages of practising the 3Rs of waste management.

11. Outline the operations at a recycling centre.

12. What is biodiesel and what are the benefits of its use?

13. Discuss the impact of environmental issues on EACH of the following:
    a land security   b food security   c human health

Exam-style questions – Chapters 14 to 15

Structured questions

1 **a)** Figure 1 is a diagram of the water cycle.

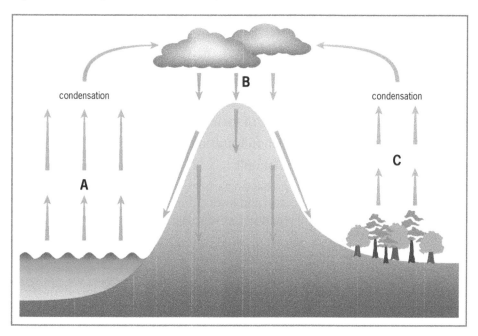

Figure 1 *The water cycle*

   i) Identify the processes occurring at A, B and C.   **(3 marks)**

   ii) Human activities can cause pollution of the water cycle. What is meant
   by the term 'pollution'?   **(1 mark)**

b) Community members were advised by health authorities to avoid polluted
floodwater after a tropical storm.

   i) Describe a test the health authorities could use to determine if the
   community's water supply is contaminated with bacteria.   **(4 marks)**

   ii) Describe ONE small-scale method of water purification that community
   members would be encouraged to use.   **(2 marks)**

c) Human activities are not only polluting water resources, but also the air.

   i) Identify TWO air pollutants.   **(2 marks)**

   ii) Suggest THREE ways humans can reduce air pollution.   **(3 marks)**

                                                                Total 15 marks

2 **a) i)** What is sewage?   **(1 mark)**

   ii) Identify TWO contaminants that can be found in sewage.   **(2 marks)**

   iii) Raw sewage is sometimes discharged directly onto the land or into the sea.
   Identify TWO ways this practice poses a threat to:

   a the health of communities in the Caribbean

   b marine organisms.   **(4 marks)**

b) The biological filter method and activated sludge method are two methods used during the treatment of sewage.

    i)   Identify the stage in the sewage treatment process that is carried out directly before the biological filter method. **(1 mark)**

    ii) Compare the treatment of sewage by the biological filter method and the activated sludge method, giving TWO similarities and TWO differences. **(4 marks)**

c) Other than by dumping raw sewage into bodies of water, outline THREE other ways water supplies can become polluted. **(3 marks)**

Total 15 marks

Structured essay question

3   **a)** Plastics can be classified as biodegradable and non-biodegradable. Distinguish between biodegradable plastics and non-biodegradable plastics, and suggest TWO ways plastics can negatively impact living organisms and the environment. **(4 marks)**

    b) Many countries in the Caribbean dispose of their solid waste in landfills.

        i)   Explain the difference between a landfill and an open dump. **(2 marks)**

        ii) Describe the daily operations at a landfill. **(4 marks)**

    c) A small village in your country does not have a garbage collection system in place. You visit the village as a Health Inspector, and notice there is solid waste strewn all over the village. What advice would you give to the villagers about the proper disposal of this solid waste? **(5 marks)**

Total 15 marks

Index

Page numbers along with 't' an 'f' refer to table and figure respectively.